D1201689

CONRAD AIKEN:

A LIFE OF HIS ART

CONRAD AIKEN

A LIFE OF HIS ART

BY JAY MARTIN

PRINCETON, NEW JERSEY

PRINCETON UNIVERSITY PRESS

1962

Copyright © 1962
by Princeton University Press
All Rights Reserved
L.C. Card: 62-11958

✤

Publication of this book has been
aided by the Ford Foundation program
to support publication, through university presses,
of works in the humanities and social sciences

✤

Printed in the United States of America
Second Printing, 1963

81152
A291xm

FOR HELEN

2-22-79 Baker & Taylor 13.75

 PREFACE

I HAVE TRIED to avoid repetitive footnotes by using the following method in referring to Conrad Aiken's work. I use his *Collected Poems* (1953) as the standard text of Aiken's poetry to 1947 and refer to works included in it simply by enclosing the page reference in parentheses immediately following the completion of the quotation, i.e. (100). When quoting from poems arranged in series (such as *Priapus and the Pool*), I shall also indicate the place of the poem in its series, i.e. (x, 100). When quoting from poems not included in the *Collected Poems*, I shall abbreviate the title of the volume, including it and the page number in parentheses immediately following the completion of the quotation, i.e. (E.T., 100). I shall do likewise in reference to Aiken's short fiction, using *The Collected Short Stories of Conrad Aiken* (1960) as my standard text, and in reference to his criticism, using his *A Reviewer's ABC* (1958) and *Scepticisms* (1919) as the sources for pieces included in them. When referring to Aiken's novels, I shall give the abbreviated title with the page number in parentheses following the quotation. Following is a list of abbreviations which I shall use to identify quotations.

A.   *Mr. Arcularis. A Play*, Cambridge, Harvard University Press, 1957.

ABC   *A Reviewer's ABC. Collected Criticism of Conrad Aiken from 1916 to the Present*, New York, Meridian Books, Inc., 1958.

B.B.   *Bring! Bring! and Other Stories*, New York, Boni & Liveright, 1925.

B.V.   *Blue Voyage*, New York, C. Scribner's Sons, 1927.

Con.   *Conversation; or Pilgrim's Progress*, New York, Duell, Sloan & Pearce, 1940.

C.P.   *Collected Poems of Conrad Aiken*, New York, Oxford University Press, 1953.

E.T.   *Earth Triumphant and Other Tales in Verse*, New York, The Macmillan Co., 1914.

G.C.   *Great Circle*, New York, C. Scribner's Sons, 1933.

H.G.M.   *A Heart for the Gods of Mexico*, London, M. Secker, 1939.

L.P.   *A Letter from Li Po and Other Poems*, New York, Oxford University Press, 1955.

N.R.S.   *Nocturne of Remembered Spring and Other Poems*, Boston, The Four Seas Co., 1917.

P.M.   *Preludes for Memnon*, 1931.

Sc.   *Scepticisms. Notes on Contemporary Poetry*, New York, A. A. Knopf, 1919.

S.H.   *Sheepfold Hill. Fifteen Poems*, New York, Sagamore Press, 1958.

S.O.   *Skylight One. Fifteen Poems*, New York, Oxford University Press, 1949.

S.S.   *Collected Short Stories*, Cleveland, World Publishing Co., 1960.

T.R.   *Time in the Rock*, 1936.

T.M.   *Turns and Movies and Other Tales in Verse*, Boston and New York, Houghton Mifflin Co., 1916.

Ush.   *Ushant. An Essay*, New York, Duell, Sloan & Pearce, 1952.

Wake   Harvard *Wake 11* (Conrad Aiken Number), 1952.

Aiken's publishers have generously allowed me to reprint copyrighted material from these volumes. Mr. Carl D. Brandt of Brandt & Brandt helped me to obtain these permissions.

I also especially want to thank the people who, at various stages, helped make this book possible. For helpful suggestions and information I am indebted to Allen Tate, Howard Babb, and John Harold Wilson. Norman Holmes Pearson helped me to get a grant-in-aid from Yale University. Willard Thorp has encouraged me by his interest in the study since I began it. R. P. Blackmur read one of the last drafts of the manuscript and spent several hours discussing it with me. Conrad Aiken himself has been the most patient and tolerant of subjects, even reading and commenting on several versions of this study. Finally, I want to express my altogether inexpressible gratitude to Roy Harvey Pearce, who alone will know how much he has taught me.

 CONTENTS

CONRAD AIKEN:

A LIFE OF HIS ART

.
.
.

And the other cricket said to the first—
fool! fool! speak! speak! speak!
speak if you must, but speaking speaking speaking
what does it get us, what does it get us, what?
act act act act give
giving is love, giving is love, give!

One cricket said to another—
what is love what is love what is love
act—speak—act—speak—act—speak—
give—take—give—take—give—take—
more slowly as the autumn comes, but giving
and taking still,—you taking, and I giving!

And the other cricket said to the first—
yes! yes! yes! you give your word!
words words but what at the end are words
speech speech what is the use of speech
give me love give me love
love!

One cricket said to another—
in the beginning—I forget—in the beginning—
fool fool fool fool fool
too late to remember and too late to teach—
in the beginning was the word, the speech,
and in the end the word, the word, the word . . .

But while they quarrelled, these two foolish crickets,
and bandied act with word, denying each,
weighing their actions out in terms of speech,
the frost came whitely down and furred them both,
the speech grew slower, and the action nil,
and, at the end, even the word was still;
and god began again.

.
.
.

CONRAD AIKEN has been one of the most prolific of modern American writers. Since 1914, when his first book appeared, he has published not only the twenty-five volumes of poetry for which he is best known, but also five novels, five short story collections, a play, and two books of criticism. His first volume of verse coincided with the beginning of the poetry renaissance in America; *Sheepfold Hill,* his latest book of poems, appeared in 1958. More recently, Aiken has gathered together selections from his short stories and poems. During his career no more than three years separate the appearance of Aiken's successive books. For these and other reasons, his literary career might be studied in several fruitful and interesting ways.

The most obvious way to deal with Aiken is to use his work as the center of a study in the dynamics of literary reputations in the twentieth century. For it would be fair to say that of our major poets Aiken has received the least critical attention. It is not surprising, then, that much of the appreciative criticism written about Aiken during the last thirty years has focused on this point. Houston Peterson's *Melody of Chaos* was written to defend Aiken's reputation against the claims of others. It is a curious irony of literary history that Aiken should have been the first writer of his generation to serve as the subject of a full-length study; *The Melody of Chaos* preceded by four years F. O. Matthiessen's work on Eliot. Successive critics since Peterson have complained about the inattention Aiken has received. In 1937 R. P. Blackmur wrote:

> An important . . . fact about Mr. Aiken is the almost complete absence of serious attention, whether from readers or critics, with which his later poetry has been received. . . . The critics have been indifferent, ignorant, inattentive, preoccu-

pied, and have dealt out kindly, and therefore irrelevant, praise for old times' sake. Many reviews have had about them that air of innocuous and mannerly illusion that flourishes in the records of class reunions. I cannot think of a more sickening consensus of unfounded opinion and hardly of a more revolting example of good will than the kindliness of inattention. The only explanation I can think of, and it is no excuse, is that most of Mr. Aiken's poems in recent years have been called 'Preludes' and have been numbered without other title, and there have been a great many of them, and that most of them have appeared in blank verse. Further than that I can only believe that the poems have been merely scanned and never read—and the reviewers have come away, like the presumed reader, with the labor-saving notion that here was more of the same, the same old Aiken, older but no different.[1]

In 1943 Delmore Schwartz complained, in similar fashion, that "each time a new volume of his verse has appeared, the same clichés of misunderstanding have been brought forward, in new dress, or in the same old dress, if the reviewer is tired."[2] Nearly ten years later, Malcolm Lowry commented upon the same failure of the critics. Whereas Aiken's contemporaries— for instance, Eliot, Joyce, and Marianne Moore—have all shown considerable admiration for his work, Lowry observed that only "the odd reviewer . . . would give the impression now and then that a certain work was outdated or insignificant or showed 'traces' of something or other: this opinion someone else would repeat almost verbatim in a given review" (Wake, 82). Samuel French Morse has recently, and with considerable vehemence, continued this complaint, insisting that "no other contemporary poet of equal stature has suffered such politely cavalier treatment, and none has been so respectfully ignored." While poets like William Carlos Williams and Wallace Stevens had been reappraised during the fifties, Morse noted that in the case of Aiken's work, "there is evidence that the limitations noted by so many of his critics have been gleaned at second hand (even to the point of compounding some errors of fact) rather than freshly discovered as the result of a fresh reading."[3]

Aiken has always insisted that the writer's only concern must be with his actual writing, not with his reputation; consequently, he has seldom complained publicly about his critical maltreatment, and he has even, in *Ushant*, expressed satisfaction with his relative obscurity. In reaction to reviews by Louise Bogan and Randall Jarrell of his 1940 volume, *And in the Human Heart*, however, Aiken wrote to Malcolm Cowley of the curious course of his literary reputation:

> Another interesting comment is to the effect that *only recently* have my books been badly treated—tacit assumption being that the earlier ones weren't. *That* line might be described as the theme song of my literary career. Each new book is panned—but in the background is the implication that all the previous ones were good. In me you behold an almost unique phenomenon, a poet who has acquired a Reputation, or a Position, or what have you, without ever having been caught in the act—as it were, by a process of osmosis. At any given moment in the Pegasus Sweepstakes, in whatever Selling Plate or for whatever year, this dubious horse has always been the last in the list of the also-ran,—he has never even placed, much less won, nor, I regret to report, have the offers to put him out to stud been either remunerative or very attractive. (Wake, 30)

An investigation of the factors in literary reputation, with Aiken as its point of reference, might certainly prove very interesting. Such a study might adduce several reasons for the critical neglect of Aiken's work. Because Aiken produced such a mass of ostensibly similar work between 1916 and 1920 he became identified with a certain style—the mellifluous, honeyed perfection of "Discordants" and the blue-flower romanticism and

Krafft-Ebing decadent eroticism of *The Charnel Rose*. Thus, his later, quite different, poetry has been judged very often in the light of the reputation his earliest work gained him. Such is the case, for instance, in Vernon Loggins's *I Hear America*. By 1937, when this book was published, Aiken had written his two volumes of Preludes, *Landscape West of Eden* and *Osiris Jones*. Yet, despite this growth, the poem by which Loggins judges him is the 1916 *Jig of Forslin*, Aiken's third volume. Aiken has suffered comparable treatment in Louis Untermeyer's forty-year series of anthologies of American poetry. Both in his prefaces and in his selections, Untermeyer has always represented Aiken by his earliest work—and Untermeyer's influence upon the formulation of a hierarchy in poetry has been immense. In short, because Aiken achieved a poetic "character" so early, his reputation has ultimately suffered. In his review of the *Preludes for Memnon*, Granville Hicks argued: "So much has by now been written about Conrad Aiken that . . . it should be necessary merely to summarize critical opinion of his previous work,"[4] in order to judge any new book. Other critics, perhaps in the main unconsciously, have proceeded similarly. Such criticism allows no possibility of the poet's progress, and ironically, as I shall show, Conrad Aiken's work can only be adequately evaluated with regard to its development. His poems are always (as Valéry and Péguy considered their poems) "Work in Progress," in which not the achievement but the growth is all-important. Arthur O. Lovejoy has spoken of "the internal tensions or waverings in the mind of almost every individual writer . . . arising from conflicting ideas or incongruous propensities of feeling or taste,"[5] and has complained about the tendency of critics to find unity of thought where there is only unity of personality. From the first, Aiken has kept his mind, and his poetry, receptive to the incongruities of his ideas and feelings. He has allowed, even encouraged, contradiction in his work: his poetry is constructed out of conflict. While Aiken presents his readers with no fixed or systematic philoso-

6

phy, then, he exhibits as the guiding principle of his development a consistent desire to explore and ever more fully to understand his own, and through him, man's personal and collective consciousness.

Such a study of the dynamics of literary reputations might also analyze with profit the changes in critical fashion during this century. In the twenties Aiken's poetry was not experimental enough—or rather, it was not bizarre enough—to attract the kind of attention which, during this decade, exalted the stylistically odd and curious.[6] Throughout the poetic revolution in the conception of the verse line, Aiken remained conservative in his language and prosody, though not in his thought. In the critical counterpart to this poetic practice, he consistently attacked both Imagism and realism, and consequently was denigrated early as a "belated and provincial Victorian,"[7] one of the enemies of the new poetry which he was helping to create and make valuable.

Reaction against poetic form elaborated as an end in itself was inevitable, and in the thirties criticism turned from emphasis upon stylistic experiment as such toward the insistence that art must reflect or react *directly* to the social and economic conflicts of the society in which it exists. Criticism that attempted "to evaluate art and literature by revolutionary standards"[8] could have little sympathy for Aiken's methods. Although Aiken steadfastly maintained that art exists primarily for the fulfillment of a social function, he insisted as strongly that the poet must stand clear from political entanglements in his personal life and expressions of political and economic dogmas in his writing. In carrying out the tradition of the nineteenth-century "sage"—which I will discuss more fully in the final chapter—he contended that art is beneficial only in its universals. The revolution it accomplishes is in its extension of consciousness, not in its improvement of institutions. Aiken's aims were therefore as opposed to the ethical emphases of the Neo-Humanists as to the revolutionary standards of the Marxists, and consequently, although he produced some of his best work during this decade, by the late thirties his reputation reached its lowest level.

So the study might continue: in the forties Aiken's emphasis upon the individual "I" was opposed to the tendency of the age, typified in Auden's poetry, to think in terms of plurals— of groups, units, classes—and therefore to adopt forms of historical or collectivistic colloquialisms.[9] In the fifties, Aiken's work was found lacking in imagistic richness, too musical, and too diffuse in texture to satisfy the intensive analyses of New Criticism. Again, his aims were in conflict with the dominant critical demands. In order to extend man's collective consciousness, Aiken has invariably endeavored to make his work as understandable as is consonant with the highest dignity of art. Much of the criticism during the fifties, however, inculcated the assumption that there must be a breach (which the critic fills) between the poet and his audience. Whereas Aiken has sought full clarity of expression, we have been convinced that whatever is clear to us must be trivial.

Such a study of Aiken's reputation would be interesting and valuable, but it would be concerned with permutations in the history of manners rather than in the history of poetry, and it is not the study that I propose. Aiken's rank in the hierarchy of contemporary poetry is, for the present, best left to the judgment of the century. At present we must only work toward a sense of his aims and the methods whereby he sought to accomplish them. I hope to show in this study that if Aiken is to be re-evaluated at all we must come to understand him in a new way. I have already suggested that his chief virtue lies not in any particular poem or collection of poems, but in his growth. More than any other modern poet except Yeats, Aiken has exhibited vigorous growth toward sureness of expression. Yet Aiken's development has never been adequately studied. His random reviewer, of course, has seldom had either the space or the detailed knowledge to make such a study possible. In his full-length study, Peterson used Aiken's work chiefly to illustrate his own theory of modern literature. *The Melody of Chaos*, moreover, was published in 1931 and deals with Aiken's work only up to *Blue Voyage*. By casting such emphasis upon his early work, Peterson's book may, ironically, have been more hindrance than aid in assessing Aiken's value. Even Aiken himself, when asked for information on his development in 1929, avoided the question:

> Now, when I am asked to say something about my fourteen years of miscellaneous literary activity, I see how extraordinarily and bewilderingly little I know about myself. I suspect, indeed, that the author himself is the last person to consult on this question. All I can say is that I seem to myself to have moved steadily in one direction. What exactly this direction is, heaven only knows; nor do I know whether it is a good direction or a bad one. Perhaps to an outsider this miscellaneous activity might present an appearance of unity, or seem to present a personality. My own feeling today, however, is that all this has been an experiment, an experiment which hasn't yet come to an end.[10]

At the same time, Aiken has been more deeply concerned in his work with the investigation, exploration, and definition of his own developing consciousness than any other of our major contemporary poets. He has sought, particularly in his novels, to achieve a precise understanding of his own growth, both as a person and as an artist. One of his comments on the work of Archibald MacLeish is particularly revealing—deliberately so— along these lines. Criticizing MacLeish's prefatory remark that "My development as a poet is of no interest to me and of even less interest, I should think, to anyone else," Aiken observed: "One might as well say that one's growth as a human being, as a tree, as a world, or even as a God, is of no concern either to oneself or to another. It simply isn't true. One *is*, and profoundly, interested in one's own growth: one cannot escape it: and to deny one's interest is perhaps merely (inversely) to over-state it. Is it possible that Mr. MacLeish is *over*concerned with his development as a poet, *just as we are?*" (ABC, 284)

Aiken *has* been concerned with his own development. It might even be said that all of his books, his criticism and fiction as well as his poetry after *Turns and Movies*, are progressive comments upon the state of his (to use one of his own titles) "changing mind." The primary purpose of my study of Aiken will be to consider how he has developed and to what end—and what problems have arisen in consequence of his need and desire to develop in a particular way. Throughout his career, he has sought the means whereby he might make his mental and emotional development articulate; and he has used various forms to do this in his search for a linguistic and structural equivalent to his mental experience. Almost every one of his books in the past forty years has approached this problem in a new way, with a new style (though, of course, with some con-stant characteristics), each intended to communicate most di-rectly the particular experience embodied in it. I should make it clear that in speaking of Aiken's development I am not also implying that his poetry has become more perfect. Each book has not inevitably advanced upon its predecessors. Probably *Senlin* (1918), the Preludes (1931-1936), and *A Letter from Li Po* (1955), separated by many years, and quite different, are all on the same level of artistic achievement. The books that surround these fall below the aesthetic culminations which they represent. But we will be tracing out an evolution: a clear movement from one work to another throughout Aiken's ca-reer. And the principle of that evolution is Aiken's deepening and subtilization of his self-awareness. As Erich Kahler defined "evolution" in general, the movement of Aiken's career has been "neither straight nor circular, but proceeds in a revolving movement, at once expanding and advancing, like a spiral."[11] How then, I shall inquire, has Aiken expanded the range of his

experience, and how, at the same time, has he successively refined his means to explore and exploit his consciousness, from
his earliest to his most recent work?

This, as it seems to me, is the kind of study which is needed
at this stage of our understanding of Aiken's work. As Allen
Tate observed in his citation of Aiken for the Gold Medal of
the Institute of Arts and Letters, Aiken has written "a formid-
able body of work with which we have not yet come to terms."
This body of work—and its form and function—will be my
one and only concern. There is no question, of course, that
Aiken's poetry is his major achievement; consequently, I shall
be mainly concerned with elucidating that part of his work. I
will, however, also consider Aiken's fiction and criticism, since
both help to illuminate aspects of his poetry. R. P. Blackmur
observed of Aiken's first novel, *Blue Voyage*—and the same is
true of his later novels—that "the novel is the prose version of
the poems. In the novel we get the psychology, and the philosophical notions behind it, in an almost pure form; in the
poems these are translated into symbols, images, and music. In
both, the poet is preoccupied with the Blue Voyage or Great
Circle Passage of the soul, the *voyage à l'infini*, the exploration
of his own heart."[12] Since the appearance of Aiken's autobiographical "essay," *Ushant*, it has been clear that Aiken himself
understands his literary career in terms of the experience he has
been able to express in his fiction. With the sole exception of
The Kid, he mentions his poems in only a cursory fashion in
Ushant, while he discusses his fiction at length. Although Aiken
does this ironically, he also intends thereby to emphasize his
fiction. For the critic of Aiken, then, the novels assume considerable importance aside from their individual merits, since an
understanding of his fiction helps toward an elucidation of his
poetry.

Aiken has also written a great deal of criticism. The check
list of his reviews and essays lists over two hundred and fifty
pieces, written from 1915 to 1955 (ABC, 395-408). Marianne

Moore has written of Aiken that "he was the perfect reviewer, Diogenes' one honest man, fearing only to displease himself" (Wake, 56). He was one of the first American critics to apply Freudian and other psychological theories to the judgment of poetry in an investigation of the mechanism of literary creation. Because he employed novel, if not revolutionary, standards of critical judgment, he was forced to develop and explain his ideas anew in each of his critical essays. More than most poets, then, Aiken constantly provides insights into the critical bases of his creative productions. Perhaps more important, he has, on occasion, reviewed his own books. He anonymously reviewed his *Nocturne of Remembered Spring* in 1917; and in 1919, at Harriet Monroe's invitation, discussed the aims of *The Charnel Rose*. Recently, in analyzing the reasons why he "drifted into criticism at all," Aiken has spoken of the relationship between his criticism and the development of his poetry. Of his *Scepticisms* (1919) he wrote: "Its effect on myself was deep and permanent. It was apparent to me that I must henceforward be concerned as much with criticism as with poetry or fiction, that it could go hand in hand with these quite naturally and easily, and with the already foreseeable advantage that one genre could thus fortify or fructify or clarify the other: they could work in tandem."[13] After *Scepticisms* we can observe an expansion in the range of Aiken's criticism. He was quite consciously using his criticism—as he used his fiction—to provide new areas of awareness for his poetry. Taken as a whole, therefore, Aiken's criticism possesses the same interest and importance as his fiction in an investigation of his development.

Although I shall emphasize Aiken's poetry in particular, then, I shall also consider the total body of his work in tracing out the continuity of his development. Other more special studies, entirely concerned with Aiken's sources, his influence, his milieu, his reputation, his "place" in the twentieth century, and so on, will, as they must, follow; but they can only follow from such an investigation as this.

12

ANONYMOUSLY reviewing his fourth book, *Nocturne of Remembered Spring* (1917), Conrad Aiken estimated his own achievement: "If he is consistent as regards his material, sticking fairly close to a preference for an objective psychological method in poetry, he is hopelessly confused as regards the problem of poetic form. In *Turns and Movies* he willfully sacrificed his ability to write in smoothly involute curves for a dubious gain in matter-of-fact forcefulness. In *The Jig of Forslin* he recanted, and, with occasional sops to downright and rigid realism, abandoned himself to a luxuriation in romantic virtuosity. And now, in *Nocturne of Remembered Spring,* he is more clearly than ever a schizophrenic" (ABC, 120-21). Since, as we shall see, Aiken's persistent emphasis upon the need for full clarity of consciousness demanded that as an artist he be fully aware of the nature and implications of his aims and accomplishments, his comments on his own work are usually suggestive. In this criticism of *Nocturne of Remembered Spring,* indeed, he correctly recognized that the chief characteristic of his early poetry, from 1914 to about 1920, is the separation between his "lyrical" and "dramatic" forms. The one form he conceived as the means whereby he might create an emotion similar to his own in the reader; in the other he presented, as he would then have said, a "philosophy" to his reader through an analysis of the mental states of his characters. In the one form he sought to enrich the emotions of his audience—in the other, its knowledge. More and more he came, in his later poetry, to see that he could only enrich the emotional life of his society by increasing its consciousness.

In part, this separation of "lyrical" and "dramatic" poetry is an aspect of the general development of American poetry during the second decade of this century. It is not too simple to say that American poets were then moving in two quite distinct directions, with very little contact between them. Each group had its own spokesman. There were those poets celebrated by Louis Untermeyer in his *New Era in American Poetry*—Masters, Giovannitti, Wood, Oppenheim, Sandburg, Alter Brody and, tangentially, Frost and Lola Ridge—for their expression of the American way: their lustiness, their glorification of matter-of-fact reality, and, above all, their democracy in speech and spirit. On the other hand, Amy Lowell, in her "evolutionary" *Tendencies in Modern American Poetry*, was "proving" that in their endeavor to create a new kind of socially free beauty, H. D. and John Gould Fletcher, or the Imagists in general, were the most highly developed kinds of poets.

Far from allying himself with either of these groups, Aiken was attracted and repelled in equal measure by each. In his early poetry, accordingly, he vacillated between them. An alternation between dramatic and lyrical themes and styles is manifest from the very beginning of his career. We may define his two modes of investigation in this way: In the dramatic, the ego of the poet as poet explores itself by seeing what kind of characters it can create. In the lyric, this ego confronts and explores itself directly. Because I shall be using the word so frequently, I want to make clear that by "ego" I mean the individual personality of a human being—in this case, of a poet. I include, but do not limit myself to, the psychoanalytic use of the word, using it interchangeably with "person" and "self." I take it that there is a definable tradition in American poetry—dominant in the nineteenth, but continuing into the twentieth century—in which the poet is concerned with exploring and defining himself as poet.[1] To this tradition Aiken belongs; in some senses, it culminates in his work. In both of Aiken's themes and methods, finally, the ego is at the center of the poem, and is defined by it.

With the advantage of retrospect, we can see that Aiken groped toward a sense of this in his first volume. *Earth Tri-*

umphant (1914) was obviously influenced somewhat by the narrative methods of Masefield and Gibson, and is essentially "realistic" in intention—concentrating upon the solid realities of earth and love, as opposed to imagination and study. Immature though this volume is, in it Aiken anticipates his later psycho-realistic interest in the corrupt and abnormal. Parts of "Earth Triumphant" itself, and particularly "Youth" and "Romance" and "Dilemma," originate in his conviction that "we must seek / In city filth, in streets that reek, / Dark inspiration for our rhyme" (E.T., 217). *Turns and Movies* (1916) as well as, more remotely, *The Jig of Forslin* and *The House of Dust* follow from this theme—in which the ego creates other selves in order to analyze and exploit them and, therefore, also exposes the self which brought them into being. At the same time, the *Earth Triumphant* volume also exhibits the opposite lyric theme—in which the ego creates and confronts, in order to understand, itself. "Laughter," for instance, embodies the prototype of *Senlin*. In this poem, a youth speaks to his own old age as he confronts it in a mirror and imagines "All the grey shipwreck of this me" (E.T., 196). He understands himself through what he imagines he must become.

The lyric and dramatic themes are distinct, and accordingly produced in Aiken's early work two easily discernible types of poetry. But it is also clear that the two themes issue from the single emotional and intellectual impulse to investigate the ego—either directly or through other selves. The fundamental problem in a study of Aiken's development, therefore, is to see how he has used these themes, separately or in combination, in order to articulate his search for self-consciousness—the search which he came to call his Divine Pilgrimage.

Even as late as 1917, after both *The Charnel Rose* and *The Jig of Forslin* had been written, the demarcation between Aiken's realistic and lyrical poems was still patent—as if he were compelled to move successively from the one to the other. As the substance, for instance, of "Twelve Good Men,"[2] Aiken

15

presented a series of psycho-realistic characterizations of the twelve jurors at a murder trial. As each juror's stream of consciousness flows from the trial to his own concerns, he is portrayed through his egotistical reaction to the woman on trial for murdering her lover's wife. One, for example, finds himself in the same position as the lover:

> Suppose, now, Grace should find it out
> That he was not, as he told her, married;—
> She'd drag him into the courts—to-morrow! . . .
> Or if she was half-mad (like this woman),
> Shoot him!—No, no, the woman is guilty! (493-94)

The poem is built upon a series of similar interior investigations—with a jeweller, a florist, an art dealer, and others revealing themselves through their random thoughts as Aiken skillfully interweaves them with the external testimony of the trial.

The lyric theme in Aiken's early poetry is closely related to his obsessive interest in the musical analogy. By his musical structure he intends to mirror the structure of particular emotions, otherwise inexpressible. In an essay, "Counterpoint and Implication," which he wrote in 1919, Aiken discussed at length his attempt to evolve "an architectural structure in poetry analogous to that of music" (C.P., 874). Nearly all of his poems up to 1920 show evidence of this interest. "Sonata in Pathos," "White Nocturne," "Nocturne of Remembered Spring," and "Nocturne in a Minor Key," all depend for their effect upon the emotional suggestiveness of a strictly personal symbolism. Aiken's general description of his procedure in the Divine Pilgrim series is actually less applicable to it than to these poems: "this method takes only the most delicately evocative aspects of [sensations], makes of them a keyboard, and plays upon them a music of which the chief characteristic is its elusiveness, its fleetingness, and its richness in the shimmering overtones of hint and suggestion" (C.P., 876). The theory that lies behind

16

them, one suspects, is that if the poet can make the symbolism important and intense enough to himself, especially by repetition and the interweaving of metaphors, it will also assume comparable meaning for his audience. "Sonata in Pathos," which well represents the whole group, is concerned with romantic frustration due to satiety, and with the nympholeptic search which served earlier as the theme of *The Charnel Rose.* It invokes such figures as "the white-breasted one who danced before me, / Bearing narcissus in your hands; / You with the mouth like jasper, you with the feet like snow." The protagonist moves with such figures through bizarre, surrealistic landscapes: "And I walk under freezing elms, whose branches writhe / Like tortured corals against a clear green sky" (N.R.S., 41, 46). Its method, obviously, is antithetic to that of "Twelve Good Men," which emphasizes ideas and undertakes the revelation of the fragmentary consciousness of modern man. "Sonata in Pathos" does not so much express ideas as evoke their emotional resonance to produce a corresponding emotion in the reader.

While Aiken's poetry constantly shifted between the lyric impulse, with its ability to convey emotion, and the dramatic impulse, with its concrete expression of consciousness, he was satisfied with neither kind of poetry, wishing to produce effects larger than either alone could give. As early as 1913 he protested against the narrow sympathies of *Poetry* under Pound's direction.[3] In criticism of the Imagists he argued that "straying too far in search of flowers of vividness and colour, [they] have ended by losing themselves in a Plutonian darkness of unrelated sensory phenomena" (Sc., 61). Indeed, from the very beginning of his criticism he contended that Imagism had produced no great poet—perhaps, even, no great poem.[4] With the possible exceptions of "Improvisations," at the beginning, and "The Crystal," near the end of his career, Aiken's own poems do not commence in an image or a visual experience. More often, they issue from an idea or from a musical phrase. As late as 1951 he

17

could still censure the Imagist's typical method. He criticized William Carlos Williams for his failure to consider "sound values, as transmitted through the eye from the page to the ear." Mnemonic values, Aiken insisted, "are of crucial importance, and just as objective as any image" (ABC, 385). In Aiken's poetry, indeed, they often take the place of the image as his particular way of defining reality.

Aiken also became more and more dissatisfied with the accomplishments of the "realists," his earliest models. He consistently denounced their too frequent reduction of poetry to propaganda. Aware that "doctrine is interesting only when new" (Sc., 144), Aiken has nearly always avoided dogmatism in his poetry. Nonetheless, he was attracted to the realists because of the freedom their method offered in the articulation and development of ideas. For this reason, he frequently argued in his early criticism that "realistic magic is quite as legitimate in poetry as lyric magic" (Sc., 74). But he became progressively disappointed with the American realists; and in 1918, calling Edgar Lee Masters "Our Steamshovel Poet," he formulated his objections to their methods. Finally, in 1922, he rejected even Masefield, his earliest model: "We feel that we have very considerably overestimated him and that what we thought was a kind of largeness in his world was a deception, the illusory largeness of a stage-scene, sentimentally lighted and somewhat tawdry."[5]

Since Aiken could accept neither the realistic (i.e. "dramatic") nor the aesthetic (i.e. "lyrical") mode entirely, in his early poetry he wrote, as it were, now with one hand, now with the other. As anyone who knows something of Aiken's later development—which grows by synthesis and addition, not drastic revision—might suspect, Aiken sought the solution to his problem of poetic method in a combination of his lyrical and dramatic forms. The result was, as he called it, the "symphony." And, after preliminary experimentation with this form in "Disenchantment," he used it as the principle of the Divine Pilgrim poems. Aiken's prefatory summary of *Forslin*, describing the

18

variability of his method, might characterize the whole sequence: "My intention has been to employ all methods, attitudes, slants . . . as a necessary and vital part of any such study
as this. Consequently, it is possible to pick out portions of this
poem to exemplify almost any poetic method or tone" (C.P.,
866). This "running of the poetic gamut" from realism to meditation was, I suspect, as much the result of Aiken's inability to
choose between the two methods as it was his decision to combine both into a new form. He was also convinced, however, of
the importance and relevance of both ways with poetry—that
"pure aesthetics will never replace psycho-realism . . . nor vice
versa" (Sc., 254). In order to be the kind of universally effective
poet he envisioned as his ideal, he determined therefore to combine the best of both methods and, in so mixing, to give each a
new dimension. However we view it, this decision is the first step
in Aiken's development toward a poetry which might articulate
the consciousness of modern man. To use the kind of psychoanalytical metaphor of which the early Aiken would approve, it
is as if he wished to blend the voices of the analyst and patient
—to have the emotional flow of the patient's lyrical, subconscious thoughts simultaneously elucidated by the dramatic, objective commentary of the analyst. The general tendency of the
Divine Pilgrim poems as a whole is toward the increasing control of the analyst over the sensorium of the patient. This line
of development would lead Aiken back to an almost strictly
narrative mode in the poems that followed them.

· II ·

I have already spoken of the problem of form which the early
Aiken posed for himself. The early division between the lyrical
and dramatic methods implied, of course, a congruent separation between the modes of thought they represent. In the "lyrical theme" the ego creates and confronts itself as it comes into
contact with the world. Although, as I have suggested, Aiken

19

tentatively investigated the possibilities of this theme as early as 1914 in "Laughter," not until *The Charnel Rose,* written the next year, did he exploit them fully. *Senlin: A Biography* (1918) is perhaps the richest example of the lyrical theme in Aiken's early work. His "dramatic theme" consists in the ego's exploration of other selves. In the shorter poems—for instance, *Turns and Movies* (1916)—Aiken's definitive form is a dramatic monologue modelled after Browning. In the longer examples of this theme—like *Punch: The Immortal Liar* (1921)—he customarily employs a related sequence of such monologues, synthesizing them in a final statement.

The two themes, of course, derive from the single desire to explore and reveal consciousness. Both peregrinate toward self-knowledge, the only goal Aiken values. Summarizing the beliefs which guided all of his work, Aiken wrote: "Consciousness is our supreme gift. . . . To see, to remember, to know, to feel, to understand, as much as possible—isn't this perhaps the most obviously indicated of motives or beliefs, the noblest and most all-comprehending of ideas which it is relatively possible for us to realize?"[6] Hence, there is no necessary distinction between the two themes. They can be, and are the richer for being combined. In both *The Jig of Forslin* and *The House of Dust* Aiken achieved fusion of the two. Here, the ego confronts itself already in the process of arising out of its own dramatization. "If there is a single theme in Aiken's work," R. P. Blackmur has observed, "it is the struggle of the mind which has become permanently aware of itself to rediscover and unite itself with the world in which it is lodged."[7] When the two themes come together in the early poetry, and almost always in the later, the self and the world are, or are meant to be, in equilibrium.

We can observe the tentative beginnings of an attempt at such a fusion in Aiken's earliest poetry. Among his manuscripts is a poem approximately five hundred lines long which Aiken wrote on January 9, 1911, for Dean Briggs's English 5 at Harvard. This he entitled "The Clerk's Journal: being the diary of a queer man." Allowed in this poem the space for development which he did not have in the poems he wrote for the *Advocate*, Aiken was able to work out tentatively the kind of variation of method which was later to point him toward his symphonies. The clerk, on the one hand, writes a diary dramatizing his inner and outer life; on the other, he looks back at his diary in order to investigate the principle of his ego; and fragments of his diary appear, as symphonic themes, in the process of his introspection.

In the early poem "Disenchantment" he was able to achieve the same kind of fusion more perfectly. Seen in the light of the two parts of "Earth Triumphant" (Part II is called "This Dance of Life") which are contemporaneous with it, "Disenchantment" reveals Aiken adding lyrical passages to the narrative of the young man disillusioned by life, a theme characteristic also of "Youth," "Romance," "Earth Tedium," and "Sophistication," all earlier poems. While Aiken groped toward musical structure in some of these poems, notably in "Earth Triumphant," he suggested a musical analogy mainly by his literal repetition of key lines. In the variable lines, stanzas, and rhyme patterns of "Disenchantment," however, there is a freer, more lyrical use of the octosyllabic couplets he had previously employed. Instead of repeating them literally, Aiken modifies lines and phrases slightly as they recur in new contexts. He is learning to radiate, not merely repeat, his ideas. With greater skill than he has previously exhibited, he modulates his rhythms to suggest the recurrence of thematic emotional tones.

Aiken was sufficiently confident of his achievement in "Disenchantment" to give it the subtitle "A Tone Poem," and to dedicate it to the New England composer and musician Lucien Crist. His chief architectonic device is the simple contrast between harmonious and cacophonous passages and sections. Aiken reinforces the contrast of the music in the poem by juxtaposing pastoral and industrial imagery (anticipating, in this, "The Waste Land" and "The Hollow Men"):

21

There were no clouds to shield this street,
No patter of large cool drops to break this heat,
Wet the limp leaves, and make the robins sing.
And it seemed to him a shame.

But the moon rose large and sleepy behind the housetops,
In the clear blue evening air.
And softly a sea-wind came among the housetops,
With the smell of kelp and sand and mermaids' hair.

(T.M., 37)

He also directly anticipates his method in *Forslin* and *The House of Dust* in his comparison of man's mind to a city. Typically, he extends the scope of the mind so that it may *contain* the city as part of its creation:

He was a giant outstretched for torture now;
And all these things, transacted in his brain,
Beat him, and wore him down, and made him bow,

.   .   .   .

In his vast mind that now contained this all.
He felt a million men through one cell crawl. (T.M., 34-35)

Certainly, Aiken also displays increased power of psychological dramatization in "Disenchantment." But knowing now what he was later to accomplish in this way, we can see what the poem has failed to do. Although there is sufficient variation along the gamut from lyricism to statement, there is no emotional tone sufficiently sustained to hold the parts together. The lyric sections seem to serve as mere decorative interruptions in the narrative. Consequently, the chief value of "Disenchantment" is that in it Aiken moved beyond the limitations of his early poems toward the more complex and original patterns of *The Divine Pilgrim*. I have treated "Disenchantment" at such length only because *The Jig of Forslin* has been usually considered to be

Aiken's first attempt along these lines, and because the poem is not included in the *Collected Poems* and tends therefore to be forgotten.

"Disenchantment," which Aiken began in the fall of 1914, preceded *The Charnel Rose,* but the later poem shows no advance over the earlier. Indeed, in the matter of fusing his two themes, Aiken shows a distinct retreat from his earlier achievement—as later, the poems in *Nocturne of Remembered Spring* are a clear falling back from *The Jig of Forslin.*

The Charnel Rose is a failure largely in proportion to its indulgence in the lyric theme, and, consequently, in its lack of variation between parts. It totally lacks the dramatic statement necessary to sustain a poem of its length. Although Aiken made major changes in the poem in both 1923 and 1948, he was unable to bring it fully under control by providing dramatic—or at least existential—substance for his lyrical improvisations. We must first understand the theme before we can properly recognize variations upon it. Originally he tried to describe his theme with a kind of preface in verse; in the later versions of the poem he eliminated this preface and sought concreteness rather in compression than in interior explanation. But the ambiguities remain. In the first words of his prose preface to the poem, Aiken implied his acceptance of this condition. We may suspect that he was not yet fully aware of his accomplishment in "Disenchantment." He wrote: " 'The Charnel Rose' needs, perhaps, some explanation. Like program music, it is helped by a program: though concrete in its imagery, it avoids sharp statement of ideas; implying the theme, rather than stating it" (C.P., 864-65). That is, the poem is concerned with emotions for their own sake, not with the situations from which the emotions arise—exactly the opposite approach from that which he was to take in *The House of Dust.* As a result, in *The Charnel Rose,* Aiken presents his reader with images from his stream of emotions. But, because Aiken is attempting to relate his protagonist to the universal search of all men, he employs only emotions of

23

the most general sort. He deliberately uses what he called the "vague phrase." While writing *The Charnel Rose* he argued, approvingly, for such vagueness: "Cannot vagueness be suggestive? Of course it can, provided the poet uses the right sort of vague word, with a true gusto."[8] In *The Charnel Rose* the frequency of the "vague phrase" suggests, nonetheless, a dimness in his conception of the poem. The protagonist of the poem has no concrete reality and cannot become all men because he is no man; and what was intended to be grandness amounts only to largeness. Later, to be sure, Aiken was to learn how to use the vague phrase—not exclusively, but in ironic contrast to the obsessive smallness of fact. In *Senlin*, for instance, vagueness is genuinely suggestive and indicates a background left dim not because Aiken was only dimly aware of it, but because dimness serves to make the protagonist seem the more gigantic; his very insubstantiality suggests his true dimensions. Since Aiken divests his emotions of their physical circumstances in *The Charnel Rose*, it is certainly true that like some kinds of music the poem needs its prefatory "program." Only the prose preface, considered as part of the poem, provides a narrative statement and the real contrast of tone which the poem otherwise lacks.

This is not to deny *The Charnel Rose* any intermittent evocative power, nor any importance in Aiken's development. There is power, certainly, in the reversal in Part III from the Divine toward the Satanic search for love—love which causes rather than suffers pain:

> Now let us walk back, slowly, as we came.
> We will light the room with candles; they may shine
> Like rows of yellow eyes.
> Your hair is like spun fire, by candle-flame.
> You smile at me—say nothing. You are wise.
> For I think of you, flung down brutal darkness;
> Crushed and red, with pale face.
> I think of you, with your hair disordered and dripping,
> And myself rising red from that embrace. (42)

24

The central symphonic "theme" of the poem—"To shape this world of leaderless ghostly passions—/Or else be mobbed by it —there was the question" (32)—suggests the problem of the organization of consciousness which Aiken would face in all of his later poems. The problem is to find a pattern in the multi-form aspects of the ego whereby to give it a center and define it. The question is no longer "to be or not to be," but *how to be.* And, of course, the basic moral question is never solved, or only, as Aiken wrote, "in the acceptance of a heuristic conation, the spiral of ascending awareness, and in a more conscious acceptance, with gioia scienza, of pluralism, and the 'ourselves but a leaf on the fountain of tree.' "[9] While later in his career, Aiken would treat the question for its value to himself and, through him, his culture, in his early poems his quest for awareness is presented diffusely, for the form's sake. In *The Charnel Rose* the ego cannot transcend, but only embrace, and dissolve into, chaos. It becomes but one more of the mob of "leaderless ghostly passions."

· III ·

Although he was later to maintain that standards in art proceed from the most, not the least, conscious persons, during the period from 1914 to about 1925 Aiken believed (at least for the purpose of his critical theory) that "it is, perhaps, a test of the greatness of poetry that it should speak as surely to the peasant as to the man of culture."[10] So he argued in 1915. In 1923, initiating a Freudian approach to literary problems, he could still write that the critic "cannot, with a sneer, dismiss the tastes of the vulgar. Those tastes are important. They give us, in clearest view, the common denominator of art" (ABC, 64). He could make this claim on the grounds of the Freudian theory that art is primarily a means of wish-fulfillment. The impact of Freud's investigations upon the second decade was overwhelming. Writing in 1915, Walter Lippmann (whom Aiken knew at Harvard) expressed the kind of enthusiasm that many other writers, including Aiken, must have felt towards Freud's theories during this period: "These researches of Freud challenge the very essence of what we call ourselves. They involve the sources of our character, they carry analysis deeper into the soul of man than analysis has ever been carried before," Lippmann wrote, then added, in conclusion, that Freud "may rank among the greatest who have contributed to thought."[11]

Despite the fact that Aiken has been called the "bard of psychoanalysis,"[12] it is impossible to measure his indebtedness to Freud accurately. He read not only Freud, but also Adler, Pfister, Ferenczi, Rank, and Wittels. And while he recognized Freud as the greatest of these, he soaked himself in "his co-workers and rivals and followers," who, he believed, "were making the most important contribution of the century to the understanding of man and his consciousness."[13] I suspect that although Aiken was deeply influenced by Freud, he was earliest affected by the popular, publicized, and, on the whole, "sensational" aspects of Freudian theory. Although his acquaintance with Freud dated from 1910, and he read the *Interpretation of Dreams* in English in 1915,[14] his difficulty in reading German virtually confined his direct knowledge of Freud to the fortuitous appearance of translations before the twenties. On the other hand, he was aided by his association with practicing psychoanalysts and no doubt benefited from conversations with them. Among his earliest friends were Dr. G. B. Wilbur, first a Rankian and then a Freudian; Dr. Grayson McCouch, a Freudian; and Dr. John Taylor, a semi-Freudian. Later, he would be influenced by Jung through Henry A. Murray. Indeed, Aiken still maintains close contact with these men, and in a sense he has always written for their inspection, according to approved psychoanalytic principles. *Among the Lost People* is dedicated to Dr. McCouch. In this sense, he "grew up with and even *in* the psychoanalytic movement."[15] By the thirties, however, Aiken had managed to fit Freud into his own belief in the extension and evolution of man's consciousness. Freud was to be a hero, but not a master, in this epic.

In any case, in his early poetry Aiken was chiefly influenced by Freud's attitude that art, like the dream, results from the suppression, or superfluity, of sexual impulses. Through fantasy art discharges the complexes thereby produced. Curiously, Aiken first received even this idea not from Freud but from Remy de Gourmont, as he indicated in a letter of 1915 entitled "What is Poetry?" Following the French critic, he wrote that the most important single instinct of civilized man is the "Will to Illusion." He defined poetry, accordingly, as "the will to illusion explicit as a praise of life."[16] In short, art serves to conceal the reader's disabilities by allowing him to indulge in cunningly contrived fantasies.

It is clear how from this definition he could postulate the tastes of the common man as his touchstone in the judgment of art. Obviously, the vulgar require vicarious experience quite as intensely as the sophisticated. The logical consequence of this theory is clear. If art is to be judged by its success in the performance of its psychological function, then the pulp magazine is as valuable as *The Divine Comedy*—perhaps even more valuable in the sense that it more widely fulfills its purposes. In *Blue Voyage* (1927) Aiken developed this view of art at length—although it must be remembered that it is here presented as part of the psychic problem of his protagonist, who argues: "If we take a functional view of art, as we must, then everything becomes relative; and the shilling shocker or smutty story, which captivates Bill the sailor, is giving him exactly the escape and aggrandizement, and therefore *beauty*, that *Hamlet* gives to you or me. The equation is the same. What right have you got, then, to assume that *Hamlet* is 'better' than *Deadeye Dick*? On absolute grounds, none whatever" (215). The inevitable conclusion for the poet is that rather than decreasing the value of his art, the employment of the typical materials of "the shilling shocker or smutty story" will add to the universality of his work. On one level of the poem he will simply use these materials to satisfy naïve tastes; on another, he will illustrate, for more complex and sophisticated tastes, how these are part of the fact of existence. In both cases, he will have enriched experience and enlarged awareness.

From this theory came the inspiration for both *Turns and Movies* and *The Jig of Forslin*.[17] The former poem consists of twenty-five sections. It begins in narrative, or, more precisely, in the narration of a monologue, and moves finally to the dramatic monologue directly presented. *Turns and Movies* is the first major example of Aiken's series poems. While each of the poems in the sequence investigates a new figure, Aiken intends to effect emotional unity, since all of the pieces are portraits of a single vaudeville troupe. Aiken has always had a curious personal interest in the theatre. Theatrical imagery has appeared in his work from *Earth Triumphant* (1914) to *A Letter from Li Po* (1955). During the second decade Aiken habituated vaudeville at the Boston Orpheum. He followed the vaudeville circuits very closely for three years, during 1914 to 1917, even reviewing performances occasionally for the *Boston Advertiser*. In a recording made in 1962 for the Third Programme, Aiken has described vaudeville in Boston during this period:

> At Boston we had any number of theatres ranging from the really rather highbrow and slightly snobbish Keiths down to the relatively vulgar low, of which there were two in Boston. And then below that to a series of nickelodeons, honky-tonks and a variety of burlesque houses which were a mixture of Vaudeville and song-and-dance. And it was wonderful. I got to know particularly the Loew circuit so well that I could anticipate practically every act before I saw it. And in those days the *Boston Transcript*, celebrated by Mr. Eliot, always listed on its front page under the entertainments column— "Turns and Movies"; which of course was where I got my title.

From this experience Aiken drew materials for some of his
stories—for instance, "Pure as the Driven Snow," "The Last
Visit," and "The Woman Hater"; the portraits in *Turns and
Movies* take their origin in real performers—"Bain's Cats and
Rats" only slightly misnames an actual act called "Swain's Rats
and Cats." Reviewing Gilbert Seldes's *The Seven Lively Arts*
in 1924, Aiken demonstrated his extensive and sympathetic interest in the various arts of Charlie Chaplin, Jim Europe, Irene
Castle, Al Jolson, and Bert Savoy. In his poems he uses the
sordid realities of vaudeville performers in contrast to the grandeur of the illusions which they embody and can symbolize.
He sees the irony when reality and illusion become inseparable—
as in the poem entitled "Vaudeville" which, though written in
1915, was not published until 1935:

> He kissed her mouth, and felt her tremble;
> Music came round them with a beating tumult;
> Madness of wings was on that air.
> And then the expected cry came from the door:—
> They started apart, turning, feigning terror:—
> A bullet smashed the glass; a woman screamed.
>
> .   .   .   .
>
> She thought she never loved him half so much
> As in that scene,—it made love seem so wicked.[18]

In *Turns and Movies* he writes wholly of such intermingling
of reality and illusion. And by analyzing a unified group in its
multiform aspects, he endeavors to reveal not merely the individual, but the collective consciousness of man. The minor narrative connections which occur between parts serve, first, as means
of economy and, second, are intended to furnish the poem
with a unified narrative framework. For instance, Zudora is
mentioned in Sections I, V, and VII; and the Russian dancer
of whom Amorosa is jealous in VIII is praised by the cornet
player in the ironic idyll of X. Although the ostensible themes

of the poems are varied, they all occur at moments when the inner consciousness is in revolt against, or is frustrated by, the facts of experience; or when the ego is vibrating in passionate unison with the senses. An example of frustration by reality is "Boardman and Coffin":

> I told him straight, if he touched me, just once more,—
> That way, you know,—I'd kill him. And I did.
> Why shouldn't I? I told him straight I would. (xiv, 16)

And of lyrical unity with the senses:

> We are alone in an immensity of sunlight,
> Specks in an infinite golden radiance,
> Whirled and tossed upon cataracts and silent torrents.
> (xiii, 16)

More characteristic of the series as a whole, however, is Aiken's presentation of a personality or state of mind perverted by experience—often, as in "The Apollo Trio" and "Bain's Cats and Rats," with an implicit suggestion as to the resultant psychic wound. Most striking, perhaps, is the ventriloquist's narrative, which relates

> how, at his father's funeral, he threw his voice
> Suddenly into the coffin; and all the mourners
> Jumped from their seats and ran, and women fainted,
> And the preacher stopped the service, white as wax.

> Zudora said a friend of hers had seen him
> Mooning alone at 'Carmen.' And at the end
> He cried like a baby: what do you think of that. (v, 7)

In this, the usual method of the poem, Aiken poses as an objective observer and recorder; he does not actually enter into an analysis of motivation, but circumspectly provides the reader with details whereby, if he wishes, he may himself conduct the analysis.

30

Certainly, *Turns and Movies* represents a clear advance in Aiken's realism over the Nietzschean sentimentality of the *Earth Triumphant* poems. Earlier, in "Youth," he could write:

> In crowds the harlots came,
> They laughed, they sang, they moved so free from shame,
> So frank in lust! These creatures knew life's taste,
> They danced it night and day, no hour to waste. (E.T., 91)

But in *Turns and Movies* he achieved a deeper understanding of the facts of experience and of human frustration. He has replaced a Nietzsche understood via Mencken with a Freud correctly understood. No longer repeating Zarathustra's doctrines, he imitates the vigor of Nietzsche's mind. We can see him moving, perhaps unconsciously, from the external to the internal narrative, from plot to meditation, from action to motive—and thus toward *The Jig of Forslin* and the poems which followed:

> She will not turn to him—will not resist.
> Impassive, she submits to being kissed. (VII, 8)

And again:

> She moved, and touched his knee,
> And when he kissed her, hated him, but
>   kissed him, passionately. (XI, 13)

It is a tragic understanding—the discovery not of the superman, but of the wasteland, within and without himself.

The chief defect of *Turns and Movies* lies in its formal limitations. Aiken has always insisted, and has been a more richly rewarding poet for the insisting, upon the variability of man's identity—that his identity consists chiefly in his motion. But in these poems he presents, instead, moments which, because they are frozen for analysis, are falsified. His desire to diagnose modern man leads him also to present abnormality and aberration too exclusively in the *Turns and Movies* poems. Perhaps in these, his first real attempts at brief psycho-realistic portraits, he assumed that he could find his drama in abnormality. This, as he knew, was Browning's strategy in "Porphyria's Lover" and "Johannes Agricola," and he adopted the same approach. But just as Browning could also dramatize moments of intense (though "normal") perplexity, moments of action, or of historical significance, so also Aiken would soon learn to discover drama in even the most commonplace of facts or events. The larger plan of *The Jig of Forslin* was to provide a form in which Aiken could achieve the complexity of design prefigured in "Disenchantment" and expressed in the preface to *The Charnel Rose*. And he could combine this with the psychological insights gained from *Turns and Movies*.

In the fall of 1915, a few months after he completed *Turns and Movies*, Aiken wrote a second series of vaudeville poems which he entitled *The Tinsel Circuit* or, as he wrote on the manuscript above this title, "Landscapes, Preludes, Portraits, and Blues." Although some of its sections have appeared separately, this poem has never been published in its entirety, as a unit, and exists only in manuscript. As in his earlier *Turns and Movies* poems, Aiken deals with lives frustrated by experience, or with the ego confronting the horror of its own emptiness. Of the woman in "Front Row," for instance, the impersonal narrator asks:

> What was it like, that unknown world of hers—
> Those endless streets, in which no lamps were lighted
> And no doors ever opened, and no voice heard?

Nearly all of the *personae* possess such endless streets. Some avoid these in alcohol or indifference; others are able to face themselves, if only momentarily, in their dreams. The woman animal-trainer, for example, in "Violet and Leopards"—

> Now, in her dreams, she sees raw meat being torn,
> And hears the cracking of bones, and a harsh purring—

32

So near, it seems to rise from her own torn heart;
And amorous soft green eyes smile up from blood.

In its variety of viewpoint, rhythm, rhyme schemes, attitude, and tone, *The Tinsel Circuit* resembles the symphonies—with the running of the poetic gamut as their principle—more than *Turns and Movies* did, and seems to be the bridge between them. In *The Tinsel Circuit*, as in his symphonies, Aiken extends his individual subject to encompass multiplicity. "Flute: 'Silent' Picture" makes concrete what is, at its best, the metaphor implicit in both vaudeville series. The collective consciousness investigated in these poems is to represent and explain the individual. In a moment of tired vision the flutist understands:

That all this huge hot theatre, full of faces
Pale in the yellow light, was nothing more
Than the high cavern of an enormous brain:
And this bright screen was the small retina
Whereon brief images, from a world outside,
Silently quivered; and all these huddled people
Were thoughts, perhaps, or dreams, or recollections.

In *Forslin* and the poems that followed Aiken would reverse this equation, beginning with the individual and resolving him into the worlds and universes which he contains.

· I V ·

In *Blue Voyage* Demarest argues that since man's consciousness has been so widened and deepened by psychology and anthropology, the old unities and forms of literature are no longer adequate, and must be replaced by a fragmentary, implicative presentation of his shifting mental states and emotions. With the possible (but minor) exception of "Evensong," *Forslin* (1916) is the first of the poems in which this is actually accomplished. "The attempt has been made," Aiken wrote in its preface, "to relate these typical [wish-fulfillment] dreams, or

vicarious adventures, not discretely, but in flux" (C.P., 866).
"Forslin," he explained in the 1949 preface to *Senlin*, is a
"portmanteau of the Latin words *forsan* and *fors* . . . [and]
means either chanceling or weakling" (C.P., 870). Since this is
the (symbolic) name that the protagonist adopts as he enters
the subconscious, we are to understand from the outset that because of his weakness, Forslin seeks particularly strong and frequent compensations in the daydream. Aiken had already formulated and used in such *Advocate* stories as "The Wallet" (1908)
and "The Cat and the Mouse" (1909) characters who similarly
lived in their dreams of fulfillment. Forslin's ineptitude makes
the larger plan of this poem possible, for it allows Aiken to
include a wide range of vicarious experience in one figure. That
this is a formal improvement over both *The Charnel Rose*,
which has no characterizable protagonist, and *Turns and
Movies*, which has too many, is obvious from the very beginning of the poem.

The first part of *Forslin* defines the structure of the whole
poem. We find Forslin sitting, at evening, in his "small bare
gaslit room," already on the verge of entering his dreams, symbolized in the image of the aquarium which extends so that he
can "reach out his hands, and swim" (55). Aiken's method in
Forslin is expressly psychoanalytic. Freud has spoken of the
random drift of mind which the analyst encourages in his patient as a method of bringing unconscious impulses to consciousness; here, Forslin's mind drifts at random on his way down to
the unconscious:

Coffee-cups and artificial palm-trees;
Cigarette-tips glowing in the shadows;
And the mellow gleams in polished marble floors.

.   .   .   .   .

The eyes of women, the fans, the jewelled fingers,
The soon-checked smiles, the swift words lost in laughter,

Coffee and cigarettes . . . He sat alone.
The sea of twilight swept his heart again. (56)

His mind sweeps onward, recalling fragments of his past vicarious experiences, first as a murderer, then as a man who committed suicide—heroically—by holding his breath. "Was I that
man?" he asks, but can answer only: "How should I know?/
Yet when I die, that man will die with me" (57). Once he has
raised the question of identity, Forslin prepares anew for identification with other figures. Stimulated by sensational stories
in the newspaper which lies before him—particularly by the
photograph of a juggler who has also committed suicide—he
loses his own personality ("I am spread upon a fog and know
no place" [58]) and immediately after, fully achieves identity
with the juggler:

> When I was young, juggling was all I did:
> I was the best of them;
> But growing older, I wanted something better.
> To do the impossible! (58)

And so follows the monologue of Forslin as the juggler who accomplishes the impossible, only to be frustrated because no one
recognizes the magnitude of his accomplishment. But before
Forslin can proceed, in his suicide, to a final identification with
the juggler, his own world intrudes once more. A light in another building goes out, and he returns, in the inevitably contrasting lyric passage, to the general level of the "coffee-cups
and artificial palm-trees," the world of artificial glamor:

I have spent years at something; and I am tired.
Let us lounge in a bright café, and listen to the music—
Music, threading the smoke of cigarettes . . .
Vermouth, then coffee . . . How much shall we tip the waiter?
Here the fatigued mind wanders and forgets. (61)

His vicarious identification with the juggler interrupted, Forslin seems scarcely to remember his daydream. Yet, as before, he attempts to recapture the wish-fulfillment satisfaction it gave him by considering the successive possibilities of past experiences: "But was that I? . . . Or was it I? . . . Or was it I?" he asks of several figures. Finally, he returns to the story of the juggler, completing it in his vicarious suicide. There follows, again, a return to the "bright café"—although now, in contrast to and in compensation for his desolate experience of suicide, Forslin not only drinks coffee, but (in a lyric section) also assumes an attitude of sophisticated ennui and "Sips a cordial, or asks his partner the time. / He straightens his cuffs, flicks off an ash, is silent" (64). So the poem continues, through his vicarious experiences with harlots, lamias, vampires, murderers, the Virgin, Salome, Judas, Cleopatra, and Helen of Troy. After every adventure he returns to full or partial consciousness, asking the inevitable question of self-identity:

> Suddenly I awake,
> And hear familiar voices, just as though
> I had dozed a second and missed a word or two.
> I see the familiar street-lamps gleam,
> Or find myself sitting, as long ago,
> In the same café among the people I knew,—
>
> .   .   .   .   .
>
> And I am amazed, I do not know
> If this is I, who drink Vermouth,
> Or whether that was I who rode the air. (101)

Rapid though this explication has been, it should suggest that by alternating and combining his lyrical and dramatic styles in *Forslin*, Aiken has also managed to fuse the two themes which they represent. As a whole, the poem is an exhibition of an ego creating itself luxuriously by imagining the fulfillment of all its secret wishes. The nature of Forslin's identification in each situation leads to a revelation of his (and so, also, man's) ego and a definition of its impulses. The consequent revelations, in turn, produce, or are intended to produce, a greater degree of self-awareness in both the hero and the reader. Forslin's own self-awareness does not, of course, increase substantially. The weakness of his character virtually eliminates the possibility that he will perceive the emptiness of his existence. He is aware only that he has moved towards self-knowledge, that "I have climbed stairs with a candle between my palms / To seek the eternal secret behind a door" (102). The reader, on the other hand, is able to observe the self in the process of its own creation. In understanding Forslin—so Aiken hopes—the reader will come to understand himself.

Aiken defines his protagonist by the illusions in which Forslin seeks compensation. But he also attempts to transcend the merely individual ego by dramatizing Forslin in terms of several *personae*. Although all the figures in the poem are a part of Forslin—and therefore define and create him—they also, taken separately, achieve independent selfhood. Many are developments out of Aiken's earlier poetry; others spring from the poets Aiken had read: the juggler and his imagery of the theatre are made possible by the narratives of *Turns and Movies*; Forslin's associations with harlots, by "Dust in Starlight" (1914); the murders and violence in the poem, by "Youth"; the "Salome" section perhaps drew upon a hint in Eliot's "Prufrock"; and the "Vampire" tale comes from, as Aiken indicates, Gautier's *La Morte Amoureuse*. Taken together, these figures and the episodes in which they participate form a composite consciousness in which Forslin can indulge. We may put it this way: Forslin's (and, to a degree, Aiken's) dramatizations of other selves are his means of creating his own ego—as if he has no other being beyond his successive identifications. In this fashion Aiken seeks to reveal at once both the individual and the generic ego—the dual concern of the major poetry which followed *Forslin*.

37

· V ·

One critic complained that *The Jig of Forslin* contains "a disproportionate abundance of harlotry." Indeed, in his early poems Aiken achieved a reputation for erotic sensationalism.[19] But while he emphasized the erotic compulsions of the daydream, Aiken also included in *Forslin* a wide range of not only sexual but also aesthetic and ethical experiences. In the symphonies which follow—with the exception of the luxurious dissection scene in *The Pilgrimage of Festus*—Aiken strives even less to dazzle his reader with violent eroticism and more to amaze him with understanding.

Although this shift in emphasis is manifest in *The House of Dust* (1920), the poem nevertheless exhibits a clear continuity with *Forslin*. At the pinnacle of his illusions, Forslin conceived himself to be divinely omnipresent, imagining (in v, 7) that the entire city is revealed to him:

> The walls of the city are rolled away;
> And suddenly all the lighted rooms are bare,
>
> .   .   .   .   .
>
> Thousands of secret lives, with unconcern,
> Yawn and turn. (112)

In *The House of Dust* Aiken fully investigated the possibilities of such a revelation of mass consciousness. Here he came to realize for the first time that in order to satisfy his sense of his and his fellows' collective humanity he must sweep inward to the full exploration and definition of the individual "I"—the situation of the poet who is writing the poem. Perhaps he was directed to the belief, on the one hand, by Andreyev's vision of mass consciousness in "The City," and, on the other, by Whitman's celebration of both the "simple, separate person" and the "democratic En-Masse."

Aiken, indeed, considered the poem as a means whereby the individual could participate emotionally in the poet's conscious-

ness. The poem, as it were, would "absorb" the presumed reader
and at the same time enable him to transcend the confines of
his solitary ego. Aiken made this notion clear in his original
preface to *The House of Dust*. In his 1948 preface, written for
the University of Georgia Press edition of *The Divine Pilgrim*
(1949), Aiken noted that the original preface to the poem had
been lost many years before. It has since, however, reappeared.
In 1948 he could look back upon the emergence of a pattern for
the later poetry in *The House of Dust*; but in 1917-1918, when
he wrote the original preface, he was trying to prepare his readers for the effects that he was then hoping to achieve. Since it
has never been printed, I give the preface in full:

Prefaces which attempt to explain are perilous affairs: in
consequence I shall not try here to explain the House of Dust,
but shall content myself with merely extending an invitation.
This may seem an odd proceeding. What I mean especially
to invite the reader to do is that he should enter the House
of Dust as casually and as self-forgetfully as he would enter
into the hearing of a longish piece of orchestral music: that
he should surrender to it as freely as he would, say, to a strange
city to which he had come for the spending of a holiday:
that he should accept it naively, in a sense, and not too seriously perplex himself, if he does not wish, with what he suspects are its philosophical or psychological meanings. I should
like him, if he can, to regard the House of Dust as a small
sort of world-in-itself to which he has been given the key for
as long or short a stay, as curious or cursory an inspection, as
he desires. The implications of it will indeed most readily be
caught if this be his attitude, for these will not be found in
the particular phrase or line or even in the particular movement, but rather, as is true of music, in the totality of emotional and sensory effect, the balancing of episode and episode, mood and mood, overtone and overtone, to produce
through diversity in unity a final impression which is rather

to be apperceived than analyzed, and which, on the first reading, will be the more vividly found in proportion as it is less
perplexedly sought. Am I not, in asking him to do this, simply
asking him to preserve in the presence of this adventure something of the attitude which he usually assumes towards the
adventure of life itself? Our lives are from moment to moment improvisations for the most part, adventures in the un-
foreseen and often ambiguous, and it is only in retrospect
that we take up the then somewhat frozen fragments of it for
the future delight of analysis and understanding. I merely ask
the reader, therefore, to postpone this analysis, and first of all
simply to live,—if it be found possible!—in this poem, no
more nor less intelligently and receptively than he would live,
let us say, in crossing a park at dusk . . . It is growing dark:
between and above the trees, among which people are heard
walking, the lights of mysterious houses can be seen. We
move towards them. What is it that life has in store for us?

As we shall come to understand, this "invitation" has its roots
in the notion of consciousness which Aiken develops in this
poem. While the preface seems to direct the reader toward the
same satisfaction that he might have derived from the affective
symbolism of the *Nocturne of Remembered Spring* poems,
Aiken has now carefully provided his poem with a sound basis
for the "philosophical or psychological" meanings to which he
refers. In his comparison of the individual mind to the collective
consciousness of the city—both Eliot and W. C. Williams were
later to adopt this strategy—Aiken is able to move in two dimensions, inward and outward, from the personal ego to its
luminous contacts with other selves and the world; and from
these, back again to the self.

Four motifs are implied by such an investigation as he conducts in *The House of Dust*. As Aiken wrote to Babette
Deutsch: "mortality is one motif, crowd-awareness another, the
inter-relation of the crowd and the individual a third," and the

fourth, an expression of the poet's identity "in terms of a huge panorama of scenes, actions and opinions."[20] The poem progresses from external, mainly dramatic themes—those which attempt to portray the individuals who combine to form the city —to the inner, lyric theme, in the meditation of the poet who attempts to understand both the city and himself. Thus, like *Forslin, The House of Dust* combines and interrelates Aiken's two themes. The methods of the two poems, consequently, are also similar. Their difference lies in the fact that the earlier poem makes its approach immediately from within, while the later one begins in the outward contemplation of the city in general: from (section i) the vantage point of "the high bright window in a tower" (116), to (ii) the less general but still unrelated and fragmentary narration of incidents occurring in the city. Not until the third section does the narrative move from the multicellular and impersonal "we" to the meditative "you" as the observation of the crowd is succeeded by concentration upon the interrelation of the crowd and the individual. This two-level analysis comes to center in iii, 9, upon the particular relation of the reader (the crowd) to the poet (the individual). As the *persona* of his own poem, Aiken seeks to reconstruct his literary development so that the reader may understand him as he understands himself and his role:

> You tried, as I remember,
> One after one, strange cults, and some, too, morbid,
> The cruder first, more violent sensations,
>
> .   .   .   .   .
>
> Then, by degrees,—
> Savoring all more delicate gradations
> In all that hue and tone may play on flesh,
> Or thought on brain,—you passed, if I may say so,
> From red and scarlet through morbid greens to mauve.
> Let us regard ourselves, you used to say,
> As instruments of music. (161)

41

Within the poem, that is to say, he supplies the reader with the information necessary to read the poem correctly. Moving ever inward in his narrative, Aiken at last speculates upon how far one can know both others and oneself. In *Forslin* he had asserted that the individual contains multitudes. Now, in *The House of Dust* he extends the comparison of the ego to a city to show further that the collective ego receives its most felicitous expression in the individual who perceives it.

The advancement of *The House of Dust* over his earlier poems lies in Aiken's attempt, in the last section, to achieve consciously the full dimensions of self-revelation, and, therefore, self-knowledge. The speaker of the monologue, originally called "Palimpsest: The Deceitful Portrait," defines his attempt at the beginning as he compares the mind to a house:

> Suppose I try to tell you
> The secrets of this house, and how I live here;
> Suppose I tell you who I am, in fact.
> Deceiving you—as far as I may know it—
> Only so much as I deceive myself. (180)

From the beginning of his career Aiken identified, apparently, the house with the person, its rooms with his ego. As early as 1911, in "The Clerk's Journal," he wrote:

> Your heart's a house—sometimes you go
> Into old rooms you scarcely know
>
> .   .   .   .   .
>
> Old papers, boxes, dust, are there;
> The broken relics of the years
> Too cold and sunless grown for tears.

Senlin says of himself: "I am a room, a house, a street, a town" (205). Even as late at 1950 Aiken planned to title his autobiography *Rooms, Streets, and Houses*. We may be fairly certain of the psychological source of this pervasive image. In an essay written for the *Advocate* in 1910, called "On Moving House,"

Aiken improvised on the importance of the house to the child. He identified himself with his houses, probably, in an attempt to re-establish the security which he had lost with the death of his parents. In *The House of Dust* he continues the comparison and makes it the center of his poem:

> Once, on a sun-bright morning,
> I walked in a certain hallway, trying to find
> A certain door: I found one, tried it, opened,
> And there in a spacious chamber, brightly lighted,
> A hundred men played music. (178)

Throughout his poem the poet, as hero, opens one door after another in search of the elusive principle of his own being. Finally in IV, 3 he has learned enough, absorbed enough, to attempt to understand and reveal himself fully. The primary goal of all of Aiken's work is self-knowledge. For the epigraphs of both *Blue Voyage* and *Ushant* Aiken quoted lines from Coleridge's "Self-Knowledge" in order to make his own purposes clear. The definitive form of his search is the monologue or the "letter to the world," in which he attempts to explain the compulsions which make that search desirable—even necessary—in the life of man.

Most important in this final section of *The House of Dust* is the theory of consciousness which Aiken develops. He says that although we live in crowds, we know little of them; we see only "the small bright circle of our consciousness, / Beyond which lies the dark" (178). The question in *The Charnel Rose* of *how* to be is refined to the question of whether one can, in any other than a solipsistic sense, *be* at all. One must learn to transcend the "small bright circle" of personal consciousness to understand and encompass the collective view of the "high bright window" in the tower. If the poet cannot move beyond the confines of his individual ego, how can he reveal the consciousness of man in general? Not until he had written his early stories and *Blue Voyage* would Aiken be able to formulate an adequate

43

answer; but in *The House of Dust*, under the influence of Henry James, he at least defines and investigates the problem. Two years after the poem appeared, Aiken wrote that James conceived of the individual human being "as standing, like a lighthouse, at the centre of his small bright circle of consciousness." Consciousness, he says, is primarily an affair of relations. Figuratively, only when another individual comes so close that the two bright circles of awareness overlap, sharing a segment in common, is there any possibility of self-revelation between them. And, he continues, we can conceive of "our two individuals as staring, fascinated, at that small segment, with its double light, and as approaching each other, or withdrawing from each other, to watch, in that segment, the permutations of shape and light —living, so to speak, almost wholly in their awareness of the consciousness shared, and having little awareness apart from that."[21] Such a theory of consciousness—whose emphasis is upon the various luminous contacts of separate selves, whose interest is in the relational rather than the individuated—provides the theory which underlies the two themes whose presence in Aiken's poetry I have been describing. In the one, the ego delves into its own mysteries. And in the other, it confronts other selves in order to cast light on both humanity and the person—or, as in *The House of Dust*, upon the city and the mind which can absorb and recreate it. The mind, in this reversal in relations, is itself created by its compounding with the city:

> You see me moving, then, as one who moves
> Forever at the centre of his circle:
> A circle filled with light. And into it
> Come bulging shapes from darkness, loom gigantic,
> Or huddle in dark again. A clock ticks clearly,
> A gas-jet steadily whirs, light streams across me;
> Two church bells, with alternate beat, strike nine;
> And through these things my pencil pushes softly
> To weave grey webs of lines on this clear page. (182-83)

Still, full revelation of self is not yet possible, and the poet-protagonist confesses finally: "for all my best intentions, / Once more I have deceived you" (186). Although the author, as the ultimate "I," gets into the poem at the final step in the process from general to particular, he can only explore—not wholly reveal—himself. Attempts at self-revelation are always preludes, never completed; success predicates the superhuman consciousness which Aiken wants to evolve towards, but could not yet even attempt to portray. As he wrote in its 1948 preface, *The House of Dust* is concerned with "the evolution of man's consciousness, ever widening and deepening and subtilizing his awareness, and in his dedication of himself to this supreme task, man possesses all that he could possibly require in the way of a religious credo: when the half-gods go, the gods arrive: he can, if he only will, become divine" (C.P., 869). Aiken came more and more to realize that in order to trace, and so accelerate, the evolution of consciousness he must first come to know, then to reveal himself. He was to attempt, in the poems that followed, to focus so steadily upon that "small, bright circle of consciousness" that man himself might be illuminated.

In *Senlin*, Aiken returns to a purely lyrical example of the self-creating ego. But now the dramatic problems of *The Charnel Rose* have been resolved: *Senlin* assumes a protagonist kept constantly before us, as in *Forslin*, by his intermittent returns to actuality. Senlin's "concreteness" is established in the matter-of-fact observation and emphatic sensory confirmations of the first two lines: "Senlin *sits* before us, and we *see* him. / He *smokes* his pipe before us, and we *hear* him" (195; my italics). The dramatic situation of the first two parts is best taken to be the same as in "Laughter": in the mirror the protagonist confronts Senlin, "the little old man," which each of us must become. Aiken was to use the mirror throughout his career to symbolize self-confrontation. The metaphor occurs in *Blue Voyage, Great*

Circle, "A Letter," several of the Preludes, and very importantly in *King Coffin* and "Dear Uncle Stranger."

In a recent poem, Aiken has employed this trope in slightly different form—as the dialogue between "The Old Man and the Shadow." Again, he investigates his own ego; the conscious invades and absorbs the preconscious self. Speculating on death, we come to terms with the principle of our being. He sees the shadow as "my ancient familiar," always constant, yet ever shifting shapes, assuming various guises and disguises, like an "old chameleon, protean ghost"; but the poet must always come to terms with his own identity:

> Old hieroglyph!
> Your name is written indelibly in the innocence of light:
> innumerable and ingenious have been your disguises:
> but in the end I always unmask you:
> and in the end I am always afraid.

In such poems as "Laughter" and *Senlin* at the very beginning, and "The Old Man and the Shadow" at the end of his career, the protagonist and his ego, youth and age, life and death, the conscious and unconscious self, are inextricably combined, *"pari passu pari passu."* The lyrical intensity consists in the discovery of this relation, as the ego is known, understood, and, at last, accepted:

> The Shadow / Perhaps we are functions, one of the other?
>   A conceit of light?
> The Old Man / Yes, it is true, you were always the intruder.
>   But nevertheless how can we speak of intrusion?
>   For which comes first, the light or the shadow?
>   And who am I to pretend to be light?
>   Together conceived, together created in synthesis,
>   shadow conspiring with light and light with shadow,
>   the rose a promise in the invisible
>   and the invisible a premise of the rose.[22]

So also, in *Senlin: A Biography*, Senlin is his ego as the protagonist confronts it in his introspective gaze into the mirror.
Thus it is inevitable and foreseeable, that the poem should conclude with the realization that "This was no man at all, /
a dream we dreamed" (222). Untermeyer observed correctly:
"The person acts as the background, the unconscious becomes
the hero."[23] The unnamed protagonist's speculations upon what
"Senlin" is and what he contains create, in dramatic sequence,
his "Dark Origins," his "Futile Preoccupations," and his
"Cloudy Destiny"; and as these receive elaboration, the "Senlin"
in the mirror disappears and the series of images which symbolize him pass into view. He is resolved into his constituent
parts by the self which speculates upon him. Only intermittently
does Senlin himself hold the stage: his emotions, his perceptions, his dreams—these are the concerns of the poem.

Each section of the poem falls into four parts. First, we are
presented with a portrait of Senlin in some physical action—
swinging his arms, smoking meditatively, looking at trees,
and so on. Next, he begins to speculate upon his action,
usually in the form of a question: "Did I, then, stretch from
the earth like these?" (196), "Is it my childhood there?" (199),
"Does a blade of grass have Senlin for a name?" (203). Third,
his speculation passes into the symbols and visualized images
which it evokes, and Senlin fades from the scene. From his immersion in his flowing consciousness, Senlin achieves a perception of part of his identity. This is usually the longest, and the
most fundamentally dramatic section of the four. Finally, we
return to physical actuality as Senlin continues his original action. He then moves on to do something else, and the process
begins anew. The best of these scenes is perhaps Senlin's "rus-
tling among his odds and ends of knowledge" (201), seeking to
find his identity in tradition or history. Implicitly, the mind is
compared to a pyramid—a variant upon *The House of Dust*
theme—and the layers of the pyramid, room by room, are
stripped away, until we reach the burial room and the sarcopho-

gus; coffins inside coffins are removed, then finally the "scented wrappings" of "Cleopatra or Senebtisi":

> And now the body itself, brown, gaunt, and ugly,
> And the hollow skull, in which the brains are withered,
> Lie bare before us. Princess, is this all?
> Something there was we asked that was not answered. (202)

Again the quest fails; for personal identity is too elusive to be confined to mere tradition—either historically (as here) or biologically, as in 1, 2. Thus, the symbols in the mirror dissolve, and Senlin once more appears, laughing and lighting his pipe.

The third major movement of the poem begins after Senlin himself has disappeared from the mirror, as Aiken's shift to the past tense indicates: "Senlin sat before us and we heard him. / He smoked his pipe before us and we saw him" (219). His search has been futile; and even insofar as it succeeded, it was incommunicable. In his successive identifications with "Nuns, murderers, and drunkards, saints and sinners, / Lover and dancing girl and sage and clown" (205), Senlin meant to symbolize the various aspects of his identity—and to present thereby:

> simple truths he found no way to explain.
> He spoke, but found you could not understand him—
> You were alone, and he was alone. (221)

Here, in his unwillingness to formulate the "ultimate" answers to the problems of self-knowledge and in his hesitancy to postulate an essence for the ego, Aiken achieved the complete freedom from dogmatism which he henceforth was to consider essential in literature. After *Senlin*, Aiken's philosophy is openended, allowing full scope for what he came to see as the infinite possibilities of man. Much later, he would insist in the *Preludes for Memnon*:

> Jesus is not the spokesman of the Lord:
> Confucius neither, nor Nietzsche, no, nor Blake;
> But you yourself. (XLIX, 556)

He entertains all ideas—his mind plays seriously with them. Beginning with *Senlin*, he realized that "the winds of doctrine blow both ways at once" (L.P., 24)—all doctrine compounds truth with falsity. But the best kind of poem, whatever the doctrine it "uses," will be true if it is made honestly, with integrity: as a possibility, not as a dogma. "In poetry," as Allen Tate has written, "all things are possible—if you are man enough."[24] One of the faults of even *Forslin* and *The House of Dust* was that, at times, they resembled too much a demonstration—of the nature of man's imaginative life in the one, of the resemblance of a city to the mind in the other. Part of the satisfaction which Aiken no doubt intended to impart in them was in the reader's (and the poet's) seeing to what heights the wish-fulfillment could be carried, or how far a metaphor could be developed.

Senlin is Aiken's earliest complete achievement. In it he adjusts and perfects his earlier themes and methods. He came to see that as yet the search for self must remain inconclusive and thereby freed himself fully from mere demonstration. In *Senlin*, such demonstration is precluded by the inconclusiveness of the search. As one critic wrote: "For this poet there has never been an incarnation; the world is history-less, and there is just a flow of endless possibilities."[25] Senlin is an Argonaut of the Ideal. His search begins in its end; daily he walks forth into his own vastness.

· VI ·

The fifth of the Divine Pilgrim symphonies, *The Pilgrimage of Festus*, presents another such figure as Senlin, Forslin, and the poet of *The House of Dust*. Aiken has referred to the poem as "an essay in epistemology." While in all of the Divine Pilgrim poems Aiken attempts to investigate the source and principles of knowledge, in this, originally the last of these symphonies, he centers on this problem. In *The House of Dust* and *Senlin* we can watch the ego as it comes to know and re-create itself. In

Festus he seeks to determine how the self truly arrives—if it can —at such knowledge. At the very beginning of the poem, Festus sets out "joyously into the world of himself" (224); and the poem ends as this line is repeated, and he sallies out again upon the same search, "forgetting the long black aftermath of pain" (276). The significant difference between *Festus* and the earlier poems is that whereas their protagonists manage somehow to return to reality, the protagonist of *Festus* is inescapably locked within the confines of his ego. Festus declares: "I will not have a god who is myself" (258)—yet he is incapable of conceiving any other. His is the psychological solipsism which is an up-to-date analogue of Whitman's transcendental idealism; he, in fact, recalls Whitman:

Yet God, though no smaller he be than the shell of the world
No greater is, truly, than the green blade of grass. (265)

Even Festus's assertion that he has transcended the ego, if only by conceiving a god or a world, is defeated by his *doppelgänger*:

Ah, Festus, think how foolish would be that mirror
Which, gazing into itself,—if it could do so,—
And seeing a cloud, and blue sky, imaged there,
Cried out: 'Behold how nobler than other mirrors
Am I, who have here conceived a sky, a cloud,
And small birds flying in a blue depth of air!'
The mirror reflects all things that pass before it,
The mind conceives those things that made and move it.
(266-67)

Festus can have no issue: it is, as it had to be, the last of the Divine Pilgrim poems—for there the very idea of the pilgrimage itself becomes futile. The poet cannot transcend the ego where he conducts his search. "Changing Mind," which now serves as the *coda* to the series is obviously an addition to Aiken's original plan, and indicates his sense, as he developed, of what he could make his Divine Pilgrim mean. Festus's dialogue with his ego flickers out with: "Where are you? I am alone . . . I am alone" (273), and the poem ends with a repetition of its first seventy-four lines, as he starts out over again on the same search for experience for its own sake. While the earlier Divine Pilgrim poems certainly stressed the search rather than the goal, even in *Senlin* and *The House of Dust*—both of which end inconclusively—Aiken postulated the superhuman consciousness which will be able (in *Senlin*) to resolve itself into its constituent parts and thus create its identity, or (in *The House of Dust*) to achieve the detachment necessary to avoid deception in self-revelation.

The Divine Pilgrim poems point, at their best, toward such insights. Aiken wrote of his *persona* in *Ushant* that in "the final phase of evolution of man's mind itself to ever more inclusive consciousness: in that, and that alone, would he find the solvent of all things" (220). At the basis of Aiken's poetry has always been this consistent desire to promote the advancement of human consciousness. When his early poems fail in this endeavor, it is due to his too frequent reliance on the always ambiguous effects of mere "musical forms," the Sonata, the Nocturne, the Symphony. What is meant to be a journey succeeds only in becoming a dance. In *Festus*, Aiken experimented with the shimmering sensibility of a mind inextricably confined within itself. As he might himself say, therefore, he was poietic while avoiding the *sine qua non* of poetry. The plan of *Festus* does not imply evolution, but rather the repetition of an egocentric insight which can neither pass from itself to the world, nor from the world to itself. Since, as Aiken wrote in his preface, Festus discovers that "knowledge is inconclusive" (C.P., 872), the possibility of self-knowledge is repudiated. Aiken has frequently quoted Coleridge's line, "What hast thou, Man, that thou darst call thine own?" But in this poem, man possesses nothing—nothing at all; for Festus, like the lover in "Priapus and the Pool," dives through himself into the void of his own being:

51

But as a diver plunging down through sunlight
To meet his azure shadow on the wide water
Shatters through it and is gone,
Thus I, coming suddenly upon your ghost,
See it but cannot grasp it: it is lost.
I stand in the dark and call you. I am alone.

(IX, 392)

Even the loved one is only a reflection of the unsubstantial self. In denying his own divine awareness, man enters the dominion of what Aiken calls (in the Preludes) Lord Zero. And so ends his value. J. G. Fletcher commented that "Aiken is interested in the play of unconscious psychology within the individual, and within man in general; but [in *Festus*] the play itself has no other purport than its existence."[26]

An even more justifiable criticism of *Festus* is that the fictive imagination which had appeared so rich and inexhaustible in *Forslin* has here run out. Seen in the context of the poems which preceded it, *Festus* betrays in its author a poverty of experience available for articulation in poetry. Perhaps the very form of the symphony had exhausted the incidents which Aiken could embody in his Divine Pilgrim.

That Aiken constructed *Festus* from far fewer incidents than he did any of his earlier symphonies might, of course, not necessarily be a defect. One might even say that by his richer elaboration of incidents in *Festus* he has given the poem a stronger, because less fragmentary, structure than any previous one. The poem is deficient, nonetheless, in that its incidents resemble episodes used formerly in his other poems—most of all, those in *Senlin*. Aiken himself was apparently aware of this tendency in his work. As early as 1919, speaking of the "economy" of *Senlin*, he wrote: "One always praises economy when one is running out of funds" (C.P., 877). For instance, both Festus and Senlin smoke pipes—not so insignificant a detail, for in the structure of both poems Aiken uses the smoke to signify the dissolution of material reality in order that he may introduce the symbols of his protagonist's speculations. The *personae* of both *Senlin* and *Festus* confront their alter egos, and both forms are therefore dialogic. Both Senlin and Festus watch the passing of horse-drawn hearses; and both observe the same details: Senlin—"On the hard pavement ring the roofs, / The light wheels softly run" (199); Festus—"From the sound of hooves and wheels . . ." (245). Each protagonist generalizes upon the particular death: "It is as if his soul had become a city, / With noisily peopled streets, and through these streets / Senlin himself comes driving a small white hearse" (199); Festus observes "That this dark world he rules is a world of coffins; / The city he rules is a city of the listless dead" (245). In this latter metaphor, of course, *Festus* also derives from *The House of Dust*, in which the same comparison is developed at length. Also, the famous dissection scene in *Festus*—Aiken's most sensuous evocation of the futility of seeking essences—is similar to the Pyramid passage already quoted from *Senlin*, in which precisely the same search is made, with the same results:

Did we that loved you love but blood and sinew?

.   .   .   .   .

Look! your hands, which lovers desired to kiss,
Are bone and flesh, your eyes are jewels of water,
Your crimson pulse lies waste . . . The steel-blue tongues
Babble in blood, cry out in a chaos of silence,
Call you in vain! . . . (241)

This scene is perhaps even more similar to one in *The House of Dust*, II, 10—the reverie of the anaesthetist over a girl who has died under surgery:

'Number four—the girl who died on the table—
The girl with golden hair—'
The purpling body lies on the polished marble.
We open the throat, and lay the thyroid bare. (140)

Senlin's famous: "It is morning, Senlin says, and in the morning . . ." (205), is echoed in: " 'It is night-time,' Festus says, 'and in the night-time' . . ." (236). In one episode, Festus seeks the traditional gods, and he himself assumes the aspect of a god—just as Forslin had; both finally become identified with Christ. Then, in both cases (as also in *The Charnel Rose*), the search for divinity ends with the discovery of Satanic woman: Salome in *Forslin*, the incarnation of the eternal feminine in *Festus*.

Even in *Senlin* the reader can observe the beginnings of self-imitation. Senlin's speculations in II, 4, upon the possibilities of his being loved are perhaps somewhat out of place in the scheme of the poem, except insofar as they imply questions about the possibility of human contact:

> But . . . is it sure she tried to attract my attention?
> She leaned her elbow in a peculiar way
> There in the crowded room . . . she touched my hand . . .
> She must have known, and yet,—she let it stay. (209)

In a poem dated 1916, "Meditation on a June Evening," which consists of the after-the-fact meditation of a frustrated lover, the same incident is more appropriate:

> Smiling, you leaned, and let your body rest
> Trembling on mine, leaning your breast
> Softly against my arm; until my veins
> Cried out with music; it is no use, no use
> To say you could not know, you could not guess
> That brush of your hand against my hand.
>
> (N.R.S., 21)

Senlin's problem is uncertainty: "Perhaps, I thought, I misunderstand" (209), he says; the lover fears similarly: "You did not know, we'll say, / That I should misinterpret this, believe / More meant than was intended" (19).

54

Another such reiteration of ideas or images in the Divine Pilgrim poems is in Aiken's use of fortune-telling. He uses palm reading both in "Earth Triumphant" (E.T., 18) and "Innocence" (N.R.S., 82), the Tarot cards in *The Jig of Forslin* (68) and *The House of Dust* (131), and a medium in *The House of Dust* (175). In each case, the fortune-telling symbol is important in the poem and is developed at length.

In the series of Divine Pilgrim poems from *The Charnel Rose* to *Festus*, then, Aiken exhausted the range of imaginative experience which he could make effective in his poems, as well as the range of possibilities of the "symphonic" form. He had been able to write *Senlin* in three weeks. But now he began to write with effort. He wrote very few poems—only *John Deth* and a series of lyrics—between 1919 and 1928, although in the six years before 1919 he had written ten volumes of poetry. We know that in this early period he composed "always in shiny black exercise-books, with ruled lines, and in a pencilled handwriting so minute as to be almost indecipherable. These books," he has said, "seemed to exercise a peculiar magic of their own, they evoked, they elicited."[27] Perhaps these books exerted too much influence upon him; his poems were not exercises, but they were becoming one poem. Only theoretically were the variations that he might play upon both experience and the musical analogy inexhaustible. Even after his later success in the Preludes he would abandon their form and subject. If in *Festus*, and even in *Senlin*, he was the victim of his tendency towards self-imitation, in any later poems along the same lines we might have expected the tendency to increase. Then too, the movement of the Divine Pilgrim poems led to Festus's full isolation in the vault of his own ego. Aiken could not possibly portray a more isolated ego—and to move back, in another poem, to the kind of search of *The Charnel Rose* would have belied the (perhaps somewhat doubtful) value of this progress. What Aiken required at this stage of his development, then, was not another pilgrimage. He needed to create a new poetic form by exploring new ranges and depths of experience.

Whatever accidents made him write fiction seriously—he needed, for instance, the money he could earn thereby—other, stronger compulsions led him to write stories as and how he did. He felt compelled to make a statement more basic than his divine pilgrims could have made for him. After analyzing the predicaments of Forslin and Senlin as Everyman, he was coming to terms with the analyst himself. The effects of this were important. He would even change his method of composition, and "from composing reviews and criticism directly on the machine, [he] proceeded to compose fiction and poetry in the same way."[28] This change, as one would suppose, was occasioned and accompanied by a shift in subject. The one region he had not explored—except for the attempt at self-revelation in *The House of Dust*—was his own private consciousness. Although Aiken had been called "decadent" and "subjective" on occasion, his poems were by no means self-revelatory in the usual romantic sense. Absorbed by the lives he was engaged in creating, he had left his own life out of his poetry. In 1919, at the same time he was working on *Festus*, he could write: "In eighteen hundred and eighty-nine / Conrad Aiken crossed the line / In nineteen hundred and question mark / Aiken's window pane was dark," and then add, "I don't know what else there is to be added. . . . What a hell of a dull life I have had."[29] Ten years later, after his attempt in *Blue Voyage* "to escape the tyrant solipsism, and to know himself" (260), he would write in "Blues for Ruby Matrix":

> I have—what have I Ruby,
> if not a phrase of ice to carve on stone,
> ambiguous skeleton of a whisper, gone
> as soon as spoken, and myself alone? (616)

Myself alone—this, his fiction taught him, would be, if fully understood, all he would need.

56

· V I I ·

In addition to his symphonies, Conrad Aiken composed two important verse narratives prior to the publication of his first book of short stories. These are *Punch: The Immortal Liar* (1921), completed before *Festus*; and *John Deth* (1930), completed in 1924, the year before *Bring! Bring!*, his first book of stories, appeared. We can see, I think, that Aiken was searching for both a new area of experience and a new form for interpreting that experience. In his experimentation in fiction he found this new field of experience in his private awareness. In the Preludes, finally, he discovered the form whereby he might articulate his new awareness; but again, that form originates, as I shall show, in the fiction. Aiken's fiction, then, is important in his progress. In its form and intention, it is anticipated only by *The House of Dust*, where Aiken had sought the material for poetry in his own self-analysis. Important in this poem is not only Aiken's discussion of consciousness, but also, in III, 9, the letter written (perhaps by his *doppelgänger*) to the poet-protagonist. It somewhat critically describes Aiken's poetic and mental development. The letter begins:

You have been always, let me say, 'romantic,'—
Eager for color, for beauty, soon discontented
With a world of dust and stones and flesh too ailing:
Even before the question grew to problem
And drove you bickering into metaphysics.

.   .   .   .

And so you went
From subtle theme to subtler, each heard once,
Twice or thrice at the most, tiring of each;
And closing one by one your doors, drew in
Slowly, through darkening labyrinths of feeling,
Towards the central chamber . . . Which now you've
reached. (161)

Throughout, the writer viciously analyzes the faults of the protagonist. We here encounter the beginnings of a change in Aiken's poetic method—occasioned, as I think, by his need for new and firmer materials. In his attempt at self-analysis, Aiken reconstructs his ego with great patience and detail in order to see himself objectively. Here is neither the solitary self-creating ego, as in *Senlin*, nor the dramatization of other egos, as in *Turns and Movies*: it is a combination of both, an essay in dramatization by the ego of a self already created. Aiken was groping toward the elaboration of such a form, clearly, in *Festus*, but with unsatisfactory results. There he dramatized an ego previously manifest, but one which never really could assume the full measure of existence because it was snared in the tangles of its own speculations. Because he could never have meaning for himself, Festus can have little meaning for us.

The writer of the letter in *The House of Dust* had observed in its conclusion that "You lean on myth, and take more credit for it. / I stand alone . . . Well, I take credit, too" (163). To rely upon myth to give his characters validity; or to "stand alone" and attempt, by the force of will and imagination, to create, somehow, adequate embodiments of the search for self—these were his choices as they became clear to Aiken. Despite his abortive attempts at self-exploitation and definition in *The House of Dust*, it was natural to expect that Aiken would turn, in a new effort at dramatization, toward myth rather than a rigorous self-investigation; for the whole development of the symphonies presumes his use of vicarious and archetypal rather than actual and personal experience. And we must remember that even after *Punch*, in *Festus* he wrote a poem which he conceived not as self-exploration, but as an essay in epistemology, the myth of mankind. His two narrative poems, therefore, "leaned on myth." *Punch: The Immortal Liar* is based upon the Punchinello of the *Commedia dell'arte*, who became the hero of the Italian and English puppet stage; and *John Deth* is drawn from the medieval tradition, specifically from Holbein's paintings, of "The Dance of Death."

The pattern of *Punch* is similar to that of Browning's *The Ring and the Book*. Aiken defines Punch's character through his "objective" presentation of interrelated monologues, not by direct authorial comment. Perhaps the fact that both its form and subject were traditional brought *Punch* the best immediate reception of any of Aiken's poems. Amy Lowell wrote of it: "There has never been any question of Mr. Aiken's poetic ability, what he has needed hitherto was not a technique, but a subject; not the power to create a style, but a theme of sufficient weight for that style to act upon."[30] Certainly the narrative has a clearer movement than in any earlier poem. With regard only to dramatic coherence, both *Punch* and *John Deth* illustrate Aiken's advance toward the kind of narrative strength which he was soon to require for his fiction. Even the highly analytical language of *Punch* reflects Aiken's growing sense that the evocative, emotive language of the symphonies was inadequate to express and forward man's consciousness.

Most misunderstood has been Aiken's "philosophy" in *Punch*; for *Punch* is the one poem (despite some critics' claims for his value as a "philosophical poet")[31] in which there is a semblance of the development of a strictly philosophical thesis. Because Punch is literally a puppet—and is controlled, therefore, by forces outside himself—as its central character he gives the poem a deterministic basis. Far from avoiding the determinism implicit in the character of his protagonist, Aiken deliberately exploited it as an inextricable theme of the poem. Indeed, he makes Mountebank, the puppeteer, develop the thesis at length in the Epilogue:

I too am a puppet. And as you are a symbol for me
(As Punch is, and Sheba—bright symbols of intricate meanings,
Atoms of soul—who move, and are moved by, me—)
So I am a symbol, a puppet drawn out upon strings. (361)

59

There is no reason to conclude from this that Aiken contends he too is determined in writing his poem,[32] any more than one would want to argue that the monologue of the second old man proves the author to be superstitious. These are merely promontories from which the poet can view his experience and translate his ideas into actions. And if he treats experience as mysterious, luxurious (as in Punch's tales of the Queen of Sheba), ironical (as in Polly's monologue), or mechanistic, he is simply presenting the dramatic expression imaginatively appropriate to the character speaking.

Punch is more satisfactorily seen, as Kenneth Burke might say, as "the dancing of attitudes," the emotional conflict between two primary views of experience—the romantic and classical, especially as T. E. Hulme had defined and given wide circulation to them in his essay "Romanticism and Classicism." The romantic, Hulme says, assumes that "man was by nature good, that it was only bad laws and customs that had suppressed him. Remove all these and the infinite possibilities of man would have a chance." The classical attitude is exactly the opposite: "Man is an extraordinarily fixed and limited animal whose nature is absolutely constant. It is only by tradition and organisation that anything decent can be got out of him." Thus the romantic writer, because he thinks man infinite, stresses human potentiality; the classical author insists upon the limits of man. The characteristic metaphor of the romantic, Hulme says, is flight—"Hugo is always flying, flying over abysses, flying up into the eternal gases. The word infinite in every other line";[33] the definitive classical metaphor is perhaps that of the boundary.

However simplified and mischaracterized Hulme's descriptions may seem to us now, this was probably his most influential essay; and the contrast which he sets forth exactly characterizes the structure of *Punch*. In its title Aiken combines "Punch"— the puppet who is strictly subject to the limitations of his master (the puppet-maker, God) whom he reflects—with "The

60

Immortal Liar"—who, in the possibilities of his imagination, is infinite. I do not mean to imply, of course, that Aiken had Hulme's essay specifically in mind during the composition of *Punch*. Aiken simply balances the contrasting attitudes toward reality which Hulme had conveniently defined for his age. Moreover, these two views of experience may be found co-existent in much of Aiken's work. In his story "Mr. Arcularis" he uses the same contrast. Mr. Arcularis's final dream that he "was beyond the moon, shot past the North Star . . . swooped in a long, bright curve round the Pleiades, shouted his frosty greetings to Betelgeuse, and was off to the little blue star which pointed the way to the Unknown" (S.S., 52-53), ends in his discovery merely of his own coffin and his death. The large contrast is paralleled, too, by the metaphor peculiar to Aiken's work in which the finite is flatly coupled with the infinite. Much of the appeal in Senlin's Morning Song, for instance, derives from this kind of metaphor. ("In a whistling void I stand before my mirror, / Unconcerned, and tie my tie" [207].) But Aiken uses the metaphor pervasively—sometimes for pathetic humor, as in "The Anniversary": "He recalled stories of men who had engaged cabs, simply saying to the driver, 'If you know a good place, take me to it. Here's a dollar. Here's five dollars. Here's a thousand dollars. . . . Take me to the Queen of Sheba. Take me to the number of numbers in the street of streets. 1770 Washington Street. No. 2,876,452 Eternity Street. Minus seven Insanity Street. . . . Anywhere you like' " (S.S., 180). Elsewhere, as in "Strange Moonlight," he uses it in order to create an effect of mystery: "an enormous jagged black wing, soft and drooping like a bat's; he had noticed veins in it" (S.S., 281).

Thus in *Punch*, the magnificent vitality and fertility of the protagonist's imagination counterbalances the determinism of the Epilogue. Indeed, Aiken's use of the implications of the controlled puppet is itself richly imaginative. One should not confuse ideas with the poetry which can be made out of them. Conceiving of poetry as the embodiment of man's total experience, Aiken has consistently widened his range to express more and more of man's inner and outer universe. He himself observed that "a poetry of despair, or tragedy, or disillusionment—even a poetry of fatalism, or determinism—might well be a great poetry, and there is no need to go into a panic simply because poets insist on doing . . . everything they can to bring all that man knows or understands into their poetry."[34] As puppet and as hero Punch combines all of man's impulses *in extenso*. His imagination frees him for heroism. He conceives, for instance, of the most heroic act of all—a contest with Satan himself. Punch wagers that even the imperious Queen of Sheba will not refuse him a kiss:

> Confusion rose. Beside her throne
> I leaned, I roared in a tempest tone
> 'Sheba, my name is Punch! I stand
> With power of darkness in my hand,—
> Power to shake your kingdom down,
> To crack your heart and break your crown!'
> And then as I stood quaking there,
> Feeding upon her eyes, her hair,
> Amazing drunkenness waved in me:
> I gallantly hopped upon her knee,
> I kissed her mouth! and straight arose
> A clamor of cries, and silence froze,
> And Sheba, quivering backward, weak,
> Tried once, and twice, and thrice, to speak;
> And flushed; and stared; and laughed; and then—
> Put up her mouth to kiss again! . . . (327)

If, then, Punch is mechanistically determined, he nevertheless can rise above his human condition by means of the freedom he conceives imaginatively:

> 'Listen!' he said.
> 'This heart that beats here,—underneath my hand,—
> All of the clocks in the world keep time with it!

Even the stars in the sky, the sun and planets,
Measure their time by me!—I am the centre!' (301)

Like the great Elizabethan heroes—a Tamburlaine or a Bussy
D'Ambois—Punch stands at the center of his world; and, as the
first old man says, "somehow, the world seemed greater for
him." If his end is fated, he lives his life only the more glori-
ously. Aiken had earlier made the same point in one of the
stories written for the *Advocate*, titled "The Huntsman" (1910).
Here, the protagonist finds a source of optimism in his particular
notion of fatalism. And so he encounters his Destiny—the
huntsman—with courage and pride.

Ultimately, then, to value *Punch* as versified philosophy, or
even to stress Punch's role as puppet, is to miss the real source
of vitality in the poem. Fundamentally, this is a psychological
novel and anticipates the kind of fiction which Aiken would
write. Punch is only incidentally a puppet—basically, he is real.
The point of the poem is the contrast between Punch's dreams
of heroism and the fact that these dreams are paranoiac compensations for his cowardice and feelings of inferiority. The puppet-
maker is thus simply the device whereby Aiken emphasized that
Punch is a universal symbol and can represent the predicament
of all men.

Nevertheless, *Punch* pointed no clear direction to Aiken; for,
obviously, the subject of *Punch* was exhausted by the poem.
Nothing more, certainly, could be done with the myth itself,
and Aiken had discovered no new form whereby he might interpret experience. *John Deth*, written during 1922-1924, returns
to mythical subject matter—but with the significant difference
from *Punch* that in this poem Aiken attempts to create, rather
than extend, myth. The framework of the poem, as I have said,
derives from the traditional Dance of Death allegory. But the
myth which Aiken used as his real subject has both historical
and personal bases. While living in Winchelsea, England,
Aiken read a history of the village and discovered that its first

three grantees of land were the ambiguously named John Deth, Juliana Goatibed, and Millicent Piggistaile. "Here [he wrote] was the dance of death, localized; and my Deth would have two complementary figures, one of whom would symbolize (very roughly) consciousness, while the other would symbolize the unconscious or the merely physical; . . . also, I saw the thing as a myth, pure and simple, but as a matter of fact, neither very simple nor very pure. I was drawn by the notion of writing a myth, of *creating* a legend: of taking something raw and rich straight out of the racial consciousness."[35] In *John Deth*, then, Aiken can see the individual in a new way, as part of his community. Instead of working from the individual dreamer, as in *Forslin* and *Festus*, he works with the myth. In their unconscious content legends and dreams are so much alike that Freud called myths "the secular dreams of mankind." But myths are shared by all the members of a culture and express their joint unconscious desires. Myth, in short, refers to man's societal existence, whereas the dream is confined to his solipsistic existence.

In *John Deth*, therefore, Aiken deliberately distorted surface reality in order to reveal the nature of consciousness. Unless the reader accepts the dream-quality of the poem as possibly a direct reproduction of racial consciousness, the poem loses part of its meaning; if he resists, it disintegrates to shimmering syllables. Aiken attempted to assure that this would not happen by supplying the poem with its own narrative explication. Especially toward its conclusion, Aiken supplements his dream-narrative with an interior exegesis:

> 'Here lies John Deth; and by his side
> Millicent Piggistaile, his bride.
> Creator and destroyer keep
> Henceforth their everlasting sleep.
> And she,—the flame between,—who drove
> Their anguish on, accursèd Love,—

Who died before, that they might cease;—
Shares with them their eternal peace.' (442)

By 1922 Aiken recognized that the terms and descriptions of psychoanalysis were metaphors which, at their best, discovered and revealed profoundly the fundamental character of man's activities. In Deth and Millicent opposites marry—death and life, sterility and fertility, weariness and vigor—the negative and positive principles of the world. By their marriage is produced consciousness (Juliana) which, as Freud had convinced Aiken in *Beyond the Pleasure Principle*, seeks unconsciousness or, as Santayana insisted upon calling it, the inertia of Nirvana[36] (Goatibed).

In being close to the a-rationality of the racial consciousness, the poem is often ambiguous, although concrete; in radiating many meanings, it withholds all. In its a-rationality it is sometimes even close to nonsense verse, which, as Aiken was convinced by Emile Cammaerts' *Poetry of Nonsense*, is "possibly poetry at its purest."[37] Aiken puns, for instance, riotously on his own middle name—"He knew her not. / Potter had turned himself to pot" (429), and does not hesitate to parody Keats—"Beauty is food,—food, beauty! there / Is all we know, and all our care!" (430). The nature which he creates is as mysterious and unreal as that of "Kubla Khan":

Look not beneath the serpent's lid
To see what seed-pearl there is hid:
What blood-drop stone, what topaz clear,
Or frozen amethystine tear!
It is the stone of light that kills. (419)

And the real power in the poem is in its dream-quality, in its movement and variability, not in its content. In both *John Deth* and *Punch*, therefore, Aiken endeavored to define the racial consciousness through the archetypal myths that can be made real to it, rather than, as in *Forslin*, *Senlin*, and *The House of*

Dust, by the typical vicarious experiences of humanity. In this sense, *John Deth* improves upon *Punch*: for by moving immediately into the dream, Aiken could reconstruct myth more effectively. The two poems present two sides of the same coin, what Aiken once called "dream" and "project." His experiment in *John Deth*, like that in *Punch*, provided him with no new method—although I suspect that it impelled a new insight into the uses of poetry. In both poems Aiken was learning the craft of poetry, its range and responsibilities. While both were accomplishments, both also continued his search in what Nietzsche called the "hiding-places of the ideal."

OF THE FICTION

FROM 1923 to 1928 Aiken was to continue this search in terms of the experience he could make articulate in his fiction. In two books of short stories, *Bring! Bring!* (1925) and *Costumes by Eros* (1928), and in one novel, *Blue Voyage* (1927), he would replace the Divine Pilgrim with the Man—Conrad Aiken himself. And he would extend his notion of the Divine Pilgrim by making "Changing Mind" its *coda*, as he came to realize that art must always spiral toward the artist who can create it. Aiken's earliest fiction, as we might suspect, exhibits only tentative progress away from the dilemma posed by his poetry. Indeed, in method and motive, early stories like "The Disciple" and "Smith and Jones," written in 1922 and 1923, are lesser versions of *Punch* and *John Deth*. "The Disciple" is based upon popular myth—the belief that Judas and Ahasver, the Wandering Jew, meet once each year on Easter Eve to re-enact together their eternal torment. Aiken constructs his story by employing narrative devices similar to those of *Punch*. Just as we know that throughout his story Punch is in reality only a puppet, so too we know in "The Disciple" that the Jewish shopkeeper is mad, and does not reincarnate Ahasver. Punch's fertile imagination carried conviction; so also, the shopkeeper's delusion that he is Ahasver is likewise so powerful and pervasive that we suspend our real knowledge about him and are beguiled, for the moment, into accepting his delusion as reality. Both depend for their effect upon Aiken's ability to make the reader momentarily believe that the illusion embodies a deeper reality. The same is true of many Aiken stories—"Silent Snow, Secret Snow," for example, in which we seem always about to break through to the truths contained in the "secret" snow. But we never, in the story, transcend the snow itself, whose

67

meanings remain secret. Just as Aiken concludes *Punch* by returning to physical reality, with the image of puppets "huddled together, / Arms over heads, contorted, just where he had dropped them" (362), so also he ends "The Disciple" when, after Easter, the Jew has returned to a normal state of mind and does not recognize Dace.

Aiken wrote "Smith and Jones" in 1923, during the composition of *John Deth*. So close is the resemblance between them that the critic of Aiken's poetry might justifiably suppose that "Smith and Jones" is the first example in Aiken's career of his fiction preparing the way for his poetry. The narrative thesis that springs forth toward the conclusion of *John Deth* had already been formulated in "Smith and Jones." Smith and Jones are, like Deth and Millicent, polarities, positive and negative, emotion and intellect, restraint and vitality. They are the plus and minus signs of the human soul; and Gleason, whom they discuss, is (like Juliana) their coefficient—their joint consciousness—who leads to self-consciousness. Smith says:

> "Suffice it to say that Gleason loved me. It was like being loved by a planet."
>
> "Venus?"
>
> "Mars. She crushed me, consumed me. Her love was a profounder and more fiery abyss than the inferno which Dante, in the same sense, explored. It took me days of circuitous descent, to get even within sight of the bottom; and then, as there were no ladders provided, I plunged headlong. I was at once ignited, and became a tiny luminous spark, which, on being cast forth to the upper world again on a fiery exhalation, became an undistinguished cinder."
>
> "To think a person named Gleason could do all that!"
>
> (S.S., 198-99)

In his *Creative Evolution* Bergson argued that the "intellect is characterized by a natural inability to comprehend life. Instinct, on the contrary, is moulded on the very form of life."[1] Jones is *intellect* ("You're all brain to the souls of your feet" [200]), and Smith is *instinct* ("I don't like these deliberate actions. Give me the spontaneous, every time" [203]). Gleason, the ego, is produced by the union of these two. In killing Jones at the end, Smith destroys the principle of negativism which seeks dominance and would altogether extinguish vital life.

Both of these stories, however, are early and derive their method and intention generally from the earlier poetry, rather than pointing toward the later. "Gehenna," "State of Mind," and "The Dark City" fall into the same category. I need consider only "The Dark City" as an example of the influence that the tendencies of Aiken's early poetry had upon his fiction. Festus had attempted to locate the source of knowledge in beauty—specifically, in a strange but celestial music which he hears. He and the old man seek its source, but ironically discover only that:

> It is the orchestra of butchers, Festus!
> Gathered for holiday . . . They wear white aprons,
> Green do they look in the moonlight, like green aprons
> Darkly spotted . . . How sweet their music is! . . .
> The hands that held the cleaver draw the bow. (273)

Beauty and ugliness are inseparable. Likewise, *Forslin*, v, 4 describes a concert whose harmonies are interrupted contrapuntally by the cacophonies of malicious gossip. "The Dark City," written in 1922, is perhaps Aiken's most impressive dramatization of the conjunction of beauty and horror. In the first part of the tale Aiken describes a simple prelapsarian pastoral life, much like that of *Conversation*. Not until the end of the story does the protagonist reveal his sense of the total and horrible corruption of the dark city hidden beneath the beauty of his apparently tranquil valley. Like the protagonist of Andreyev's "In the Basement," he has a vision "such as ordinary people do not see":

69

Its people are maggots—maggots of perhaps the size of human children; their heads are small and wedge-shaped, and glow with a faint bluish light. Masses of them swarm within those walls. Masses of them pour through the streets, glisten on the buttresses and parapets. They are intelligent. What horrible feast is it that nightly they celebrate there in silence? On what carrion do they feed? It is the universe that they devour; and they build above it, as they devour it, their dark city like a hollow tomb. . . . Extraordinary that this city, which seen from here at dusk has so supernatural a beauty, should hide at the core so vile a secret. (S.S., 326)

The relation between Aiken's earlier poetry and his stories might be an appropriate subject for further studies. We might well discover that the kind of fiction which Aiken wrote for the *Advocate* during 1908-1910 led him toward the kind of poetry which he was to write from 1915 until 1920. A story which Aiken entitled "Corpus Vile," written in 1909, already embodies many of the characteristics, and even the central plan, of *Forslin*. Aiken's protagonist is an unsuccessful poet named Simon Plangian who, half-starved and frozen, is mysteriously beckoned into a house on Christmas Eve. Surrounded with the satisfactions of Christmas and stimulated by wine and the emotional suggestions of the three doctors who are in fact conducting a psychoanalytical test on him, Plangian dreams that he returns to Egypt to sing to Cleopatra; to Troy, where he encounters Andromache; and finally to the house of his birth, where he sees himself as a child celebrating Christmas. This story constitutes Aiken's first explicit self-investigation as he moves, in Plangian, from his generic to his specific past to discover that it is impossible to change history; one must simply, as he later argues in his play *Mr. Arcularis*, understand and accept it. This story, contemporaneous with poems modelled both in form and content after the Victorians, clearly looks forward, more than his college poetry does, to Aiken's use of self-encounter through wish-fulfillment in his Divine Pilgrim poems.

I want, however, now to turn to the fiction which influenced the later poetry, and first to that in which Aiken discovered a new area of experience. After 1925, he would not deal with the vicarious experience of mankind, nor specifically with the myths which issue from the racial consciousness. He would explore his own ego—already created, but also in the process of creation. That is, in coming to know himself he would grow beyond himself; all such investigations, therefore, are preludes, never complete since they do not—until *Ushant*—include the growth which they themselves occasion. While his personal experience may be the source of many of the episodes in his symphonies and *Turns and Movies*, it is there generalized and detached from the personal in order that its significance might be universal. Later, he would be able to treat his personal experience without transforming and translating it. He did this first not in his poetry but in his fiction. The critic who knows something of Aiken's biography and reads his work from its beginning is struck by his deliberate exploitation of his *personal* mental and emotional history, for the first time, in his stories. Malcolm Lowry (perhaps the writer who best knew Aiken) has observed that "for a writer who has been accused of being 'subjective' ... Conrad Aiken has left, save in the very greatest of his poems where for that matter any picture of the man perhaps is irrelevant, very little impression of himself. . . . Nor has Aiken himself, who has even written a poem called 'Palimpsest a deceitful portrait,' that is perhaps least help of all, ever pretended to be other than unhelpful" (Wake, 84-85). And Lowry is perfectly right with regard to Aiken's early poetry. Nevertheless, it is also true that Aiken deliberately conceived of fiction as a means of defining himself in such a way as to provide a new stock of experience for his poetry. In order to understand the relation of his life to his fiction, we might first consider Aiken's own view of the elements of which fiction is composed.

71

In a story curiously entitled "Life Isn't a Short Story," Aiken deals with the problem of the genesis of a literary work. How far, he asks, are we justified in saying that experience can become fiction? He argued in 1923 that "biographical criticism . . . has proved itself indispensable to any critic who is not content simply to accept art unquestionably as a blazing gift from God." By biographical criticism he meant "the effort to see in an artist's life and personality the origins of his art" (ABC, 59, 58). And in his long essay on Keats, as well as in several essays on Dostoevsky, he applied biographical apparatus at length, convinced that one's art originates in his mental, emotional, and physical existence. On the other hand, he could also write that life contains "no story—at best, only the materials for a story. Life seldom arranges itself in an obvious pattern. It may surprise us—and often does—or it may shock us, or turn swiftly from melodrama to comedy, or from the humdrum to tragedy; but how few lives do we know in which there is any perceptible 'form,' any design of the sort that novelists employ" ("Thistledown," S.S., 245). "Life Isn't a Short Story" simultaneously entertains both of these views and shows how they may be reconciled.

The story itself is simple enough. It deals with a short-story writer who has run out of ideas, who "was feeling as empty as a bath-tub and as blue as an oyster" (S.S., 327). But when a middle-aged woman walks by the window of the cafeteria in which he is eating breakfast, he finds that he has already begun thinking about a new story. It occurs to him that she might serve as the physical model for the story which, unnoticed, has been germinating in his mind. Only when the woman gives a concrete form to his emotion does the idea arise from his unconscious.

The "story," or the emotion from which the story is to spring, derives from two phrases which he had heard as fragments of greetings in the lobby of a theatre: *as I live and breathe!* and *in the flesh!* (329). But juxtaposed, and therefore combined

72

in his mind, they expressed, as he sees, the wonder of being alive: "We haven't seen each other for a long while, we didn't know whether we were dead or not, but here we are" (330). Like his short-story writer, Aiken is able to recognize the ultimate in the immediate and thus understand the person in terms of his tradition. His characters transcend tragedy because he sees revealed in their situations the dignity of the human condition. Dealing with the life of Everyman—with its hopes, fears, successes, failures—Aiken also triumphantly perceives in actual life the eternal formulas of existence. Men may act as if they have just emerged into space and time from nothingness, but he knows and proves that man incarnates and includes his past. Committed to his culture, he nevertheless puts it in its proper perspective—not as a denial or imitation, but as a creative exfoliation of history. This area, where the commonplace and eternal meet, or where one can discern the eternal in the commonplace, is the distinctive province of Aiken's stories. Of the trite phrases he comments: "One witnessed, in the mere hearing of them, innumerable surprised greetings, innumerable mutual congratulations on the mere fact of being still alive. The human race seemed to extend itself backwards through them. ... [If] one pursued the thought one came eventually to a vision of two small apes peering at each other round the cheeks of a cocoanut and making a startled noise that sounded like 'yoicks!' " (330).

This, at least, is what the short-story writer sees in the phrases. And since his story originates in this equivocal emotion, the story, as he begins to see it, is itself similarly equivocal. The writer himself sees into the unalterable, while his main character—a plump, blonde woman named Gladys seems right —sees only the commonplace in the trite phrases. So the story arises as the conflict between Gladys, who prides herself on her superiority over clichés, and her simple husband, Sidney, who epitomizes the commonplace, but who partakes of the timeless.

While he is half-consciously developing his essential character conflict, the writer casually observes the scene outside the cafeteria window. A horse and wagon draws up to the curb, and the writer watches the shabby horse. He characterizes him: "The horse waited patiently, was absolutely still, didn't even stamp a foot. He looked as if he were thinking about the rain. Or perhaps, dismayed by the senseless noise of all the traffic about him, he was simply thinking about his stall, wherever it was. Or more likely, not thinking about anything at all. He just stood" (333). By the end of Aiken's story we know that just as the writer drew Gladys' character from the trite phrases he overheard, Sidney's character arose from the writer's emotional response to the patient horse. And the futile atmosphere which pervades the tale derives from the dismal, rainy scene outside the window.[2]

Life, then, isn't a short story. But life can become a short story, or a novel, or a poem. Aiken deliberately illustrates here the means by which we may properly read his fiction. For the work of art transforms the materials of life; it imposes a beginning and end upon them, and so gives them form. The short story, then, is life; for it is rooted physically, emotionally, and mentally in reality. Hypothetically at least, the critic who knew every fact and emotion of a writer's life could trace to its source every detail in his fiction. This, at least, is what Aiken contends about his own work. No such critic, of course, exists or could exist; he would have to know more than the author himself. The problems in treating the relation between Aiken's life and work are far more basic. No adequate biography of Aiken has been written. The only attempt of this kind, Houston Peterson's chapter "Biographical Fragments" in his *Melody of Chaos*, is neither complete nor detailed. Lacking a dependable biography, we cannot study the relation of his life to his fiction fully or systematically. Even *Ushant* (1952) is not an autobiography in the usual sense. Only in part of the book does Aiken explore his own life. And in *Ushant*, as in its prototype *Blue Voyage*, Aiken uses *personae* in order to preserve his integrity in telling the truth. Nevertheless, used with caution, *Ushant* reveals, to a large extent, the autobiographical substance of his fiction.

For instance, in *Ushant* Aiken mentions an incident connected with his last visit to his paternal grandmother,

> in the forlorn nursing home on Palfrey Hill. . . . He had gone from his last visit to the nursing home by street-car and subway . . . to one of his clandestine meetings with Marian . . . [which contrasted to] the horror of the final visit—for he never again saw grandmother alive—the shrunken body lying motionless under the sheet in the hot room, while the sad head, with its two little braids of grey hair, turned in misery from side to side on the pillow, the tears running down the sunken cheeks. . . . 'I can't die—I can't die—I want to die and I can't—and my teeth hurt me and I can't wear them any more—' . . . [She] had adored . . . the children of Lorelei and himself, that very minute playing in the sunlight on the beach at South Yarmouth—and, above all, little Jean, little Jean! (104-105)

In his story "The Last Visit" he had very nearly translated this incident directly into fiction, except that the protagonist of the story is a woman, Marie Schley (whose name has perhaps some relation to the "Marian" of the *Ushant* account). The nursing home, again, is on Palfrey Hill; Grandmother turns her "small shrunken face on the pillow. . . . [with] the forlorn little braid of streaked hair" (26). She complains " 'It's my teeth— I can't use my teeth—that's why I talk so badly. The dentist was here last week. He said my jaw had shrunk, and this set of teeth wouldn't fit anymore' " (27); and also, "I can't die! I can't die! . . . I want to die and I can't!" (31). She asks for the children—"Especially little Kate! She's always wanting to see your little Kate" (28), the nurse says.

Then too, details which Aiken mentions elsewhere in *Ushant* in connection with his grandmother he also uses in "The Last Visit"—the fact, for instance, that her house was in Watertown

(Ush., 101). He describes the furniture of her house in both: In *Ushant*—"The florid Victorian furniture, of embossed and filigreed curly walnut, the marble-topped tables, the hassocks, the antimacassars" (102); in "The Last Visit"—"the queer musty old furniture, the antimacassars, the tussocks" (23). Aiken mentions "the parlor organ" and Grandmother's "favorite son, who had died young" in his story. The favorite son is, of course, Aiken's father, "the beautiful son, her golden-haired Apollo, her genius, her beauty, [who] was early marked as one of those whom the gods would destroy" (103), and the organ is his (101). Aiken himself had come from Savannah, after the death of his parents, to Boston and New Bedford when he was twelve. Correspondingly, he gives Marie Schley the same background. Finally, the climactic incident of both accounts is the same; if Aiken (as he relates in *Ushant*) had gone with a woman to the Orpheum after the visit, Marie met a man "in the little alley that led to the theatre"; both hear the same blackface singer crooning "*Hot lips . . . That are pips . . . and no more conscience than a snake has hips*" (S.S., 32).

Aiken turned to such self-exploitations in his fiction, I believe, in an effort to "*be* himself, and to *know* himself, as, perhaps, preliminaries to speaking as he must."[3] In ten volumes of poetry he had proved his ability to create fables or to use the materials of myth. But in writing his fiction he came to insist that the writer "will impregnate [his fiction] deeply, if he is successful, with his own character. The novel is the novelist's inordinate and copious lyric: he explores himself, and sings while he explores, like the grave-digger" (ABC, 347). One might certainly argue with his definition of the novel. He has confined its scope wholly to that of the *Bildungsroman* in the midst of an argument that "there are no canons for the novel." It is important, however, only to observe that his conception of fiction governed his practice. From the beginning of his career, including his work in the *Advocate*, he had never, in the usual romantic sense, written "personal" poetry; his stories are his earliest lyrics. Basically there are two kinds of fiction, aspects of the two main traditions of modern literature in general. We may call these "aesthetic" and "confessional" fiction. Proceeding aesthetically, as did Henry James, Huxley, and Joyce, the artist disparages his subject in order to stress the importance of his form, the way he presents his subject. Defining his artistry by what he can make, he calls attention to the design so that we may admire the beauty of his technique. Such a procedure defines the human in terms of its periphery, by the art which can give shape to the individual experience.

Conrad Aiken proceeds in the other fashion. In "confessional" fiction the writer conceals his art because he is primarily interested in elucidating the experience itself. He will ferret out the crucial moments of a life when the individual—arriving at what Carl Jaspers calls "frontier situations"—is able to understand momentarily the basic things of the soul. Life, as he sees it, is not a problem to be solved, but a reality to be experienced. In his fiction Aiken penetrates to the mystery and inexhaustibility of his own personal existence. Such stories would provide a richer poetic substance for the poems that followed them. In 1930 Yvor Winters could write of the early poetry: "Mr. Aiken's long poems in a sense achieve form or at least cohesion—that is, they are not obviously falling apart from line to line. . . . The lines cohere not because they have any common intention or direction, but because they have no intention or direction; there is nothing to force them apart."[4] Almost from its very beginnings, Aiken's fiction exhibits a central intention. And shortly after 1930, his self-analysis was to provide his poetry with a unifying hero: Conrad Aiken himself.

Although it was by no means his most recent story, Aiken placed "Your Obituary, Well Written" last in his collected *Short Stories* (1950). Aiken has always attempted to give his books— even his collections—a spiral form, moving ever inward; that he placed this story last, then, suggests that he meant it to carry special emphasis—to provide the reader with *his* figure in the carpet, as a means of explicating his fiction. For the thinly veiled central character of "Your Obituary, Well Written" is Katherine Mansfield, whose example guided much of Aiken's own short fiction. The story is concerned, as it had to be, not so much with her work, but with Katherine Mansfield as a person whom Aiken has known. After her death, he described her as "an extraordinary woman—not a woman with whom . . . one could easily be comfortable. She was too direct, too truthful, for that: too much a creature of smoldering and violent loves and hates. Shams and polite conventions shriveled away in her presence. One discussed essentials with her, or one discussed nothing. One knew her intimately, or one knew her not at all" (ABC, 299). Of the Reine Wilson in his story he made very nearly the same comment—that she revealed "a burning intensity of spirit such as I have never elsewhere encountered. . . . It seemed to me that I had never met anyone whose hold on life was so terribly *conscious*" (403).

In this study, of course, I am more concerned with the influence of her fiction than the impact of her personality upon Aiken. He was sure enough of Katherine Mansfield's literary power to write: "Taken as a whole, her short stories form the best group of short stories which have ever been written in the English language" (ABC, 297). It is important to understand why Aiken should have rated her stories so highly. In Katherine Mansfield's fiction Aiken discovered the element which suddenly began to appear in his own stories in about 1923—the drive toward complete self-revelation. At least, this is the view he consistently took of her work. In 1923, as he was himself beginning to write fiction, he wrote of hers: "Miss Mansfield, far more identifiably than most short-story writers, used the short story as a medium for undisguised confession. She was essentially what one calls for convenience a 'subjective' writer; . . . she was invariably at her best when a theme, a scene, a character, most closely and intricately invited her own unclouded personal confession."[5] Somewhat later, he used Katherine Mansfield's example to denigrate Virginia Woolf: "It is easy to understand why Katherine Mansfield distrusted 'Mr. Bennett and Mrs. Brown.' She felt a kind of sterility in this dexterous holding of the raw stuff of life at arm's length, this playing with it as if it were a toy. Why not be more immediate—why not surrender to it?" (ABC, 390). Mrs. Woolf's method, in short, was antipodal to Mansfield's and Aiken's. She avoided an "immediate" presentation of life, "as if she never for a moment wished us to forget the *frame* of the picture, and the fact that the picture was a picture" (392). They, to the contrary, conceived of only one kind of fiction, in which the author imbues his narrative with confession.

Katherine Mansfield, however, influenced Aiken only by her example, not by her stories as such. Aiken had learned elsewhere —and earlier—how to write fiction. From Chekhov, and perhaps even more from Andreyev, his favorite short-story writer, he discovered how to dispose of the barrier of art between author and audience, and to establish actuality by striking at once a convincingly colloquial tone. The beginnings of the first three stories in his *Collected Short Stories* demonstrate this admirably —"Bring! Bring!": "Miss Rooker dreamed that she was on board the *Falcon* in Marblehead Harbor"; "The Last Visit": "Marie Schley sat in the Watertown car by the open grilled window"; "Mr. Arcularis": "Mr. Arcularis stood at the window of his room in the hospital and looked down at the street." In each of his stories—and this is true, also, of his poems, *Senlin* and others— he begins with the tactile, then moves into the center of his characters' beings where their everyday actualities are resifted and redefined. We discover, for instance, that Mr. Arcularis is not looking from the hospital window at all: at the moment of his death on the operating table he is dreaming his life. He relives it in order to understand it. Like this, many of the stories move from the colloquial to the inexpressible, the mundane to the marvelous. In "Field of Flowers" the protagonist discovers the beauty which his love affair should have had mysteriously

79

embodied in a Hiroshige print. "The Professor's Escape" seems to begin as a smoking-room story, but approaches, at its conclusion, a revelation of the essence of love and the guilt involved in all choice.

As I have already suggested, many of Aiken's stories are autobiographical—but all appear to be so. The effect of personal revelation is guaranteed by Aiken's frequent use of the first person singular, the "I" which communicates immediately with the reader. Even in his casual method of composition Aiken has encouraged this seeming artlessness, the presentation of life for life's sake. He wrote his fiction directly on the typewriter, and, as he has said, "the first script was, with very rare exceptions, the last: a short story would usually go out, and quite uncopied, just as written."[6] By his use of the first person, his easy familiarity, his colloquial pitch, his puns, Aiken assures us that he is up to no tricks. Like the hero of Andreyev's story "The Man Who Found the Truth," Aiken emphasizes truthfulness rather than artistry, insisting: "Not endowed with literary talent, which in reality is an indomitable inclination to invent and to lie, I shall attempt to introduce myself . . . exactly as I was at that remote time."[7] He invites the reader—and his own ego—to enter the darkness of his past.

· II ·

Since in my remarks on "The Last Visit" and "Your Obituary, Well Written" I have suggested the kinds of fictive translation he made of his own history, I want to show very briefly that (and to what extent) Aiken's fiction often issues from his own experience. I should first make it clear that Aiken drew details from his own life not as an easy way to fill in his narrative, but that he might relive (and so understand) the inner experience associated with those details. The autobiographical impulse had, to be sure, appeared tentatively from the beginnings of Aiken's career in fiction and poetry. With "Tetélestai" and the "Deceitful Portrait" section of *The House of Dust*, this impulse became more immediate. Thenceforth, Aiken would enrich not simply his awareness of himself, but also his ability to articulate that understanding with greater intensity. What experience he would use had, for the most part, been already stored up. He had now to explore and perfect by art what he would call in *Ushant* this "gold-mine of consciousness." He would make a myth out of himself.

Fewer than a quarter of the pieces in Aiken's *Collected Short Stories* are not based upon actual fact. Of these, several are stories describing mental states. "Gehenna," "Smith and Jones," "By My Troth, Nerissa," and "State of Mind" in themselves constitute Aiken's experiencing of the mental states which he describes in them. "The Disciple" and "Bow Down, Isaac," stories dealing with religious aberrations, were invented, as were "No, No, Go Not to Lethe" and "Impulse," in which the hero decides to carry out his impulse to steal a worthless object and so be "a Columbus of the moral world" (162). Although it had its origin in greetings actually overheard in a hotel lobby, "Life Isn't a Short Story" thereafter is constructed from Aiken's imaginative speculation upon the implications of the phrases. Chiefly the product of invention, "The Bachelor Supper" was suggested by a bachelor party which Aiken attended at T Wharf in Boston. Finally, "Hey, Taxi!" although generally imagined, was suggested by a taxi driver's telling him about a freak trip from Boston to Hanover, Massachusetts.

The remaining stories are all more or less based on actual occurrences. In some, the plots are invented while the portraits are true. Some are stories based on experiences told to him by friends, or are actual incidents which he learned about in other direct ways. Others are autobiographical reflections, often distorted, of the facts of Aiken's personal life. I am concerned not with writing Aiken's biography, but rather with demonstrating the range, purposes, and origins of his fiction. I wish to make clear that although most of his stories begin with real incidents, these are transmuted and translated by the art which organizes them. Aiken uses the devices he had learned as a poet to shape and express the experiences which he had as a human being. He lives as Everyman; his art makes him into a Representative man. Aiken has himself spoken of the "mercurial substance" out of which his fiction was wrought—"mercurial, yes, because it was so seldom the merely factual elements—in the loves, the loves, the loves!—that would be of any use to the artificer, but rather the by-products of these, in animal drive, or psychosomatic; the renewal of the sense of wholeness and unity" (Ush., 314). In an ultimate sense, perhaps, the kernel of experience which initiates the story is unimportant beside the perfected artifact which the poet as maker can construct out of his life. But we can understand the degree of perfection in the artifact only by recognizing that a chaotic actuality serves as its matrix. For this reason I want simply to indicate the relation of Aiken's stories to his experience.

"The Anniversary" and "The Dark City" are stories in which the plot is entirely invented, while the portraits are truly drawn. Knowing and seeking to understand the people who serve as the chief characters of these stories, Aiken investigates their reactions, their attitudes, and ideas in moments of crisis—at times of self-confrontation which they never actually, but only ideally, experienced.

Other stories are based on fact in both plot and character. "Bring! Bring!" "The Professor's Escape," "The Fish Supper," "Pure as the Driven Snow," "The Woman-Hater," and "Fly Away Ladybird" are all amplified from experiences of Aiken's friends; their experiences, of course, were all resifted and recreated as Aiken's imagination acted upon them. In "The Moment," for instance, Aiken combined the experiences of two friends. "West End" details and extends a similar story told to Aiken by a woman in London. "The Necktie" retells an experience of an uncle. In a book he was looking at in a friend's library Aiken found an actual letter with the same intent as the

one which makes up "I Love You Very Dearly." "A Pair of Vikings" describes motor-cyclists whose performances Aiken watched
in Rye during 1933. Observing a brief scene in a garden from the
back window of Jeake's House, Aiken imagined the rest of the
incidents which he writes of in "All, All Wasted." "Round by
Round" describes a newspaperman writing a report on a cham-
pionship fight and, at the same time, trying to compose a letter
which will make clear to his unfaithful wife the kind of integrity which the beaten champion's fiancée seems to share, odd-
ly enough, with the James family—Henry and William and
Alice. This combines the experience of a newspaperman-friend
of Aiken's with Aiken's own reporting of a middleweight cham-
pionship fight involving Vince Dundee.

Aiken's two most famous stories, "Silent Snow, Secret Snow"
and "Mr. Arcularis," have only slight and peripheral relations
to his own experience. Aiken conceived the original idea for the
first story from his own listening each morning for the steps of
the postman as he turned the corner and started down the hill.
"These footsteps, once muffled by a mirage of snow, had given
him the idea for a story" (Ush., 206). The details of Paul's life
and situation were invented in extending the initial image. As
Aiken has described in his preface to the stage-version of "Mr.
Arcularis," this story began "with Mr. Arcularis himself, that
odd, pale, shabby little man, who by chance sat opposite me,
years ago, at the dinner-table—Third Class—of an Atlantic
liner. . . . I thought of him as somehow having the air of a
somnambulist" (v). His meeting the real Arcularis aboard ship
coincided with his dreaming the dream of "frost and stars"
which he attributes to the fictional Mr. Arcularis.

Like these two, other stories are inventions out of the casual.
"Hello, Tib" documents Aiken's observation of the actions of a
kitten, while the preceding situation was invented in order to
give the perceptivity meaning. "Thistledown," "O How She
Laughed," "Spider, Spider," "Farewell! Farewell! Farewell!,"
"A Man Alone At Lunch," "A Conversation," "Field of Flow-

ers," and "The Night Before Prohibition" all draw upon Aiken's reactions or relations to various women in real life. Again, I should emphasize that Aiken's experience is always changed, often beyond recognition, in the act of creation. One could not know merely from the stories, for instance, that Miss Rooker of "Bring! Bring!," Eunice of "The Night Before Prohibition," and Nora of *Conversation* all began with the same real woman. Whoever she was in life, the process of artifaction has made Miss Rooker/Eunice/Nora three separate characters in the fiction. No story *reproduces* experience. The very act of such an investigation involves a conscious ordering and evaluation which random reality never includes. Life merely provides us with the material: we make our own myths.

In "Strange Moonlight" and "The Orange Moth" Aiken speculates upon his own childhood and youth. The former depicts the bright, peripheral consciousness of a child for whom a series of incidents and emotions—receiving a medal at school, the death of a playmate, a trip to the beach—all seem to be aspects of the same inner experience. The story details Aiken's memories of disorder and early sorrow. The "jungle graveyard, turned park" is Colonial Park in Savannah, Georgia, where Aiken was born and spent his childhood. In "The Orange Moth" he describes the attempt of a young author to "capture" Beauty itself. He is living in the boardinghouse on Twenty-Third Street in New York, where Aiken lived during one summer. Among the characters are Van Wyck Brooks and the elder Yeats, "who invariably, when asked if he was the father of the great Yeats, replied, 'I am the great Yeats!'" (Ush., 71) Cooke's dream, that an orange moth settled on the pages of his copy-book, and that "when he opened the book he found that the pages were soft orange moth-wings; and incredibly fine, indecipherable, in purple, a poem of extraordinary beauty was written there" (S.S., 519), was an actual dream of Aiken's.

In *Ushant* Aiken discusses his novels at length and makes clear for us to what extent their substance is autobiographical.

The whole situation of Demarest in *Blue Voyage*—his journey to England in pursuit of Cynthia, only to find her already engaged and sailing on the same ship with him—is based, with many changes, on fact. All of the ship's passengers, including Faubion, Cynthia, Silberstein, and Smith, are modelled after real people.

Great Circle may be properly termed a psychological invention from biographical and autobiographical elements; but much of the personal material has been altered to suit the thematic purpose. Andrew Cather's unhappy discovery that his wife is unfaithful was invented to supply the jealousy motif; Uncle David was invented for the same reason. As in "Bring! Bring!" Aiken uses his childhood recollections of Duxbury.

King Coffin, on the other hand, was completely invented. The protagonist was named after "a singular character in my apartment house in Cambridge, odd name something *like* Ammen, and an air of mystery and superiority. And there *was* a Dr. King Coffin living in Boston."[8]

Aiken's remaining two novels are both largely autobiographical. Never published in the United States, *A Heart for the Gods of Mexico* deals with the train-ride of three people from Boston to Mexico. The trip to Mexico draws upon Aiken's memories of his own Mexican journey. The character of Noni—soon to die—inadequately portrays, Aiken says in *Ushant*, a woman whom Aiken knew in Boston. Among the characters is the writer Malcolm Lowry, called Hambo, a student and friend of Aiken's who lived for some time in Mexico.

Finally, all of the characters in *Conversation* are based upon real people, even to the "Robin Hood fur-thief" and the poets whom he supported. One of these, of course, was Maxwell Bodenheim—the Karl Roth of *Conversation*—who also wrote a novel about the thief, John Coffey, entitled *Crazy Man* (1924). Aiken's prefatory statement: "The characters in this novel are entirely imaginary, and any resemblance they may bear to real persons, living or dead, is therefore quite accidental," is, of course, ironical, and as much a comment upon the novel as are the passages which he quotes from the *Journal of the Pilgrims.* One might add that the resolution of the quarrel was an invention.

Such novels as *Blue Voyage* and *Conversation,* and stories like "The Last Visit" and "The Night Before Prohibition"—indeed nearly all of his fiction—explore the ego to reveal failures of honesty, kindness, and integrity. They are Aiken's attempts to remember, by setting down, the pain he has caused both to others and to himself. In his consciousness of his failures he seeks forgiveness for them; and, more than forgiveness: the understanding which will allow him to transcend them, in life as in art. Of his protagonist's weakness in the climax of "The Night Before Prohibition" he wrote: "He groaned as he thought of it; he could never think of it without closing his eyes" (355). By concentrating upon his selfishness, he seeks to achieve generosity. In writing of his failures as a person—and in *Ushant* he would discuss only failures—he hopes to attain success as an artist. All of Aiken's characters are themselves engaged in precisely the same effort. The protagonist of Aiken's story "Round by Round" looks up, in desperation, at a picture of the James family: "The three good faces looked forward at him with an extraordinary integrity. Integrity! Yes, that was it, it wasn't only the intelligence, the wisdom, it was the profound and simple honesty of all three faces" (S.S., 240). Throughout his career, Aiken has striven to incarnate such "profound and simple" integrity. He has often parodied, for its sentimentality, Holmes's famous aspiration, "Build thee more stately mansions, O my soul"—in "The Orange Moth," for instance. But his aim has been as fundamentally simple as this, though not as easy to accomplish as Holmes thought it was. His approach is a revitalization of Emersonian self-reliance—an attempt, by better *knowing* oneself, to better *be* oneself. In singing his failures, he sings the self into existence:

86

much evil, and so little kindness, done,
selfish the loves, yes all, the selfless none;

illness and pain, ignored; the poor, forgotten;
the letters to the dying man, not written—
the many past, or passing, great or small,
from whom I took, nor ever gave at all!
          ("Dear Uncle Stranger," 811.)

· I I I ·

It will be instructive, now, to consider the poems Aiken wrote
in 1925, after his immersion in autobiographical fiction. These
poems discover a new immediacy of tone, a less reflective, more
stringent note, and, above all, an emphasis upon personal revelation. Although it is a minor poem, "Cliff Meeting"—which
Peterson says "was transcribed by Aiken rapidly, word for word,
from a dream"[9]—illustrates these qualities. Since the poem falls
into two distinct sections, it would probably be more exact to
say that the dream consisted of the cormorant section, the second half of the poem, and that in the first part Aiken consciously supplied the existential matrix of the cormorant symbol in
his dream. Like his stories, this poem arose out of Aiken's
anguish over a personal failure. In this case it was his treatment
of a woman whom "he had taught . . . how to love, but at the
expense, to her, of heartbreak, and, to himself, of a fearful complex of pity and guilt, but mostly pity, which had made him
physically and morally ill. It had given him a new concept of
the terrible—almost evil—power of love, its power for destruction and horror" (Ush., 308). In the dream section of the poem
the love-starved woman is transformed into a cormorant; her
last letter turns into bird claw-marks on the sand. The symbolic
value of the cormorant lies in the food-love equivalence: just as
this bird is typically voracious for food, so the woman was for
love. She is symbolized, therefore, by the starved cormorant

which the protagonist finds. And in a desperate effort to repair the damage he had done to the woman and thus rid himself of guilt, he seeks to save the bird, and lifts it "Between my hands, and laid against my breast, / Striving to warm her heart." But just as he had utterly and hopelessly (according to *Ushant*) destroyed the woman by teaching her to love, so also he realizes that his effort to help only accomplishes the bird's destruction: "seeking to make her eat, I did but hasten / Her death" (457).

"Cliff Meeting" indicates a significant development in Aiken's poetry. From 1922 to 1925 Aiken experimented intensively with fiction. He discovered two things—first, that he could increase man's awareness only by first achieving awareness of himself; second, that in his own past failures of awareness lay the appropriate area in which he might conduct his investigation. "Cliff Meeting" issues from these insights. It is the first poem in which he clearly exhibits his ability to illuminate his personal history and to embody in poetry the intellectual and emotional attitudes which accompany it. "Changing Mind," also written in 1925, is a far fuller and even more revealing example of this new direction in Aiken's poetry.

When Aiken gathered his early symphonic poems into one volume under the title of *The Divine Pilgrim* (1949) he included "Changing Mind" as the *coda* to the whole series. As *Senlin* provided the series with a generic "I," "Changing Mind" supplies it with the specific "I" of the artist at a particular moment of his experience. As early as 1919 Aiken had tentatively planned *The Divine Pilgrim*. And that plan included *The Charnel Rose, Forslin, The House of Dust, Senlin,* and *Festus* —but not "Changing Mind." For Aiken's earlier poems dealt with humanity's, not the individual's, experience. As late as 1924, he could still claim in his criticism that the artist should even, if he must, be false to his own ego so that he might be true to the universal experience of mankind. Accordingly, he condemned D. H. Lawrence for too exclusively asserting his individual personality.[10] By 1929 he had incorporated into his

criticism the insight he gained from his fiction. He then praised
D. H. Lawrence, noting that his "peculiar virtue is his terrific
endowment of 'consciousness.' If we like, we can see his whole
literary career as one prolonged and desperate and exhausting
effort to be as conscious as possible" (ABC, 267). Aiken realized, in other words, that in creating an ego to conform with
mankind, the artist must inevitably falsify the "I" which is the
sacred basis of poetry. Only after his experience in fiction did he
see that the individual as well as the generic consciousness must
be explored, and, in some ways, offers the greater challenge.

Thus, as Aiken was to point out in his Preface to the poem,
"the wholly anonymous hero of 'Changing Mind' . . . and perhaps anonymous with reason,[11] is not only particularized, he is
also shown to be the willing participant, and perhaps to some
extent even the instigator, in the process of seeing himself
resolved into his constituent particles" (872). Like *John Deth*,
"Changing Mind" is a dream poem, the invitation to "enter
the darkness" of the self and be dispersed—"Dissected out on
the glass-topped table, / The tweezers picking up syllables and
putting them down" (278). Whereas in his 1917-1918 preface to
The House of Dust Aiken had invited the reader to enter the
poem as he would a life, he now accepts that invitation himself
and enters the dream of his own life. And in the dream the protagonist confronts and attempts to understand the elements
which have created him. He discovers he is not self-constituted,
but an " 'Inheritor!'—this word my father said / And Doctor
Wundt said also" (280).

The poem is therefore a pilgrimage—the final pilgrimage, as it
is now the final poem of the Divine Pilgrim series—epitomized
in the journey of Childe Roland, whose Dark Tower is the ego.
But not all of the elements of the ego can be absorbed into
poetry, and for the first time in his work Aiken combines a prose
passage with his verse. He could not yet adequately translate the
lesson of his fiction into poetry, and, since he endeavors not to
falsify his experience, it remains prose.[12] In *Turns and Movies*

and elsewhere, he had dramatized a series of vaudeville performers in order to suggest a collective ego; he now turned in this new autobiographical direction and dramatized them as aspects of himself. He understands their identities in himself, and not vice versa as before:

Here I was Glozo, the card eater, the ventriloquist . . . and Mrs. Glozo, the plump-rumped assistant. Here I was Tozo, the Jap, and his family of little Tozos . . . lying on their long backs and twirling purple barrels. . . . Here I was Nozo, the hobo. . . . I was each of these in turn, and then also I was Bozo, the muscular trapeze artist, and all the while I was Harry cocking his left eye over his fiddle, and Tom rubbing sandpaper together . . . and three thousand yellow faces perched in rows like birds, and a humming marble foyer with gilt mirrors, and O'Dwyer crowding into the same telephone booth with Mrs. Harry Frank (naughty-naughty) and the electric sign in Bosworth Place—

All this I was, and also the amphitheatre itself,
All this, but also a small room, a forest. (284)

And he moves into another series of details in which he defines himself as a "highly complex and self-conscious contemporary individual" (873)—Socrates, Christ, and Hegel all contributing. Finally, he becomes a boxing ring in which he destroys himself: "Daily I fight here, / Daily I die for the world's delight / By the giant blow on my visible heart" (287). Here, then, is the same process we have noted in "The Last Visit" and Aiken's other short stories—the celebration of suffering through memory. He dies daily that the past ("Inheritor!") may live in him, and that therefore, he and his audience may live daily:

Father and mother, who gave
Life, love, and now the grave,
What is it that I can be?
Nothing but what lies here,

The hand still, the brain sere,
Naught lives in thee

Nor ever will live, save
It have within this grave
Roots in the mingled heart. (288)

This, in the fourth and final section, is a moment of terrible directness, perhaps the first of its kind in the poetry of Conrad Aiken. In *Senlin* the ego asked generically, "how is it that I am I, Senlin, and not someone else?" (870); but the hero of "Changing Mind" is able to adopt no such guise. He is inexorably, irretrievably himself—and, as consciously as possible, asks only: "What is it that I inherit?" (287). What, in the whole history of the world, and in my specific history, has made me as I am?

It is almost as if in this poem Aiken were recreating, in order to understand, the whole process of his development: beginning with his early psychological interest in *Forslin* (section 1: "Sell him to Doctor Wundt the psycho-analyst / Whose sex-ray eyes will separate him out."); then moving to the mythical poems (2: "Childe Roland, leaving behind him the dark tower, / Came in the evening to the land of kites."); to, in the third section, his prose; and finally, in section four, to a new restraint and control. In both subject and form, the poem constitutes Aiken's first real self-investigation in verse. In the fourth section he moves through and out of his earlier sense of the divine pilgrimage. With Childe Roland he has discovered the Dark Tower. But he has gone on alone to explore the darkness itself.

· I V ·

Perhaps, in the light of what I have been saying, *Blue Voyage* (1927) is best entered at its conclusion; or rather, near its conclusion, in the six unsent letters to Cynthia which constitute Chapter VII. Aiken had moved toward the letter as the defini-

91

tive form of his short stories. We will recall that in an attempt at self-revelation in *The House of Dust* he employed the device of a letter to a friend. Properly understood, his use of the letter assumes considerable importance in a study of his development. Demarest's first letter to Cynthia, in fact, is an extension of a piece called "The Whale-Ship," which Aiken took from his manuscript and published separately as a short story.[13] It is necessary to observe, then, the effect which Aiken wished to achieve in the epistolary form.

Perhaps influenced by Emily Dickinson's "letters to the world"—he had edited her *Selected Poems* in 1924—Aiken struck upon the form at once in his first volume of short stories, in a piece called simply "The Letter." The hero of "The Letter" is a voyeur who ever desires, but is always unable, to reveal himself; as he says: "I am at the same time exceptionally sensitive and exceptionally incapable of expressing my feelings" (B.B., 186). In his relations with people, nonetheless, he has "a private and all-devouring *curiosity* as to the lives, the intimate secret feelings, of others" (189). This is, of course, a symptom of the megalomania which he shares with the later protagonists of "No, No, Go Not to Lethe" and *King Coffin* (1935); perhaps all are descendants and extensions *in extremis* of Coverdale of *The Blithedale Romance*. "The point is this—[as the hero of "The Letter" explicitly says] that the sight of a human being undergoing a crisis, victim of powerful emotions, thrills and delights me, provided that I can be a concealed witness, watch the drama unobserved" (190). Thus the supreme event of his life is the receipt of a letter not intended for him personally, or for anybody in particular, but written by a man who, having discovered that he has only two years to live, feels compelled to tell someone, anyone, about himself—to make a full confession at his moment of crisis. The moment of crisis—that is what Aiken's fictive letters consistently deal with. Unlike "normal" letters they are not primarily, often not at all, concerned with events. Their intention, rather, is to serve as examples of intense self-revelation.

So also in "Round by Round," the sports-writer attempts to write a letter to his faithless wife—not a letter, he says, "in the ordinary sense of the word" (S.S., 243), but one in which he might become conscious of and, by defining, escape the emotions which are destroying him. Prompted by a photograph of the James family, he writes, finally: "What I really want to tell you about is these three people. I would like to tell you what they mean to me, what art-shape they made of their lives, what it might mean to you or to anybody to *realize* what they are as they sit there—" (244). But like Senlin and Demarest he fails; for since he despairs of revealing his ego, the writer seeks refuge in symbols. The same situation obtains in "The Fish Supper"— with the same failure: "How [the protagonist asks] could you sum up in one letter all your feelings about ten years of married life?" (S.S., 297). Although these characters cannot possibly succeed, yet they must attempt to define their egos. Perhaps they can never be fully understood because they never fully understand themselves. The hero of "By My Troth, Nerissa" is more successful in perceiving and ruthlessly exposing his own defects. So too, the writer of the letter which comprises the whole of "I Love You Very Dearly" has, through time and the experience of suffering, achieved the kind of serenity which allows him to hope in conclusion that "this blather of confession of my own worthlessness, will be excused maybe if it helps you out" (S.S., 316). In *King Coffin*, Jasper Ammen concludes his public life with a self-revelatory letter, "with the impediment in my speech removed" (338), in which he reaches his highest level of self-understanding.

When the letter itself does not appear in Aiken's stories, it is often replaced by another form used in a very similar fashion. A common variant is the extended soliloquy, as in "Soliloquy on a Park Bench" or Chapter IV of *Blue Voyage*. Another is the description of a person's response to the climactic crisis of

93

his life. The hero of "The Moment," for instance, "believed that one's life consisted of at most half a dozen moments of supreme experience, or perhaps not even as many as that" (S.S., 465). In this story, and in others like "The Professor's Escape," Aiken reveals a *persona* by analyzing his actions during a moment of "supreme experience." In each case the possibilities of self-revelation are uppermost; the "plot" itself is negligible. The obituary notice in "Your Obituary, Well Written" is of course a striking variant upon these forms—its question being: "which one, of all the innumerable events of a well-filled life . . . would [I] choose as revelatory?" (401). The story, in this sense, consists of the protagonist's composition of his own obituary notice, the only one which would truly define his life, by reducing it to its quintessential experience.

Blue Voyage is, as might be expected, an extension of the methods adumbrated in the short stories, as well as the fruition of Aiken's earlier autobiographical explorations. Considering the way in which Aiken composed *Blue Voyage*, one might argue that he wrote the stories partly in order to learn how to write his novel. He composed the first chapter of the novel in 1922-1923, then "felt at some loss to go on, [due to] certain technical weaknesses, and decided to strengthen his hand by trying a volume of short stories."[14] The result, *Bring! Bring!*, preceded *Blue Voyage* by two years. He did not complete the novel until 1926, after he had written many of the *Costumes By Eros* (1928) stories. In his stories, then, he developed the form appropriate to his novel. Aiken was to write in 1931 that "Ulysses was a landmark in my life,"[15] and many critics remarked on the similarities of Aiken's to Joyce's novel. But *Blue Voyage* was only slightly influenced by the methods and psychological schemata of Joyce and Dorothy Richardson. Rather, it issued from the Divine Pilgrim—itself a psychological novel—and Aiken's recent short stories. Obviously Aiken was trying to fuse the confessional with the aesthetic novel, to move simultaneously in two directions: in the confessional novel, from his art to his life; and *via* the aesthetic construct, in the tradition from Flaubert to Joyce, from his life to the work of art which can be made objective from it. One feels the conflict between these intentions in *Blue Voyage*; they force the novel apart from chapter to chapter. In *Ushant*, consequently, Aiken would face—and, I think, solve—the problem of working in those two directions, while yet holding the book together. To do this, however, he would have to create a wholly new form, not merely combine the old ones. The attempt in *Blue Voyage* is the measure of his success in *Ushant*.

Blue Voyage, to be sure, succeeds in its own right as a revelation of the artist who can both live and write about his life. The plot of the novel, in brief, is built upon a descending then ascending curve. And, as in *Great Circle* and *Conversation*, novels to come, Aiken was able to adapt the assumptions and methods of his earlier symphonies to the necessities of the novel. He counterpoints facts, emotions, and tones as correlatives to the inner conflicts of his protagonists. Sailing to England (Chapters I and II) in pursuit of Cynthia, Demarest discovers that she is on the ship with him (III)—and that she is engaged to be married. At its very beginning, then, his journey is futile. His actions lack ultimate cause, and he must therefore seek their motives in himself. In Chapter IV, consequently, Demarest retreats into himself as a person and, in a preconscious monologue, explores his relation to Cynthia. In Chapter V, Aiken deals with Demarest's dilemma as a writer who has discovered that he is a failure. These two chapters are paralleled by VI and VII; in VI, Demarest sublimates his love for Cynthia by transforming her into "a tall Gothic window, where motionless, in frozen sentimentalities of pink, white and blue . . . [she] was turned to glass" (267). In VII he seeks to solve his problem as a writer by writing letters to her. These six unsent letters to Cynthia are clearly meant to serve the same revelatory purpose as similar letters in Aiken's short stories. Because they carry with

them associations from the whole novel, they are more sugges-
tively luminescent in their meanings. The book ends (VIII) as
Faubion—the incarnation of the earthy, and therefore antithetical to Cynthia—is about to enter Demarest's stateroom.

After meeting Cynthia in III, Demarest immediately seeks
refuge in the unconscious. Thereafter he becomes progressively
more conscious; IV constitutes his unconscious, and VII, his conscious self-exploration and confession. In the first of his letters
Demarest relates a boyhood experience at New Bedford, believing that "whatever is true—I mean *idiosyncratically* true—of
me, is also deeply true of you; and my confession would therefore be your—accusation" (272). Like many of Aiken's other
fictive letters, this is inconclusive; for Demarest is unable to
bring the childhood episode into any real, communicable bearing upon his personal situation. This is not to say that the story
does not have meaning or evocative power—only that its symbolic and emotional values resist Demarest's attempt to apply
them to a definition of his personal situation. Aiken thereby
succeeds brilliantly in revealing Demarest's character, while
Demarest fails utterly to reveal his own to Cynthia. Thus, the
letter is "Not Sent." In his second letter, he tries self-revelation
along different lines. The first was concerned with what kind
of person he was and *is*, the second deals with what he *does*; and
he is, of course, a writer. From the question, "Why should I
be writing you letters at all?" (288), he moves naturally to an
analysis of his literary production:

> What if . . . in choosing this literary method, this deliberate
> indulgence in the prolix and fragmentary, I merely show my-
> self at the mercy of a personal weakness which is not uni-
> versal, or ever likely to be, but highly idiosyncratic? That is
> perfectly possible; and it brings me back to my starting-point.
> I *am* like that—I do think and feel in this confused and fluc-
> tuating way—I frequently suspect that I am nothing on earth
> but a case of *dementia praecox, manqué,* or arrested. Isn't all

this passion for aspects and qualifications and relativities a clear enough symptom of schizophrenia? (290-91)

This is precisely the criticism which Aiken directed toward his own work in his review of *Nocturne of Remembered Spring*, entitled "Schizophrenia." Like the narration of the childhood episode, Demarest's analysis of his failure as a writer results from his desire for self-revelation—if Cynthia cannot identify herself emotionally with the man, perhaps she can sympathize with his predicament as an author and respect his integrity as he ruthlessly exposes his defects. His discussion in the same letter of the hallucination he had in Chapter VI presents further, and even more concretely, the mind behind the writing. We see him casting out various ways of making his confession complete; yet we see too that all of them are failures. In his third letter he retaliates with anger and a defense of his own actions— "I am simply too shy" (303)—so inadequate that it is not even finished. The fourth letter moves to irony; the fifth consists simply of the minimal confession of a pun ("Sick Transit!"); and the last letter gives up entirely the desire for confession— it is, in short, "Not written." Altogether, the six letters document the progressive degeneration of self-knowledge in Demarest; introspection failing, he moves toward Faubion and the conclusion of his book.

As in "Round by Round" and "The Fish Supper," then, Aiken concludes in *Blue Voyage* that complete self-revelation is impossible. Of ourselves we know only a little; of others, nothing at all. Repeating the classical admonition *Know Thyself*, Demarest comments, "That was the best joke ever perpetrated" (16). Personal identity is viewed simply as a series, with no continuous, constant existence. It is "a steaming universe of germ-cells, a maelstrom of animal forces, of which he himself, his personality, was only the collective gleam" (16). This view constitutes, of course, an emotional and intellectual solipsism— in which man is, as in *Festus*, both the reflection of the world,

97

of all things, and is still confined within himself. But Aiken as author has moved beyond the limits of self in creating, and thus standing aside and objectively analyzing, himself in Demarest. Aiken can write the book, but Demarest must forever project himself into the infinite in order to discover and comprehend his own individuality.

In this sense, the "Blue Voyage" is the voyage of Demarest's soul, or of his consciousness, into the infinite, and therefore into itself. As soon as he enters the ship, Demarest is "launched into the infinite, the immense solitude," while at the same time he is "alone in a cage with a world of tigers roaring outside" (3). It is this double, paradoxical movement which defeats Demarest; for, catapulted into the infinite, he loses his ability to act as a person and is therefore reduced to passive mental projections of his own ambiguity. As we see in his letters to Cynthia, he has not managed to reveal the ego—though his attempt is heroic. All he has discovered is the utter frustration and desolation of existence. Setting the emotional tone, the preconscious reverie which comprises Chapter IV repeats the word "Misery" throughout as its recurring motif. Because of his isolation, he finds misery as the center of creation. "MISERY . . . Misery is consciousness. Misery is death. Misery is birth. Misery is creation" (119), he says at the beginning of his descent toward the unconscious, giving direction to the whole of the soliloquy to follow.

The notion that at the heart of things is suffering or misery was not an unfamiliar theme in Aiken's poetry before *Blue Voyage*. In 1917, for example, he had written "Tetélestai," his first approach to the shortening of the symphonic mode. The title is Greek for "forsaken," and the poem deals with:

> The one who went down under shoutings of chaos,
>   the weakling
> Who cried his 'forsaken!' like Christ on the darkening
>   hilltop!. . . .

This, then, is the one who implores, as he dwindles
            to silence,
A fanfare of glory . . . And which of us dares to
            deny him? (299)

Demarest is himself plunged into chaos and at last, in his letters, "dwindles to silence."

Following the narrative elements of time, place, and scene
which open the book, the preconscious monologue of Chapter
IV constitutes Demarest's attempt to escape from obsessive concreteness. Structurally, it parallels the concluding letters, the
one being the protagonist's conscious and the other his subconscious attempt to impose his own identity upon the infinite. In
his monologue, of course, he approaches self-revelation differ-
ently than in the letters. He is engaged both in pointing up the
misery of all mankind (through the symbol of Goya who *"drew
four slatterns, in an attic, Heavy, with heads on arms, asleep:
And underscribed it. 'Let them slumber! Who, if they woke,
could only weep!'"* [122]) and in himself expiating (as Christ)
for this misery. After the long catalogue of misery and self-casti-
gation produced by this effort, he reaches the point of summary
atonement, and sets the world right by casting himself into the
role of the crucified Christ:

> Smith, star-wandering, cigar in hand, will find his mother.
> For the fly with torn wings, I will make new wings of an
> even more daedalian beauty. The clairvoyant I will deliver
> from his torment of vatic dreams; and Goya, touched by my
> hands, will at last close his eyes. . . . From the whole earth,
> as it rolls darkly through space around the sun, will come a
> sound of singing. . . . I will permit myself to be crucified.
> MY SELF. (188-89)

The prophecy of the clairvoyant that someone on the ship
would die is fulfilled. Spiritually, Smith dies in his lack of human sympathy ("This was the death of Smith" [316]); and in

the same spiritual sense Demarest is crucified. His separation of the body and soul in his love for Cynthia results in his loss of his own identity; he exists only in the image he has created. In so sacrificing his selfhood, he ceases to be.

At the same time that Demarest is moving toward infinity—Cynthia—he is descending into himself. While he is crucified generically, as universal saviour, he is also, on the personal level, a scapegoat. One reviewer observed that the book "is intrinsically sincere—indeed, almost too directly cathartic in motive to be of value as a work of art."[16] If this is a fault, it is also, from the point of view of this study, a virtue, and constitutes a primary value in the novel. In its cathartic motive lies Aiken's development; for in his self-inflicted crucifixion of Demarest he exorcises the part of his poetic self which held him to a proliferation of divine pilgrim poems. He is able to use "his protagonist as the scapegoat for his own life,"[17] and thus to free himself from his earlier work. He can leave behind the "popular" Freudian view that the artist does nothing but lie in order to satisfy man's desire for wish-fulfillment, developed in Chapter v of *Blue Voyage* as fully as in "A Basis for Criticism." One suspects that Aiken had been initially misled by a loose understanding of Freud, though by the middle twenties he came to understand Freud more deeply. Whereas Freud had emphasized the ability of psychoanalysis to study the artist, not to analyze his art, Aiken had earlier confused the two. But in *Blue Voyage* he shows a new, more mature sense of Freud's notion of the human character and its motivations. In Demarest Aiken shows the dilemma which results from confusing the art-work with the artist. As a result, he attains the freedom to allow the possibility "that the whole ["popular"] Freudian idea, as thus applied to art, is wrong" (218-19). Regarding his intentions in *Blue Voyage*, Aiken wrote to Malcolm Cowley: "And it seemed to me a useful thing to do, at this point in my life: I mean, to give myself *away*, for the benefit of any stray psychologist of literature who might be interested in diagnosing the case of the

100

author of Forslin et al" (Wake, 28). Perhaps Aiken meant only that the novel is an example of conscious self-revelation. But in "diagnosing the case of the author of Forslin," he also expelled that author from his ego. Never again could he write the kind of poems he once wrote. The author of *Forslin* expelled, the author of the fiction remains. Neither Demarest's voyage into the infinite, nor his "Blue Voyage" into himself—one and the same—has been successful. Aiken, on the other hand, has disposed of the Demarest and the Cynthia of his early poems. It is Aiken's Blue Voyage as well, for the book was admittedly an attempt, and a successful one, to explore and reveal his own psyche at that moment. The Cynthia story, then, serves merely as a vehicle for an interim statement on Conrad Aiken, aged thirty-five. Thus, in conclusion, Aiken can ask the all-important question: "What shall I do? Shall I go on, half-civilized liar that I am, and add a few more reefs of flowery coral to my already disgracefully massive production, and thus help deluded mankind to add delusion to delusion? Or shall I turn back, and do my best to destroy this terrible structure of hypocrisy? . . . I think . . . I will turn back. I think I must turn my back on you" (B.V., 301-02). In doing so, he could turn to the Preludes.

THE LONG POEM has been modified in our time by the antithetical attempt of the Imagists to delineate sensuous reality through single, precise shocks upon the nervous system. While we can think of many important long poems—*The Bridge, Paterson*, the *Cantos*—even these are made not from unified and harmonious world-views, but rather, grow from what Erich Kahler called the "all-embracement of discontinuity." Our poets in general have accepted and used a world populated by the disparate and fragmentary. Prose fiction has assumed the responsibility for the epic, even for the meditation, and poetry has confined itself to the visual or tonal titivation of the sensations. In a sense, this is what poetry had to do for us, to relate us once more to our universe in a physical way. But it is not, as Aiken and others felt, the whole speech of the whole man. Influenced by the Imagists, yet wishing to do something larger than a concentration upon observational sensibility alone allows, Aiken became interested in presenting poems in a seqence or series. As the musician constructs something meaningful out of a sequence of notes, working finally to the complex composition, the quartet, the symphony, so also Aiken hoped to expand the meanings of single poems by arranging them in series. Thereby he would move beyond the limitations of the Imagists and present the whole man. Written in 1914, "Discordants" indicates this interest at the very beginning of his career. In later years there followed *Turns and Movies*, "Variations," "Improvisations: Lights and Snow," *Priapus and the Pool*, and "Sonnets I-IX" (included in *John Deth*). The Divine Pilgrim poems, of course, were an elaboration of the series idea. In all, much of the interest lay in "the possibility of variation, whether by contrast of tone, theme, or form, within the frame of a unifying reference."[1]

Such variations within unity is at its simplest in "Discordants" (18-20). In the well-known first poem, "Music I Heard With You," the tone is deliberately sentimental and meditative; the poet conceives of his love as a sacrament. The tone of the second poem is more stringent—its rhythms less fluent and its line more definitely end-stopped than in the first. Here also, Aiken employs city imagery ("And tunes from a hurdy-gurdy that coldly rejoices"), and emphasizes the "I" in contrast to the "you" of the first poem. The third poem, in contrast to the second, directs us toward tradition and luxurious imagery ("Dead Cleopatra lies in a crystal casket"). In its emphasis upon union, it combines the persons of the first two poems— "you and I." The theme here is derived from *Earth Triumphant*, with the union brought about by earth ("Close well above us, that we may rest forever, / Sending up grass and blossoms to the sky"). In IV, there is an inner contrast between the city of II and the sea, recalling Arnold's "Marguerite." The accompanying separation of the lovers ("You on the farther shore, and I in this street") contrasts to their unity in III. As a whole, "Discordants" is inconclusive simply because Aiken was interested in the process of working out variations, not in the possibility of "completed" statement. "Discordants" may be best seen as Aiken's first experiment with the kind of connotative language and personal symbolism that was to dominate the poems in *Nocturne of Remembered Spring*. "Variations," was also, "an experiment in modulation of emotion-tone" (C.P., 877). In both poems, nothing but the implication of contrasts in emotion holds the parts together in a series. And in the sense that each poem ever written is different from all others, there is no actual justification, other than the poet's arrangement, for considering these poems to have emotional unity.

Therefore, Aiken sought in "Improvisations: Lights and

Snow" to adapt (or adopt) a form which would suggest unity
while at the same time allowing for diversity in the series. In
"Variations," of course, he had achieved a certain simple cohesion by making Autumn the basic scene of all the poems. He
continued this device in "Improvisations," employing Winter
in the same way. But in order to give his sequence a firmer
unity, Aiken also attempted to suggest in it a predictable, basic
form upon which he could play variations. The form, as is clear
from the very first poems, is that of Waley's Chinese translations or of Pound's *Cathay*; its emotion is subdued by the conjunction of sharp images with a deliberate flatness of tone. It
uses too, the foreshortened blank verse characteristic of the
Imagists:

> Like an old tree uprooted by the wind
> And flung down cruelly
> With roots bared to the sun and stars
> And limp leaves brought to earth—
> Torn from its house—
> So do I seem to myself
> When you have left me. (xɪv, 295)

Although the line lengths both within and between poems are
varied, the rigidity of the form chosen allows less variation than
that exhibited in "Variations." Here, Aiken gained unity by
surrendering the primary intent of the series—emotional contrast and variation.

Priapus and the Pool (1922) is, with the exception of the
larger Divine Pilgrim poems, perhaps Aiken's first successful use
of the series. The form is fairly constant, but the standard quat-
rains are sufficiently open to be varied, as in v, ɪx, and xɪv—
the last moving into the broken couplet. Chiefly through his
use of a new device—the dialogic preface which asks the central question of the whole series—Aiken achieves unity in
Priapus:

But can a pool remember its reflections?
That is the thing that troubles me!
Does it remember the cloud that falls upon it,
Or the indignation of a tree?
Or suppose that once the image of Priapus
Fell quivering in ferocious sunlight there
As he came suddenly upon it from his forest
With fir-cones in his hair—
Would the pool, through the silence thereafter,
Recall that visitation and be stirred? (384-85)

The question is, What can the ego remember? Is it simply, as in *Festus*, a surface, a sea-surface full of clouds—a pool or mirror which reflects the fluid world that passes by it; or has it any identity of its own—if only an identity whose principle is the ability to create itself in conjunction with the world? Can it somehow absorb into itself the energy of its racial history—symbolized in Priapus and his ancient forest—and thereby transcend its own limits? The poems which follow are memorials of the ego creating itself, much in the same fashion as in the sections of *Senlin*. The poems, then, give various answers to the single question posed by the preface.

Aiken also accomplishes the kind of variation within unity which he had previously sought by his use, for instance, of companion poems. Number IV, originally published as the "Portrait of a Girl," envisions the girl as the meeting of three pilgrims under a tree: "This is the shape of the tree, / And the flower, and the leaf, and the three pale beautiful pilgrims" (388); VII was first entitled "Portrait of a Man," and, in contrast, pictures him as a desert over which passes "a faint wind, slow, exhausted" (390). In these poems—as in most of the others—the shape-shifting ego is created through memory in its various guises and disguises, by the sets of symbols which evoke it. In XIII, Aiken epitomizes his manner of self-creation by comparing the poet's method to the sculptor's:

See, as the carver carves a rose,
A wing, a toad, a serpent's eye,
In cruel granite, to disclose
The soft things that in hardness lie,

So this one, taking up his heart,
Which time and change had made a stone,
Carved out of it with dolorous art. (395)[2]

Just as in his carving the sculptor reveals the inward shape of
his granite, so also the poet discloses the secrets of his heart by
shaping his ego into poetry. Above all, he must be true to that
shape which comes from within. Only in this way does the ego
become more than a passive pool—it becomes a world which
reflects both inward and outward.

Priapus and the Pool received little attention, and it is re-
grettable that Aiken did not include it in its original form in
his *Collected Poems*; for part of its design is lost in the dele-
tions. Nevertheless, even as the sequence now stands, one can
observe its pattern of self-creation in accordance with a central
question or theme. The question provides the basic unity, while
the various answers contrast and set emotions or ideas against
one another. Its publication in 1922 is significant; for it is clear
how in Aiken's development the theory of the poems like these
combined with the beginnings of his work in fiction. Both seek
to memorialize the ego by setting down the details important
to its creation and continuity.

Priapus led to no immediate fruition in Aiken's poetry—
probably because it was not sufficiently formed in the sense
that *Senlin* was, or the Preludes were to be. For this reason,
Aiken's important literary development during 1920-1925 is in
his fiction; in his major poetry Aiken turned to the mythical
form and substance of *John Deth*. We should not forget, however, that during this period Aiken was also experimenting in
poetic form, and developing a blank verse poem in which his

range and freedom of expression might be greater than earlier. The results of this experiment are the thirteen poems which now follow *John Deth* in the *Collected Poems*, although they first appeared in the 1925 edition of *Priapus and the Pool*. Of these experiments Aiken wrote: "The great flexibility of the form attracted me, with its range all the way from lyric or narrative to contemplative or analytic. . . . It was my idea to keep the *terms* as simple as possible, and merely to let the chosen theme *act itself*: a mere reporting of a thing done and seen."[8] He made no attempt to put these poems together as a series. Each poem comprises an individual experiment in technique. Not all would be usable in Aiken's development. The result is often bizarre, as in "Sea Holly," which explores to their fullest the possibilities of repetition; the word "rock" is repeated twenty-two times in forty-eight lines. "God's Acre" plays upon tombstone epitaphs:

> In Memory Of. In Fondest Recollection Of.
> In Loving Memory Of. In Fond
> Remembrance. Died in October. Died at Sea. (450)

And the poem moves, without warning, into a dialogue of dead men trying to rise: " 'Try once again—together—NOW!' " (451) In other poems Aiken experiments with the dialogue of the self with itself—for instance, in "King Borborigmi" and "The Wedding"—or of the self with others, as in "Elder Tree"; with the fragmentation of the stanza, as in "An Old Man Weeping"; and with the shortening and compressing of the symphony, as in "Electra," a decided advance upon his earlier similar attempt in "Tetélestai." These thirteen poems range from the traditionally poetic (from Trumbull Stickney's "Be Still. The Hanging Gardens Were a Dream," which Aiken anthologized):

> And in the hanging gardens there is rain
> From midnight until one, striking the leaves
> And bells of flowers. (447)

107

—to the creation of (in Aiken) a "new" grammar and imagery in "Dead Leaf in May":

> Human, who trudge the road from Here to There:
> Lock the dry oak-leaf's flimsy skeleton
> In auricle or ventricle; sail it
> Like a gay ship down red Aorta's flood.
> Be the paired blossoms with dead ribs between.
> Thirst in the There, that you may drink the Here. (455)

In general, the kind of form which these poems are pointed toward is the *parable*. Aiken wrote to Peterson in 1924 that in them he "decided in advance that a *parable* form, a kind of symbolic narrative might lend force to one's ideas which in a more strictly reflective manner would be lacking."[4] In this Aiken was influenced, he has said, by the work of Jean de Bosschère, a now little-known Flemish writer who still continues, however, to be one of Aiken's favorite poets. Aiken had enthusiastically reviewed de Bosschère's *The Closed Door* in 1918—noting that he was "a poet who happens to be highly developed on the cerebral side, as well as on the tactile, a poet for whom the most terrible and most beautiful realities are in the last analysis ideas, who sees that as in life the most vivid expression of ideas is in action, so in speech the most vivid expression of them is in parables (ABC, 138-39). Both *Festus* and *John Deth*, perhaps, had been somewhat influenced by de Bosschère's poetry—especially by the poems in which he created a myth out of a hint in legend. Bosschère's "Ulysse Bâtit Son Lit" combines, as *John Deth* does, surface comedy with underlying tragedy and suffering. But it was his more personal poems which were to have a lasting influence upon Aiken, poems like "Doutes," "Homer Marsh," or "L'Homme de Quarante Ans":

> Alone, with death alone,
> My inner companion,
> Faithful wife, daughter and son, father and mother,

All my ancestors;
And always my monstrous, cruelly thought-out child.[5]

Aiken would deepen Bosschère's narration of parables into his own characteristic meditations *in* parable.

It is easy now to see the direction in which Aiken has been moving in the effort to create an adequate form to sustain his exploration of consciousness. I should quickly add that I do not mean to imply that Aiken's work to 1930 is important only as it contributed to his increasing awareness. Individually his poems and stories make their own claims upon our attention. Nevertheless, Aiken himself has always been concerned with his own development, and in a sense his whole work is one continuous series progressively working toward a full clarity of consciousness, within and without himself. The first step in this direction was in his essay at self-revelation and definition of the limits of consciousness in IV, 3, of *The House of Dust*. A development of this monologue was the idea of the document developed in *Punch*, whose subtitle is *Documents in His History*: the facts of a life are set down from various viewpoints, contrasting with and complementing one another. In his short stories and *Blue Voyage*, he used the letter form toward the same end of self-revelation. In these thirteen poems the letter is deepened into the parable: the poems become letters to the world in a symbolic narrative, or narrative symbol. With this development, he was able to write his Preludes, the coherent series use of his earlier experiments in form and self-investigation.

Aiken wrote most of his *Preludes for Memnon* before the dramatic poem which was published almost simultaneously with them, *The Coming Forth By Day of Osiris Jones*. The later poem, however, makes clear what Aiken sought to accomplish in both volumes of the Preludes. It is his own sense of what his efforts meant. In the same way that Aiken explicated, for instance, *The House of Dust* and *John Deth* toward their conclusions, so also with *Osiris Jones* he gave to the Preludes their all-encompassing *raison d'être*, the myth by which they have meaning. For this reason, I shall consider *Osiris Jones* before the Preludes. Explaining why he placed *Osiris Jones* ahead of the Preludes in his recent *Selected Poems*, Aiken wrote in the preface: "For one thing, it helps, I think, to explain those two sequences; and for another, it enables me to put them together, as they were meant to be—to all intents, they are one poem."[6] These, taken together with *Landscape West of Eden*, make up the central poem in Aiken's career.

· I I ·

In a note to *Osiris Jones*, Aiken quoted from E. A. Wallis Budge: "In all the copies of 'The Book of the Dead' the deceased is always called 'Osiris,' and as it was always assumed that those for whom they were written would be found innocent when weighed in the Great Balance, the words 'true of voice,' which were equivalent in meaning to 'innocent and acquitted,' were always written after their names" (C.P., 878). The dead man is called Osiris in the book of justification interred with his body, "since Osiris, overcome by Set the Liar and reconstituted by eating the eye of Horus, was the first to be delivered from the Devourer and be adjudged 'true of voice,' his individuality perfect, his soul divine, his words exquisite."[7] Since the act of judgment is essentially an act of knowledge, the deceased must fully report the facts of his life to Memnon so that he may be judged true of voice and step forth from the darkness into the light. As Aiken conceived it, then, "the judgment is not upon the good and evil a man may have done in his life, but upon the completeness of the accounting."[8] He must, in other words, be fully conscious of what he has done, for such consciousness serves to balance the feather of truth and justify his life.

Thus, while Aiken had been searching for a form adequate to full self-definition—successively in the monologue, the document, the letter, the series of answers to a single question, and the parable—there was a ready-made form available to him since the Egyptians. But it was one whose possibilities, I should quickly add, he could not have realized had he not gone through this agonizing search. Here, then, his interest in myth and self-revelation unite. Using the form of a late dynastic or Empire funerary roll or grave book, he once more prepared a report on his life. And the report is a document, a letter, a parable: its material is all life, since everything and anything may go into the book in order that the deceased may be wholly forgiven by being wholly understood. It is, as John Holmes observed, "salvation by total recall."

He therefore sets down the memories of his consciousness from several different viewpoints. In the ninth section, "Mr. Jones Addresses a Looking-Glass," he makes a distinction realized through *Priapus* and the cathartic action of *Blue Voyage*. The self is not merely a passive mirror of the world. By the act of memory, Jones becomes conscious: "but I remember / what I see / and that, in mirrors, / cannot be" (591); and by his consciousness he becomes divine, acceptable to Memnon as "O angel soul, O memory of man!" (574). The mirror can only preach, through passivity, oblivion and the avoidance of suffering: "well, Mr. Jones, perhaps it's better / to be, like me, a good forgetter" (591). But it is precisely through suffering and, as in the short stories, the celebration of his failures, that Aiken, or Jones, achieves salvation. To the sins against him—which he does not fail to include—he simply says: I have done much evil in my time, but I have not forgotten; I have remembered, and, therefore, suffered, understood, and accepted.

Thus in the second, third, fourth, sixth, seventh, and eighth sections he leaves in his tomb memorials which trace his various careers from birth to death. Osiris Jones leaving actual articles in a real tomb, or Aiken setting his memories down on paper—these acts are one and the same. In "The Things" section he leaves articles from the youth which he spent both in Savannah

111

("magnolia trees with whitehot torch of bud" [575]) and in New England ("Indian-pipes, and cider in the shed" [576]); and he transforms them, by his act of memory, into "the stars that make Orion's galaxy" (577), hoping to follow them into infinity. In "The Costumes" he leaves in the tomb the clothes he wore, from the "pair of infant's socks two inches long" (577) to "a coffin" (578). Here also he does this with an instinct for continuance; if the coffin is sinister ("I also serve who only lie in wait" [580]), the heart balances the beam by continuing, after death, to make an apology and justification, a final affirmation of the life so lived: "I will" (580).

So the rest of the sections continue. "Remarks on the Person of Mr. Jones" are written testimonials placed in his funerary roll. These include not only his nurse's remark, "it's a fine boy, not a blemish, God bless him" (581), but also critical comments: "you're an angel and a devil, too / and amateur at both" (582). Throughout the poem—in "Characteristic Comments," "Remarks on the Person of Mr. Jones," "Various Rooms"— Jones's mother appears in her several aspects, as a face, in the nursery, symbolized as music. In each case she responds lovingly, rapturously, to the child who has now come for judgment as a man. Like Jones's books, her love counterbalances the weight of analytic truth against him.

In "Inscriptions in Sundry Places," the poet lists the laws by which Jones has lived—another way of defining his personality. But he must be completely honest. Only the way he lives his daily life is important. He recalls, accordingly, the mottoes "Smoke Sweet Caporals" imprinted on a billboard; "e pluribus unum" on a coin; and, in the double-entendre "give yourself a weigh" (583) written on a scale, emphasizes his chief concern with self-revelation.

The last section but one, "Speeches Made By Books, Stars, Things and People," makes the final plea for continuity. Jones is, after all, a writer, and his books—the chief products of his consciousness—are included in his tomb and speak on his be-

half. Whatever he has done, he has been true to his ego. Aiken
is contrasting the weaknesses of the body with the integrity of
the mind. The earlier denigrations of Jones are now repeated
contrapuntally against the testimony of the books, in a "Negative Confession" similar to that in Chapter cxxv of the *Book
of the Dead*:

> *The books*
> I have not done an evil thing, but live
> on truth, and feed on truth, and have performed
> behests of men, and things that please the gods.
> *The things*
> Pull out the plug. (602-603)

In this section the testimony of the books is reinforced by the
reappearance of the mother as Aiken deepens the theme of
"Changing Mind." The books are the products of his consciousness; she is its producer, always immanent in its product, who
"follows the moving memory like a shadow,/ and only rests, at
last, when that too comes to rest" (594). Her speeches are the
pure lyrics for which Aiken had always sought; they are verbal
utterance uncontaminated by logical substance—pure affect:

> Wonder of wonders in a world of worlds
> o heart that beats beneath a larger heart
> quick hands to beauty born in helplessness
> and love of loveliness with tenderest touch—(607).

Thus Jones is wholly understood as he wholly understands, completely accepted as he completely accepts.

Aiken's second novel, *Great Circle* (1933), is the human, non-
mythical version of *Osiris Jones*. Although in point of composition it falls between the two volumes of Preludes, it is perhaps
better considered in anticipation of those poems; for it shows
the other side of the coin of *Osiris Jones*—and both sides make
the Preludes. Like Demarest and Peter Jones, like the Conrad

Aiken who is the personal hero of the Preludes, Andrew Cather of *Great Circle* is studied at the instant of his greatest agitation; and that crucial moment lays his soul bare and brings his whole lifetime into the focus of consciousness. Cather, like his earlier counterparts, seeks to become aware of the elements in his life which have produced this crisis. Aiken's work characteristically moves from an event to its cause, from motion to motive and emotion. As one critic says: "In each novel [Aiken] has begun with the unquestioned world of the senses, only to push gradually down through the different planes of being to the 'well' where the world of atoms, heat, blood, and digestion entangle with spiritual abstractions like love, honor, hope, beauty, and God."[9]

Having discovered that he is being deceived by his wife, Cather seeks to avoid consciousness so that he will be able to blame the whole affair upon others. "I get drunk," he says, "because I don't want to be wholly conscious. Because, I admit it, I'm partly a coward" (68). That he has one glass eye (he is called One-Eye Cather) symbolizes, of course, the blockage in his vision. He can only see half of any truth; he is acutely aware of his own private suffering, and yet strenuously avoids any insight into the pain whose cause is within himself.

Great Circle consists chiefly of Cather's interior and exterior monologues. These are often fantastic, for he distorts the real contents of his consciousness by falsely dramatizing them. At the very outset of the book he decides that "If life chooses to imitate a cheap melodrama, why then it is obvious enough that you have to behave like a character in a melodrama—a ridiculous hero" (7). But subconsciously he undergoes the inevitable, concomitant effort to make the roots of his problem conscious. He considers early in the book the possibility of taking a trip to Duxbury—the scene of his first rejection—but refuses consciously to admit his need to do so. At last, however, a long and detailed flashback into, and reliving of, his youth (Chapter II) and his partly drunken confession (III) to an amateur psychologist, Bill (who is William Demarest, Cather's alter ego), force

114

him to self-confrontation and the realization that he must go to Duxbury "to touch, for the last time, that agony, and to exorcise it—to drown in it derisively, savagely, or even, at last, indifferently. No, not indifferently—at last with acceptance" (334).

Both the flashback and the discussion with Bill are forms of confession and bring Cather to consciousness. The flashback into youth is an extension of the method of *Osiris Jones*—with its compulsive piling up of details in the effort to remember and thus to understand everything. To understand the original betrayal, the wound he sustained in Duxbury, he seeks to reconstruct the entire scene. Chapter II, then, is not merely a dream-sequence; Aiken intends it to be real, an exact and complete account of his experience insofar as it entered the consciousness of the boy. And Cather's imagination, as it returns to the scene, re-creates it with the sensuous imagery of youth—in contrast to the adult wasteland surrounding this chapter, with its cigarette ashes, cockroaches, and tired obscenities. He relives his youth by descending into the maelstrom of details, all clamoring for a place in his consciousness: "—particularly the smell of the pine-wood walls, soaked in sea-fog, but pine-smelling also in the strong sea sunlight, smooth to the touch, golden-eyed with knot-holes, and the wind singing through the rusty wire screens, fine-meshed and dusty, or clogged brightly with drops of dew, or drops of rain, or drops of fog" (86). Elsewhere he recalls his youthful botanical expeditions with his uncle: "Shad-bush, wild sarsaparilla, St. John's Wort, sand spurrey, wild indigo, and checkerberry. The goldenrods belong to the composite family, there are forty kinds in New England; but this sort, *solidago sempervirens*, which grows in the salt marshes, or near them—the heaviest, the strongest, the most fragrant—the one that the bees love, and the flies" (107-108). Again, he remembers details of the household:

—particularly also the food . . . the great jugs of rich cocoa, the great deep dish of blue-misted blueberries, the piles of muffins with their warm fragrance under the fresh napkins, the hot sweet corn wrapped in damp linen, the mountain of steamed clams. Porper beating with his spoon and saying second help, third help, fourth help, fifth help. The floating island pudding with the little white islands of stiff-beaten white of egg, which vanished on the tongue like sea-fog, and the brown column of griddle cakes, Molly laughing as she brought in a new batch. This is the grub that makes the butterfly. Every time we had griddle cakes Uncle David said that. (133-34)

Such lyric passages follow in series, periodically interrupting the narrative progress of the sequence which Cather seeks to relive so that he may understand his first rejection. They are the means —the only means—by which he can finally come to accept his mother's original betrayal of him, which he is now re-experiencing in his wife's infidelity. In a sense, there are no details in these passages that are relevant to the incident itself; but in the more important dramatic and psychological sense, of course, there can be no detail that is not relevant, so long as it is remembered clearly and can therefore be the means whereby he can re-create the suppressed contents of his consciousness. Cather is seeking the same kind of salvation as Jones, and in exactly the same way.

Like the characters in "A Letter" and "No, No, Go Not to Lethe," Cather resists revealing himself to Bill in fear of losing his virtue. In various ways he conceals his confession. But he has at least achieved self-understanding. And he awakes from his argument with Bill feeling calm and refreshed in his sense of having confessed, having realized that "to be aware is to suffer" (255). Bill's function is to prime Cather's consciousness with approved psychoanalytic answers, and then politely step aside (or even fall asleep) so that Cather can have the security of the confessional. That is, Bill can define Cather's problem in psychological terms—"In every one of your love affairs, you've tried to make your sweetheart your mother" (217)—and he can

116

then fall asleep in order that Cather may securely bring the details he keeps remembering to consciousness by speaking about them.

It was probably the great attention which Aiken paid to dreams and the analytic situation that caused Freud to call *Great Circle* a masterpiece and keep a copy of it in his waiting room in Vienna.[10] But perhaps Freud also understood that Aiken was dealing with a situation whose memory was as important to him as to Cather. Its personal significance became obvious by 1957 when Aiken published his play, *Mr. Arcularis*. The genesis of the play is important. Diana Hamilton, an English authoress, adapted Aiken's story of the same title to the stage. Among other changes in the story, she supplied Mr. Arcularis with a wife. Of the evolution of this character, when the play at last came to production in 1946, Aiken recently wrote:

> She refused to make sense. What to do about her? It was now that it first occurred to me that if a *mother*, Mr. Arcularis' mother, a mother towards whom . . . he had ambivalent feelings of love and hate, were substituted for the wife, it might conceivably be made to "work." And so I lifted almost bodily, from my own novel, *Great Circle*, the episode of the unfaithful mother, to whose misdemeanors her only son had been an accidental witness. . . . It would not only provide a recognizably logical explanation of Mr. Arcularis' sense of guilt—guilt, as it were, by identification and substitution—and a guilt not otherwise explained; it would also have the effect, at the moment of his absolution, of freeing him for the love which he had all his life denied himself. He could now, at last, die with a knowledge of supreme acceptance. (A., viii)

In the last scene of the play, Mr. Arcularis constructs the myth of his life and at last reaches back into the *Great Circle* scene to re-create his mother and Uncle David in order to accept

117

them and their betrayal as a fact of experience, so that he too may be acceptable. In a revision of the final scene in 1952-1953, Aiken allowed Mr. Arcularis to construct his mother's *apologia* with the sympathy derived from his abruptly acquired knowledge of the power of love. She explains:

> Children don't understand these things—how can they? Or they half understand . . . which is worse. . . . You see, your Uncle David meant a very great deal to me: meant everything: we loved each other very dearly. How could you possibly understand that we were all *young*—? all of us *young*? Only too late does the child understand that: only too late, too late either to help him, or to help them. For they need help too. . . . Don't you see, now that you're even older than we could ever be, that . . . it was just as cruel and dreadful for all of us?[11]

Likewise, *Great Circle* indicates that in going to Duxbury and accepting the whole situation, Cather will also be able to return to his wife. Mr. Arcularis more fully completes his "great circle" journey than Cather; for he lives his life so that he achieves his moment of acceptance coincidentally with the last instant of his existence—as Peter Jones does also—while Cather continues on to an existence more equivocal.

That Aiken should have used precisely the same situation as the crucial episode in both the novel and the play clearly suggests its personal importance to him. We can, I think, leave an analysis of this problem to the professional psychoanalyst; for, equating Aiken himself with his characters, we might think him, as Cather claims to be, "one of those talented fellows who combine all the madnesses in one—paranoia, dementia praecox, manic depressive, hysteria—name another" (191-92). One must differentiate between using Freudian concepts to analyze Aiken, and using them to understand the motivations of his characters. It is sufficient to note the resemblance between this mythos and the actual occurrence of his being awakened by revolver shots

118

and discovering, at the age of eleven, that his father had killed his mother and himself. Perhaps Uncle David is substituted for the father in the novel and the play, since Aiken had already carried through a "re-appraisal and exoneration of father, and the tacit admission . . . of his genius" (Ush., 103). It was only his mother who required understanding. And the experience was so dreadful that he had to re-create it, re-shifting the details, in order to wrest the necessary understanding out of them.

Indeed, Aiken had originally considered beginning *Mr. Arcularis* by arranging the first section, "Stage Direction," of his *Osiris Jones* chorally. He also concluded this 1950-1951 version as Mother and Uncle David—the "Two Voices" of Scene One —appear on stage and deliver the epilogue in verse borrowed from the mother's (music's) speeches in the penultimate section of *Osiris Jones*:

MOTHER

Angel of nothing in a world of nothings,
palmetto leaf in sunlight, time and tide
divinely moving, and the lighthouse bright
against the golden western sunset light—

UNCLE DAVID

O phrase of beauty in the darkness born,
spoken and stilled; swiftness against the cloud;
cloud against starlight, heartbeat in the blood,
memory of the dust and gods of dust.

In creating the characters that can so richly remember, he too remembers; and in their absolution he is absolved:

Give us this day our daily death, that we
may learn to live;
teach us that we trespass; that we may learn,
in wisdom, not in kindness, to forgive. (T.R., II, 666)

119

· I I I ·

"One of the 'perils of the soul,' " Jung wrote, "is, for instance, the loss of a soul. This is a case of part of the psyche becoming unconscious again."[12] *Preludes for Memnon* (1931) and *Time in the Rock* (1936) constitute Aiken's chief attempt to preserve the soul in the flux and chaos of a changing universe. The two volumes are meant to be taken together as one poem, and they are therefore his most extended use of the series form. Of the connection between these two volumes Aiken wrote: " 'Preludes for Memnon' and . . . 'Time in the Rock' are really, in effect, all parts of one poem. . . . Originally, I planned to entitle the two companion groups 'Preludes to Attitude' ('Memnon') and 'Preludes to Definition' ('Time in the Rock'), and I have always regarded them as belonging together and as constituting one unit."[13] They are the very center of his work, its core, emotionally and intellectually. To them all his earlier works lead; and from them his later work would issue. The first volume deals with the attitude we should most profitably take both toward the internal and external world, and the second with an attempt at defining its fluidity. They are built around a central philosophic concept, as we shall see, which gives core and unity— even if affective rather than logical—to the whole. Though their subject gives these poems a wider range than *Osiris Jones*, their method is fundamentally the same. In both cases the theme is "to put down, to fix in the eternal form of words, the fragments of consciousness, as many of them as possible, so that the life which the consciousness reflects may be known and judged."[14] The range is perhaps equal to the combination of *Osiris Jones* and *Great Circle*—self-investigation and revelation existing on both a universal and personal level.

Many critics have complained that Aiken has written preludes, but has reached no goal. This criticism results from a misunderstanding of the mythical basis of the poems. In the same sense as the fragments in *Osiris Jones*, his preludes commemorate

120

moments of consciousness before death. The ego in these poems builds the ramparts of memory against the terrors of extinction. The Preludes are speeches written for Memnon, the Colossus at Luxor which, because of a fissure caused by an earthquake, was the god who "sang the day before the daybreak came," and reminded the Greeks of Aurora's son Memnon slain at Troy, waiting for his mother, the Dawn, and fighting the powers of the darkness. Like Memnon or Peter Jones, the individual must accept the conditions of darkness in order that he may come forth into the light:

> Go back again, and find the divine dark;
> Seal up your eyes once more, and be as tombs;
> See that yourselves shall be as Memnon was.
>
> .   .   .   .   .
>
> Stone feet in sand, stone eyes, stone heart, stone lips.
>   (P.M., xxxviii, 543)

The poet must weave his song out of doubt and despair and chaos and change in order to achieve knowledge and hope and order and permanence; for, as Aiken insists in *Time in the Rock*, v, out of all things come their opposites: "Is hell your kingdom? / you know its privies and its purlieus? keep / sad record of its filth? Why this is health" (668). In descending, one ascends—toward himself.

The scheme of the whole series, then, is this: In human life we suffer the vicissitudes of doubt, despair, boredom, lack of understanding, the ravages of time, the confusions of chaos and change, the futility of endeavor, the loss of childhood illusions, unfaithfulness in love, self-deception in friendship, fear, terror, and so on. Only in consciousness of these things lies the salvation of life; for the consciousness of them transcends them. And thus these, the most important concerns of man, make the subjects which appear over and over, seen in their various aspects, in this series of one hundred and fifty-nine poems. The acknowledgment of futility, for instance, is the way by which

121

one moves beyond futility to value. In this program Aiken replaces orthodox religion with poetry, traditional ethics with aesthetics, so that he can better satisfy his notion of man's dignity in the face of a chaotic universe; he calls for:

> Mysticism, but let us have no words,
> angels, but let us have no fantasies,
> churches, but let us have no creeds,
> no dead gods hung on crosses in a shop,
> nor beads nor prayers nor faith nor sin nor penance:
> and yet, let us believe, let us believe. (T.R., XI, 674)

To put this in another way, Aiken writes preludes commenting on the failures of life. Some deal with people (for instance, "Good virtuous son, adviser to the poor" [P.M., XXXVI, 540], and "This biped botanist, this man of eyes" [LIX, 568]), but are different from the characters in Robinson's *Tilbury Town* or Masters' *Spoon River*. He writes especially, however, of his own failures, in order to prepare them for their transformations into successes as they are brought forward into the light redefined. They are, taken together, the full portrait of the man as an artist, with all that this involves and implies.

At the center of the Preludes is the mind which can so variously—in one hundred and fifty-nine poems—engage itself. The series is thus not "organized": it is free to become what that mind can make of it, and in consequence it becomes an inner portrait of the artist-man. In the very first poem of the series Aiken illustrates for his readers the method and assumptions of the poems to follow. The poem begins as "Winter for a moment takes the mind"—and continues as Aiken shows how, in turn, the mind momentarily considers winter, ponders its implications, and envisions it in terms of snow, icicles, wind, and frost, all seen in concrete, particular ways. So also, the mind compounds, at other moments, with spring, summer, autumn. All exist not only externally but also internally—in that they can symbolize internal states. In a sense, these exist only as they exist within. "What is frost?" the poet asks, and answers:

> It is not the sparkle of death,
> The flash of time's wing, seeds of eternity;
> Yet it is these because you think of these. (499)

He has in mind a notion similar to, but more complex than, Walter Lippmann's well-known distinction between "The World Outside and the Pictures in Our Heads." We think and act, individually and collectively, in accordance with the pseudo-environment which we have created. This is, of course, the traditional predicament of Plato's Cave. As Lippmann says: "The real environment is altogether too big, too complex, and too fleeting for direct acquaintance. . . . And although we have to act in that environment, we have to reconstruct it on a simpler model before we can manage with it."[15] Aiken is concerned with the models we create, and particularly with making these, through his poetry, more richly rewarding models in their subtlety, complexity, and beauty. He knows that even in the models there are many degrees of truth. In *Preludes for Memnon*, XVII, for instance, he characterizes the man who, understanding the self only superficially, laments his inevitable death in terms of traditional clichés, the commonplace models. But suddenly, his awareness deepened in a moment of vision, he sees in himself a "dumb, tumultuous, all-including horror," a "Caliban of rocks" (519). Never again will he take lightly the seriousness of his own impermanence. Aiken attempts to bring us to such reappraisals of our attitudes toward reality. Always moving beyond merely inherited, received knowledge, he challenges all of our beliefs. Whereas the Metaphysical poets, for example, found their means of doing this by discovering and proving paradoxes (like Donne's "Death, thou shalt die"), Aiken accepts such paradoxes as commonplace and investigates their implications. He can begin a poem by calmly imagining:

123

death being dead, and love to hatred changed,
The fern to marble, and the hour to snow. (P.M., xxvii, 531)

He concludes the poem by trying to understand properly the way death gives life its fierce vitality. If tradition supplies him, at its best, with paradox, these poems are preludes to a proposed reconciliation.

In *Ushant*, a clairvoyant tells D.: "At least two or three times you will have . . . the blessed experience of coming suddenly upon a veritable gold-mine of consciousness, seemingly inexhaustible, too, and with the words already hermetically stamped on the gold" (131). Both volumes of Preludes constitute Aiken's extended documentation of such an experience. The poems flowed, as it were, fully formed from his consciousness. He has said that he felt himself to be undergoing the same kind of visionary experience as did Blake when he composed his prophetic poems. The poems are "arranged" in the order as written, and with very little revision. Just as the first poem begins when the mind ponders winter, so also in the others, a theme, an idea, an attitude, a feeling, or a definition momentarily engages the poet's mind—and the poem takes shape as a testimony to the seriousness and vigor of this involvement. The same basic "themes" continuously appear, disappear, and reappear, but always in new ways; for Aiken observes the aspects of ideas as one turns a gem to watch its flash and sparkle from various angles. The series of Preludes is thus the poet's journal of his daily encounters with reality. "What shall we do—what shall we think—what shall we say—?" he asks, and then sets down the reports on his daily answer.

There are other days, other themes, as the omniscient consciousness invites all reality to make its contribution to the one Poem which the series ideally presupposes. He composes preludes in which even the act of writing poetry becomes the subject for the poem as written. In *Time in the Rock*, xcii, for example, the poet, seeking an objective correlative to his emotion,

124

rejects numerous possibilities—the "familiar symbols," the "coarse grassblade," the "silver pencil," his thumbnail, and others—and only at the end of the poem arrives at the image of "a single light, far-off, which is suddenly quenched" (754). *Time in the Rock*, XL, begins with a two-line fragment. We can tell from the manuscript that Aiken began his fortieth prelude with these two lines, but could not complete the poem. Instead, he wrote a prelude dealing with the causes and implications of his inability to finish the original poem; it begins: "False beginnings will lead you to false endings" (704).

In all of the poems he attempts to renew our awareness of the world from which man was separated by his discovery of personal identity.

Thus one kind of poem among the Preludes presents, as in *Osiris Jones*, the mere fragment of consciousness, the observation of details filtered through the poet's sensorium:

> And then the trains that cried at night, the ships
> That mourned in fog, the days whose gift was rain,
> June's daisy, and she loved me not, the skull
> Brought from the tomb—and I was there, and saw
> The bright spade break the bone, the trumpet-vine
> Bugled with bees. (P.M., LII, 560)

Here, the poem celebrates the bright memory of emotionally related details. In other poems, the poet laments as he remembers and itemizes his failures—especially those in which he has deceived himself or others, "holding the candle nearer that you might see / the essential horror" (T.R., LXXV, 735). In most cases, the setting down of the fragment leads to a speculation on value or definition. Not all of the poems, of course, deal with pain or failure. Often, at their best, they celebrate the great loves at moments in which they lead almost to the mystical rapture:

> Merciful God—
> This is a wondrous thing; that if she touch

125

My fingernail with but her fingernail,—
Or if she look at me, for but the time
It takes a leaf to fall from leaf to leaf,—
I become music, chaos, light, and sound;
I am no longer I: I am a world. (P.M., xvi, 518)

In such poems as these, Aiken interrupts the mind-stream in order to make an instant of memory concrete. He sees life, he wrote in 1931, as a "kaleidoscopic series of incandescent instants—sometimes apparently meaningless, sometimes profound" (ABC, 82). Through the eternal forms of words he preserves the incandescence in all its profound or meaningless beauty. Not precisely surrendering to the spontaneous overflow of his emotions, but rather guiding and controlling and measuring their overflow, Aiken accepted and made poetry of the possibility that the meaningless would necessarily be mixed inextricably with the profound.

Contrasting to poems in which he sets down the fragments of consciousness are those in which he deals with the unselfconscious child who is simply, as Festus was, "that frail mirror of the sky" (T.R., xxii, 686). Such poems, occurring chiefly in *Time in the Rock*, define awareness by portraying the lack of awareness (as in lviii), or show awareness in the process of development. For instance, in xli, there is the set comparison of descriptions; of the child:

> In the clear shaft of light the child so standing
> alone, but his aloneness yet unknown,
> all things accepting, all things at random heeding. (706)

and the man:

> In the clear shaft of light the man so standing
> alone, but his aloneness known,
> all things accepting, all things gladly heeding,
>
> .   .   .   .   .
>
> and marvellous with understanding. (707)

126

So also in LXXIV there is the dramatization of the first wavering flicker of consciousness in the child, as his whole world changes from the simple contact with the physical, to the physical maintained only by his memory of it ("Of this you may keep only what you remember" [734]). Perhaps the best poem of this kind —the one which most clearly gives, also, the rhyme and reason for such poems—is XXXVIII, originally titled "The Miracle in the Garden," in which the poet confronts himself as a child in order to recapture and retain the illusions and innocence of childhood. At the end of the poem the transformation is complete; the child becomes man, the man, child:

> the holy innocence became unholy
> the younger hand grew older and stronger
> the world-stained hand grew fairer and younger
> together sharing the adulterous union
> which is the dreadful secret of communion. (703)

Innocence and experience come together and exchange "stained hand and immaculate feather." In one sense, of course, this poem goes beyond the notion of a "prelude," for defeat is replaced by success, and the poet steps forth transformed. But it might be said with equal justice that in the poem Aiken only imaginatively considers the possibility of such a transformation in anticipation of its fulfillment. His consciousness of the possibility will make it an actuality.

To analyze further the kinds of poems which compose the Preludes—those dealing with time, chaos, despair, and his other concerns—would be fruitless. Aiken composes all upon one basic pattern, and, as Blackmur commented, achieves, "like the Elizabethan sonnet or the heroic couplet, a definite and predictable form of thinking."[16] The need to grow both in self-awareness ("Be conscious, for a fraction of the world" [P.M., XL, 545]) and in self-revelation ("Let us be reckless of our words and worlds" [P.M., LVII, 566]) is everywhere constant, though not everywhere explicit. The Preludes effect the program which goes as far back as "Changing Mind"—that the poet "must make his experience articulate for the benefit of others, he must be, in the evolving experience of man, the servant-example" (873). The entire effort is given its most admirable expression in the final lines of the Preludes, for all the poems have pointed to this:

> when will you learn the flower's simplicity—
> lie open to all comers, permit yourself
> to be rifled—fruitfully too—by other selves?
> Self, and other self—permit them, permit them—
> it is summer still, winter can do no more
> who brings them together in death, let them come
> murderously now together, it is the lifelong
> season of meeting, speak your secret. (T.R., xcvi, 756-57)

Thus the division between the lyric and dramatic themes, which characterized the earlier poetry is resolved. The ego achieves its most fruitful identity, its ultimate self-creation, in compounding with other selves and the external world. It must be continually resurrected in the universal non-ego in order to be fully itself. The schizophrenia of his poetry about which Aiken complained in both his review of *Nocturne of Remembered Spring* and in *Blue Voyage* is here resolved by the total effort of the Preludes. He has freed himself of the logical fastness of the theories which prevented the compounding of the individual with other egos, and now replaces logic with a constant piety of emotion. At the same time, it is obvious that in the combination of the lyric and dramatic themes he has also combined the corresponding manners, and produces a harder and clearer imagery than in any of his earlier poetry—although the process from, say, "Samadhi" to "The Room" and "Sound of Breaking" to the Preludes is clear. The form remains similar, but now thought (drama) and emotion (lyric) come even closer together and issue in the action and meditation—or meditative action—of the Preludes.

Criticizing Pound's poetry in 1934, during his work on the

Preludes, Aiken wrote: "At all events, one wants more freedom, one wants the freedom—among other things—of a greater severity, a harder outline; and also a deeper synthesis of emotional and conceptual attitudes. We can't go on forever talking in the loose language of 1917, which Mr. Pound appears to desire; times have changed" (ABC, 326-27). His sense of style inseparably reflecting the artist's mode of thought, Aiken's recognition of the need for a new kind of language was caused by his combination in the Preludes of his earlier themes. Thus the question of language or communication assumes as important a place in these poems as do his efforts toward consciousness and self-revelation.

The problem of language is of necessity crucial in the scheme of the Preludes for the obvious reason that if by consciousness the poet can transcend the terrors of existence, his exploration and revelation to mankind of his consciousness can only take place in language—never, as he might wish, on the level of pure conception. The evolution of consciousness, therefore, is concomitant with the evolution of language. Experience becomes reality only as it achieves form in speech.

Although like most artists he avoids the logical implications of the theory, Aiken's view of language begins in a fundamentally Platonic framework. Plato, who has no significant place in his philosophy for language, considers its problems briefly in the *Theaetetus* and the *Sophist*, and at length only in the *Cratylus* dialogue. In the last he endeavors to discover the function or essence of language. He is therefore concerned with "the correctness of names," or words, and attempts to determine whether they are naturally predetermined by reality, and, as Cratylus says, have "truth or correctness in them"; or whether they are arbitrary and possess truth only by "convention and agreement," as Hermogenes maintains. His final decision in the dialogue is that "Cratylus is right in saying that things have names by nature." Since naming or language-making is a part of being, the nature of the world dictates the way we are going to

129

speak about it. The best kind of language, according to Plato, is that which is interchangeable with the object to which it refers: the word and the world, in this ideal language, are the same. "The written word," as Plato says in *Phaedrus*, "is properly no more than an image."[17] It is, as best it can be, an image of reality. I do not mean to contend, of course, that Aiken consciously adopted his attitude toward language directly from Plato. The Western tradition is, in this regard, Platonic. Very nearly the same correspondence theory is implicit in the notion which Pound borrowed from Fenollosa, that because the original pictographic nature of Chinese writing persisted, the reader actually *saw* the image in the complex ideogram. The correspondence theory was simply articulated first by Plato; and, however inadequate we may now see it to be, its dispersion was wide, its influence immense. The view that is everywhere constant in the Platonic theory is that ontological must precede linguistic truth. Herein lies the crucial motive for Aiken's drive toward full clarity of consciousness; we must understand the world fully before we can properly talk about it at all.

Of the Platonic theory of language Aiken adopted at least the notion that words should reflect the reality to which they refer. As early as 1917, he criticized a writer for "his inability to associate words precisely with the ideas for which they stand" (Sc., 131). And as late as 1942, he suggested: "In this [primitive] trial-and-error evolution of consciousness, a new word meant, to all intents, a new feeling; a new cluster of words meant a new complex of feelings" (ABC, 109). In both comments he clearly has as his ideal an isomorphic correspondence between language and reality. So too, in 1923, in "A Basis for Criticism" he stressed the same referential quality of language: "The poet . . . when he chooses words and phrases and rhythms (or, to be exact, is chosen by them) is not primarily choosing the mere word, phrase and rhythm—primarily he is choosing the thought, feeling or emotion which they represent" (ABC, 63). Aiken, like Plato, holds the notion that words are predetermined by the nature of reality. Thus the poet is "chosen" by the words he uses, rather than himself arbitrarily choosing them, for they are dictated by his concept. He must choose the right words in order that his concept may be directly "given" to the reader without change: "What the writing of the poem does to the poet, the reading of it does to the reader" (ABC, 187), he wrote in 1934.

Traditionally, the formula works only in one way: reality determines the way we are going to talk about it, and never vice versa. But Aiken adopted the correspondence theory *in extenso*, arguing that through language we create reality—that the word and the world are interchangeable, because identical, and one may work in either direction. He described exactly the method of his poetry in a passage of "A Letter from Li Po":

> It is the self becoming word, the word
> becoming world. And with each part we play
> we add to cosmic *Sum* and cosmic sum. (18)

Quite simply, Aiken maintains faith in the instrument of the poet as opposed to the analysis of the logician, and so frees himself from Plato's strictures. His most extreme statement of this interchangeableness of language and reality is in a criticism of Herbert Read: "Mr. Read is really suggesting that the writing of poetry is a kind of *translation* of an emotional experience into a suitable language. We have the experience (he says in effect) and *then* set to work to find for it an objective correlative in language. But I venture to suggest that the process is not like this at all: that it is itself a direct emotional experience, which happens to be in terms of language rhythmically arranged, and that it is just as true to say that poetry is a *translation of language into experience* as to say the opposite."[18] The poem is experience becoming language or language becoming experience both for the poet and his reader: it does not matter, for both are the same thing.

How to distinguish between poetry and prose, or between good and bad poetry does not, even assuming this interchangeableness, present insoluble problems. In the first case, Aiken originally distinguished prose from poetry by characterizing prose as denotative, "merely accurate, hard and clear," and poetry as connotative.[19] He soon, however, saw that this distinction was inadequate, since the language of prose and poetry, as he was persuaded by the Imagists, is essentially the same. He refined this distinction, therefore, with the notion of rhythm— "the most powerful single *artifice* of poetry which is at [the poet's] disposal. . . . Rhythm is persuasive; it is the very stuff of life. . . . Things can be said in rhythm which otherwise cannot be said at all" (Sc., 80). Believing that nonsense has a place in poetry, he had to postulate rhythm as carrying a large part of the meaning. Very early in his career he held out for rigid forms against the trend toward free verse; he wrote, for instance, "I think we shall find that free verse, the fetich, the illusory promiser of complete freedom, will rapidly take its place as one of the lower, more primitive, less organic forms of poetry, to be used therefore only on suitable occasions: for translations, for instance, or for moods more colloquial, and less intense."[20] In insisting upon the importance of rhythm in communication, Aiken again moved beyond Plato, and in defending poetry argued that, like language, rhythm reflects in its structure the structure of the world or of the individual emotion. As he writes in *Time in the Rock*, LXXXIII, rhythm may communicate beyond the capabilities of language:

> But verse can never say these things;
> only in music may be heard
> the subtle touching of such strings,
> never in word. (743)

It might be reasonably maintained that from this idea, expressed as early as 1918, proceeded much of Aiken's early "symphonic" poetry. As I have shown, however, after his fiction Aiken began moving toward a verse line less "poetically" musical. In consequence, by the time that he arrived at the Preludes,

132

he seldom argued for music as the distinctive element in poetry. Instead, opposing I. A. Richards' famous distinction, he defended poetry by arguing that it combines analytic with emotive language: "Remove the logical statement from a poem, an important part of the 'meaning' would still remain—the affective. And it is precisely in this way that poetry makes the highest use of language, as it perhaps also represents the highest degree of consciousness of which man is capable: the most complete. It combines the logical or factual with the affective" (ABC, 188).

We never find in Aiken the complaint, so often heard, that language is debased, inadequate to embody conceptions unambiguously or completely. Especially as it may be rhythmically organized, language is, for Aiken, all we could desire it to be. It evolves with the evolution of our consciousness. In order to maintain the theory that language is at least potentially ideal, Aiken plausibly found the cause of inferior poetry not in the bad poet's inferior language, but in a defect in his sensibility. He contended that "the difference between a poet who merely echoes the ideas and rhythms of the past, and the poet who creates something new, is simply that in the former instance this verbo-motor mechanism [of language] is not deeply related to the poet's specific sensibility; in the latter, it is" (Sc., 181). It is therefore a failure of self, not of language, for "many such [imitative] poets have, even among literary folk, exceptional vocabularies [but] they lack any peculiarity of sensibility" (Sc., 44). What he is saying is that such poets have no experience at all of their own—so that their language is a reflection of nothing at all; it gives us no reality since it corresponds to no experience. It is sheer emptiness, a mere multiplication of the language which in other poets had meaning. Perhaps it was Aiken's fear of being or becoming such a poet that drove him to the fiction, in which he investigated and created his individual area of experience. Language, through it all, retained its sacred character inviolate.

133

The unique part of Aiken's theory of language is the psychological analysis which he imposed upon his Platonic foundation. In developing his psychoanalytic view, Aiken was strongly influenced by N. Kostyleff's *Le Mécanisme Cérébral de la Pensée* to which he turned after dissatisfaction with Freud's contention that poetry arises from the desire for emotional satisfaction, through wish-fulfillment, of erotic complexes. To satisfy his already developing emphasis upon the poet as an extender of consciousness, Aiken needed a theory which would understand poetry as speech intensified; that is, as a cerebral, not solely an emotional mechanism. In Kostyleff he found such a theory ready-made, and accepted it almost wholly. Reviewing Kostyleff's *Le Mécanisme Cérébral de la Pensée* in 1917, Aiken considered Kostyleff to have advanced in some ways beyond Freud in the treatment of art. "Most critics," he said,

> at least, are familiar already with the theory of Sigmund Freud, that poetry, like the dream, is an outcome of suppression, a release of complexes. To the curious-minded this, however erratic or inadequate, was at any rate a step in the right direction. . . . M. Kostyleff, in the chapter devoted to poetic inspiration, takes as his starting-point a belief that Freud's explanation of it as due entirely to hidden complexes, largely erotic, is insufficient. . . . M. Kostyleff here concludes, it appears wisely, that after all the writing of poetry is, like speech itself, a purely cerebral affair: and that it is not the result of a discharge of an excess of emotion in the poet so much as a cerebral reaction to external stimuli. (ABC, 34-35)

He added: "We can subscribe without reluctance to the main tenet of M. Kostyleff's thesis" (39). Almost at once Aiken began to employ Kostyleff's theory in explicating and criticizing poetry. Of the essays included in *Scepticisms*, Aiken uses Kostyleff's theories as the basis of his criticism in "Possessor and Possessed," "Confectionery and Caviar," and "Magic or Legerdemain?" No other person is given such authority in *Scepti-*

cisms. Aiken mentions Freud more frequently, but also with a stronger sense of the limitations of his theories.

For Kostyleff, poetry arises as a cerebral reaction to certain stimuli, often accidental, but nearly as often self-induced. The stimuli set off "de décharges verbo-motrice," or a series of linguistic associations; for, according to Kostyleff, words, in common with other sensory impressions derived from contact with reality, are stored in the unconscious in chains of association, whence they are released when the appropriate stimuli again call them into consciousness. Thus, although the stimulus may be emotional, poetry is not basically the product of emotion:

> If poetry were merely a discharge of emotion, it would be far less complex than it is. In reality, the emotional shock finds, in the poet, cerebral mechanisms preformed by study, by meditation, by life. These are chains of reflexes which are not themselves kept in the brain, but the paths of which are traced there, and are easily reproduced. In a poet, these reproductions are particularly easy and the chains [of reflexes] very numerous. The cerebral reflexes, linked together at the will of unforeseeable connections, draw him along beyond the emotional stimulus. . . . Indeed, what does the extent of the emotional power matter, since the principle does not lie there, but in the chains of cerebral reflexes, and since the latter can be initiated by a wholly cerebral stimulus? . . . This obliges us to admit, finally, that poetic inspiration has *two sources*: *the sensibility of the poet* and *the preformed mechanism of verbal reactions.*[21]

To be sure, Aiken did not accept Kostyleff's argument in its entirety. He recognized that by basing his study solely upon lyric poetry Kostyleff had thereby limited the application of his conclusions. In narrative or "philosophical" poetry, poetry arising from and embodying an idea, Aiken argued, "the poem would not be dictated by the automatic unfolding of associated verbal chain reflexes, but, on the contrary, the verbal mechanisms themselves would be directed throughout by the original poetic theme" (ABC, 40). He realized that poetry is not essentially nonsense, but that, on the contrary, it is a supremely articulate statement; "its *only* being is in its meaning" (ABC, 101). Nevertheless, Aiken's poems sometimes—but not frequently—fail precisely because he is unwilling to distort or disturb (by controlling) his free verbal associations; for instance, *Time in the Rock*, XC:

> And in the wide world full of sounds and nothings
> of faces and no faces and no sounds
> of words and wounds and in the words no world
> but only you whose face we cannot fathom
> and you whose word is what a word is only—(752)

One suspects that here the individual chain of linguistic and, therefore, conceptual associations which produced much of the poetry in the Preludes is given for its own sake: it is language communicating itself alone—which is, in effect, no communication at all. But Aiken realized early, and almost always remembered, that a poet grows and is measured by his achievement of control over the wealths which his subconscious offers. Throughout his career he called attention to the disintegration of communication in modern literature, writing in 1924: "It is hardly a step from the compulsive iterations of religious mania to the stammerings of Miss Gertrude Stein, or Mr. Pound's 'Spring . . . Too long . . . Gongula'; and even so fine a poem as Mr. Eliot's *Waste Land* is not untainted" (ABC, 259); and, returning to the subject emphatically during his composition of *Time in the Rock*: "If language is communication, poetry is simply communication (or language) working at its highest pitch. Poetry cannot communicate itself alone, any more than language can communicate itself alone—Miss Stein to the contrary" (ABC, 187).

While he could not fully accept Kostyleff's conclusions, they provided a basis upon which he could develop his own theory of the relation between the person and his poems. In the two sources of poetry for which Kostyleff argues—the sensibility of the poet and his preformed verbal mechanism—we can see the root of Aiken's program of consciousness (which calls the sensibility forth) and his insistence that language is the means by which man is perfected and saved. His emphasis is upon the poet's memory, what he can store up, and, when the time comes, make conscious. Not until Aiken had worked out the form of the prelude in the progress I have outlined could this theory achieve fruition. It, like his language and sensibility, was waiting unconsciously until the stimulus of the prelude form called it forth.

I can now return to the Preludes and complete my discussion of their scheme. I have said that, although, for Aiken, consciousness is necessary to transform a chaotic world into final order, the poet can express his awareness only through language. Since in *Osiris Jones* Aiken dealt only with an individual reporting his life for judgment, his single subject was the elucidation of that communication. But the Preludes deal with both the mythical situation and the human condition. They are speeches written for Memnon; but they are also letters to the world. Consequently, the second major theme of the Preludes deals with language, the means whereby consciousness may be elucidated. Nearly three dozen of the Preludes are concerned incidentally or chiefly with the problem of language. The poem thus contains a theory of language built into the structure of the communication itself. Along with Aiken's revelation of consciousness, he indicates the way in which such fragments are made articulate. "Rashly we give them both,—the wound, the word" (T.R., VIII, 672), he says, indicating the two directions of the series of poems; or elsewhere, "your word was only self" (T.R., XXXVI, 701), and "Word is only Hand" (T.R., XLII, 707).

Preludes for Memnon, V, begins the analysis of language with a discussion of the symbol. In order that he may effect understanding of his poems Aiken must teach the reader—as society would previously have taught him—what attitude to take to-

ward the poet's communication. And he cannot do this externally, but only by providing his poems themselves with an
indication of how they should properly be read. He begins, then,
with the simplest lessons: "If poetry says it, it must speak with
a symbol," the poet instructs us, and continues in primer fashion:

> What is a symbol? It is the 'man stoops sharp
> To clutch a paper that blows in the wind';
> It is the 'bed of crocuses bending in the wind,' the
> Light, that 'breaks on the water with waves.' (503)

He concludes, as in *Senlin*, that the symbol in itself leaves "the
whirling You unknown," and the analysis of language must be
carried beyond this simple stage. In the next poem, he encounters an objection to his poetry—that his language does not
correspond, or is not equivalent to his subject; word does not
equal object, complains the woman whom he is describing. The
poet had described her in terms of a bright leaf, "gold fruit /
Burning amongst the leaves," a bird, a bough, and the sky. He
considers her objection, and attempts to re-create her essence
through a new set of symbols. But again she objects. And the
poet:

> This is not you? these symbols are not you?
> Not snowflake, cobweb, raindrop? . . . Woman, woman,
> You are too literal, too strict with me.
> What would you have? Some simple copper coin—
> I love you, you are lovely, I adore you?
> Or, better still, dumb silence and a look?
>
> No, no, this will not do; I am not one
> For whom these silences are sovereign;
> The pauses in the music are not music,
> Although they make the music what it is.
> Therefore I thumb once more the god's thesaurus,
> For phrase and praise, and find it all for you.

He points out that in insisting upon literalness, she has not understood the lesson of the symbol or the language of poetry. Then, having clarified the symbol by illustrating its action ("I find you written down, between / Arcturus and a primrose and the sea" [P.M., VI, 504-505]), he proceeds in VII to illustrate how the poet renews our feelings about familiar reality by renewing his language. For instance, by praising the rain in a new way, with new language, he revitalizes our emotions about the rain. From this matrix the other poems proceed: the fact of communication established, the following preludes are allowed, theoretically, to operate with optimum meaning.

Time in the Rock follows a similar pattern. In XIX, Aiken comments on the images which, at random, pass into his perceptions. These memories, he argues, must be preserved "before the idea of self is lost." Since only language can preserve them he pleads once more for the language which will correspond to the world:

> Walk with me world, upon my right hand walk,
> speak to me Babel, that I may strive to assemble
> of all these syllables a single word. (684)

The correspondence of language to the world is complete. But the task is no easy one—only the poet can truly accomplish it. "Not every man," as Plato says, "is an artificer of names, but he only who looks to the name which each thing by nature has, and is able to express this name in letters and syllables" (49). The separate facts of life correspond to syllables in language; a complete emotion, which is the synthesis of details, corresponds to the word—the one magical word which will directly "give" its mirrored reality. Thus, as he explains in XXIV, language can create and shape the world anew just as the world predetermines speech. For him, as for Plato, the two are interchangeable:

> and to know also that the word is action,
> the word is murder,

139

to know also that the act is speech,
the kiss a word. (xxx, 695)

He stresses the same fact, that the landscape and the language are the same, in LVI; then in LXXVIII, the inevitable conclusion follows:

What miracle is this? that she who reads
here in a simple room of time and chairs,
can watch a bough dissect an arc of sky?
can feel the current of the wind that lifts it?
can hear, and see, and feel, that wound in air?
As the bough dips and flurries, she reads and breathes;
as move the leaves, her hands upon the page;
as lives the tree, or as the poet lives
in living with the tree, so lives her eye. (739)

Finally, Aiken tells us, poetry is a directly physical experience in which the reader receives, through the experience of the poet translated into speech, the precise experience of the tree or the bird, or whatever other fragment of consciousness is made concrete.

The Preludes, then, constitute Aiken's synthesis and re-evaluation of the tendencies of his early poetry. He puts the intensive self-investigation of the fiction to use; he fruitfully combines the lyric and dramatic themes which he had too frequently separated, with the consequent division of thought from feeling; he achieves the form toward which we have seen him working; and he confronts the problems of communication which had left *Senlin* and other poems inconclusive. If the Preludes constituted a new beginning, it was a beginning immanent in the completion of the old. More than a new beginning, in their sheer lyric beauty, in their complexity and subtlety, and thus in their power to involve the reader, they are an ending, an achievement.

· I V ·

Landscape West of Eden (1934) is Aiken's narrative continuation of the Preludes. Or perhaps, since he here attempts to create the myth of man's arrival at consciousness from the stage of simple innocence, this poem might be considered as an after-the-fact prologue to *Osiris Jones* and the Preludes. *Landscape West of Eden* is probably Aiken's most difficult poem. Its complexity arises from the theory upon which the poem is based—that consciousness can be shown only in its development. Its character lies in its motion. In his narrative, accordingly, he continuously shifts from one level of consciousness to another; for at no point can we say: Here we arrive at awareness. Theoretically the poem can have no end, for consciousness has had none. Moreover, Aiken's presentation of expanding consciousness is further complicated by the fact that the poem exhibits three planes of consciousness, all in the process of development: the angel's, the poet's, and Adam's and Eve's. The poet-protagonist is the pivotal figure in this scheme, for only he can communicate with the other two levels: to Adam and Eve, he is God; to the angel, he is as Adam and Eve appear to him.

Given this complexity, a brief analysis of the way in which the structure is developed will be helpful. Aiken was to write in *A Heart for the Gods of Mexico* that "landscapes are like states of mind, like feelings, like apprehensions" (124). *Landscape West of Eden* is based upon this metaphor. As the *personae* travel westward through various landscapes, they grow in awareness. The landscapes are the reflections of their own souls. In the first section, the poet is already sailing with Adam and Eve westward from the Eden of childish innocence and unself-consciousness. He regards their lack of awareness with benevolent, fatherly tolerance: "Eve and Adam, from Eden come with flowerbuds, / and roots of flowers, and acorns in their hands, / and words for worms and flies" (622). Since they have hardly begun to develop self-awareness, they are chiefly concerned with

141

instinctual pleasures; and their language mirrors their stage of consciousness. It exists on the most accessible level of communication. They even resist the poet's attempt to instruct them in knowledge and cling "with small hard hands [to] their buds and flowers / and precious seeds from Eden" (623). He himself wonders whether there would be any value in increasing their awareness—and giving them the pain which inevitably accompanies it—for although his own awareness is deeper than theirs, it is still rudimentary; he does not know that, as Freud had shown, only increased awareness can help us prevent pain. Nevertheless in II, both he and Adam refuse the temptations of the angelic anti-self, who encourages them to give up the fruitless (because inconclusive) search for consciousness and embrace the comforts of the south. Thus the journey continues.

In the third section, the poet turns back to the concrete reality of the room in which he is sitting—the device made so familiar by *Forslin* and *Senlin*. He speculates upon his memory, which has created both Adam and Eve and the angelic anti-self. Which is the ego, he asks, that which remembers or that which is remembered? Or does the principle of the ego lie in its ability to transform reality—the simple sea-shell to a jewel, the grain of sand to a desert? But he reaches no answer—only "thou art and hast," for he has reached the stage of consciousness appropriate to the asking, not to the answering of such questions. He is enraptured, however, by the newly discovered pleasures of his memory and, in IV, asks, "what need I more than this?" At that moment, the angel of the west, who is continually prodding him on,

> the angel with the lantern
> held his light against my eyes so that I shrank back,
> my eyes hurt by the cold full horror of light,
> but too late turning back, for the light held me. (626)

Since man can never return to the Eden of simple innocence, he must reach toward a new spiritual land which his soul can-

not yet fully grasp. He must move from the brightness of outward things, the clear world of instinct, into the darkness of the
ego; thence he will finally come, as does Peter Jones, back into
the light again, fully transformed, complete and whole. In this
sense, then, the journeys, the divine pilgrimages, of Adam and
Eve on the one hand, and of the poet on the other are fundamentally different; for while Adam and Eve are moving into
the obscurity of the ego, the poet is attempting in several different ways to ascend from the ego in whose exercises he is
caught. He transforms himself into a tree and postulates death
as the ultimate goal of being—and is again rebuked by the
angel (v, vi). In consequence, he moves in the opposite direction and sees creation as his purpose. Like Festus, he creates
the world anew (vi, vii) by renewing himself. Next (viii) he
walks in a graveyard and considers the relation of the ego to
its heritage, as in "Changing Mind," and at last (ix) sees his
purpose clearly:

> Dreaming thus I saw
> the god of wrong, the downward-going god, which
> Eve and Adam
> were doomed to be; and for myself alas I saw
> the upward-going thought. (632)

Through this dream (or dream-vision) he learns the folly of
his pride, the pride of the "poet who thought himself (alas) a
god" (633). Since he had become aware of the purposes of
consciousness, he can be instructed in section x by sages of
language. That is, only after he understands the world can he
learn to use language. The first sage offers him language parsed
into nonsense by philologists—its meaning so dispersed "that
(on a careful estimate) it will take / a thousand years to as-
semble (of such sounds) / enough to make one meaning" (633).
But such a language is useless, and is scorned by the angel; for
if language may be the means whereby reality is created, the

dispersal of language constitutes the destruction of reality. The
second sage then offers him another kind of language:

> 'It is a language
> in which the meaning is so concentrated, so
> terrible, so godlike!—
> that one quick syllable is a thousand years.' (634)

The synthetic language of the mystical rapture is opposed to
the investigations and divisions of analytic science. The angel
derided the first sage: "One more of these, by God, and we shall
have no sense, no sense at all" (634). But the angel and the
whole world with him are transformed by the words of the second sage. For by such a language as he postulates, the world is
ordered out of chaos. But both sages are right: the world is both
chaotic and controlled, all things are relative. From their lessons
the poet learns the complexity of reality.

Having learned the lessons of consciousness and language, the
poet can go on to new flights of the ego, each of which advances
his awareness, though each is likewise inconclusive. If he can
never learn all, like Forslin he is nonetheless "wiser only / in
facing the unknown" (642). Throughout his development there
is the contrapuntal theme of Adam's and Eve's progress in their
simpler, but no less important, journey. Adam continually prods
Eve onward: " 'Woman,' he said, 'would you know nothing?
would you be / ignorant all your days? dawdle here forever?' "
(644). That the angel is in the same process of evolution is suggested by his lesson in section x that everything is relative. Of
course, the point of view—in the poet—precludes an observation of the stages of the angel's developing awareness, since the
poet would have to understand all that the angel does, if not
more, for such an analysis to take place. The process of the
personae on the three levels—and especially on that of the poet
—in subtilizing and deepening their understanding is the subject
of the poem from x onward. At the conclusion, Adam has

reached the stage at which his efforts in search of knowledge, although woefully brief, are nonetheless manfully vigorous. The poet has moved even more rapidly, for he began in the poem far beyond simple innocence. In the best section of *Landscape West of Eden* he conceives the possibilities of dimensions which transcend logic. Logic is symbolized by the chessboard, which is the world reduced and simplified—and thus falsified:

> 'suppose this board, in which all logic so clearly lies
> in one bright plane, though now by shadow altered—
> suppose this board, this game, had other dimensions?
> If kings and queens had wings—
>
> .   .   .   .   .
>
> 'If all were on one plane, how easy! If sorrow
> were sorrow only for a single reason, not for
> a thousand things! And if, for but a moment,
> alas, for but a moment, we might know
> the countless planes of feeling, or of knowledge,
>   or of guess,
> of which a moment's awareness is the intersection!
>
> .   .   .   .   .
>
> If we might know, at the instant itself of speech,
> the atom's disaster in the blood, the new decision
> made in the nerve cell!' (646-47)

Here is the final answer to the determinism of *Punch*. The world is never so simple as the logic of the chessboard. There are dimensions beyond dimensions in reality, just as in language, and not a primary, predetermined pattern of motivation. In its perception of this freedom the ego is liberated to create its being more fruitfully in the eternal interchangeability of word and world. "The word is intricate, and we are nothing. / The world is nothing: we are intricate" (P.M., L, 557), Aiken wrote in the Preludes. In the final revelation in *Landscape West of Eden* the angel tells the poet:

'Why not go farther still?
what of the kidneys, the liver, the heart, the stomach?
Your speech is these: it is the sum, also, of these:
you are the sum of worlds within and worlds without.' (647)

This knowledge, that language creates the world by making in-
choate awareness concrete, constitutes a new level of consciousness. The poet himself takes on the aspect of his angel, as Eden,
to which he can never return from experience, is closed forever.

All of the works considered in this chapter, then, issue
from Aiken's need to bring the ego into awareness of itself.
Only in *Landscape West of Eden* does Aiken deal, as he did
in the earlier poems—*Senlin,* for example—with the ego in
the process of creation. But *Landscape West of Eden* acts as
the preconscious mythical exploration of the fact from which
all the other works proceed. The remaining pieces all assume an
ego which, however shadowy and difficult to perceive, is available for exploration and confession. Their great circle voyage
leads at once outward and inward and, finally, to self-expression,
as the two directions meet and are discovered to be one and the
same:

> Move outward, and you only move, poor biped,
> and atom's atom from here to here, never
> from here to there—again your 'self' you meet,
> it is yourself that waits outside the door. (T.R., v, 673)

And with that discovery, the ego assumes its full stature at the
center of its world, the world within and world without. And
it can speak.

FOUR · CARITAS—

PERHAPS "No, No, Go Not to Lethe" was excluded from Aiken's 1950 collection of short stories because in its plot and protagonist it resembles *King Coffin* so closely. The S. Pierce Babcock of the story desires above all to be at once conscious and amoral and to "surround" other people with his awareness, to absorb them, as it were, by osmosis, "as a kind of psychological octopus; a vampire" (S.S., 433). He tries to "absorb" the consciousness of a girl so completely that he will know what she is thinking at every moment. But she forces him into a confession of what he has been doing. And he realizes that in exposing his own motivations he has lost his divinely unconcerned omniscience; he is no longer the center of awareness. "Good God—suppose, now, she was to *reverse* the roles—and make a remorseless study of *him*? . . . He was at her mercy" (444). And this, of course, is precisely what happens. They have reversed roles, and too late he discovers that in knowing her so completely he loves her, who had earlier confessed her love for him.

"No, No, Go Not to Lethe," then, is an example of the ego moving out of itself, discovering that egocentric self-consciousness is inadequate, since awareness must inevitably lead to understanding, and thence to love. In 1934 Aiken criticized MacLeish for his "always remaining, in his progress, equidistant, on the one hand, from the ego and, on the other, from the world" (ABC, 284). In the series of poems which Aiken wrote in the early thirties, he fully committed himself to egocentrism. Beginning in the mid-thirties he was to alter his emphasis and show how the ego, guided by love, inevitably moves outward to humanity. In their theory of the "willing loss of self" the Preludes and *Great Circle* anticipated this new direction. Near the climax of the novel Cather considers "surrounding" Bertha and Tom with his awareness of them. He will be a third conscious-

147

ness, present in everything they do. In this way, he believes, he will revenge himself upon them. But his alter ego modifies and deepens this notion by suggesting: "This idea of the surrounding consciousness—there's something in it. . . . Suppose you do it with real kindness—I mean, real love—for both of them. . . . Go ahead and be conscious . . . but let them feel that you are there in the rôle of the person who most loves them . . . and as a result of it, you will grow: you will become the wisest of the three: and the strongest" (265-67). But that Cather may attain such a level of awareness is only suggested in the novel. In brief, all of the works considered in the third chapter are concerned with the means by which the ego comes to know and express itself. The work which followed this discovered its subject in the world—for the most part, the world of people, not of nature—which created this consciousness. Aiken came to believe, following the myth of *Landscape West of Eden*, that consciousness is not self-generative but grows out of the luminous contact with others—in mutual awareness. The self is a product of relations; and as Bill advises Cather, it is most fruitfully created in the relation of loving kindness: *caritas*.

With the exception of "No, No, Go Not to Lethe"—which is slight and inconclusive—*King Coffin* (1935) is the first of Aiken's works stressing the necessity of the ego to embrace the world. Even in *King Coffin*, self-extension is not the ostensible theme. One critic, for instance, described the novel as "the crisis-chart of a paranoid psychosis, complete with narcissism, megalomania, sexual symbols and a psychopathic inheritance."[1] Surely, the book can be read—as can *Blue Voyage* and *Great Circle*—as a psychological casebook; at one time it was even required reading in psychology courses at Harvard.[2] But such a reading concentrates wholly on the character of Jasper Ammen and ignores the structure of the book. Only with the hindsight gained by reading Aiken's later works can we see self-extension as the significant new element which *King Coffin* manifests in Aiken's development. To understand how this is so, I must be-

148

gin by considering the novel's ostensible subject. For, from the point of view of this study, in *King Coffin* Aiken did not write a strictly "psychological novel"—he wrote a parody of one. In *Great Circle* Cather argued: "That's what makes me sore with you [psychoanalyst] fellows—you seem to think that merely by driving us back from one set of phrases to another by a series of historical substitutions, you've settled everything. . . . Childish. I say sweetheart to you, and you reply, brightly, mother. I say drawers, and you say diapers. I say whisky, and you say breast. All wrong. All completely wrong. Mere jugglery" (256-57). It is not necessary to suppose that Aiken has rejected psychoanalysis. He has merely achieved sufficient artistic freedom to imagine how one might be compelled to reject it. By the time of *King Coffin* he had gained the further freedom which allowed him to play lightly with a serious psychological subject, while still retaining a real sense of its dignity and importance.

King Coffin is similar to Aiken's "Silent Snow, Secret Snow" in placing the point of view in a protagonist who is ambiguously mad. Jasper Ammen is diseased and abnormal, and the situations of the novel are filtered entirely through his mind. The effect is thus different from, say, that of Benjy's monologue in *The Sound and the Fury*, for Benjy is openly acknowledged to be psychopathic. Ammen presents himself, however, as not only normal but even super-normal. He seems to have achieved a high degree of self-consciousness and to have become more aware than his associates. On more than one occasion, Toppan calls him "the great Jasper," and he customarily views himself as the embodiment of Nietzsche's "Exceptional Man." Thus we are, for the moment, persuaded to turn reality about: the abnormal is taken as an epitome of the normal; and, through Ammen's eyes, the normal becomes increasingly perverted and malicious. Moving back and forth between them, Aiken gives the reader intermittent glimpses into the normal through the journal which Toppan keeps, and which Ammen reads periodically in secret.

The interest of the story does not lie in how Ammen came to

be mad; for, if we accept the novel immediately on its own terms, he is not acknowledged to be so. Much of the success of the story depends on this reversal of reality, the degree to which we are temporarily convinced that the abnormal is the true normal. We are led progressively into Ammen's paranoia, which, were it to be shown all at once, we would see as obviously psychotic. In the beginning of the novel, for instance, Ammen suggests that his actions might be construed as mad. Speculating about what he might read in Toppan's journal, he supposes: "Saw Ammen tonight and am more than ever convinced the man is a megalomaniac: he evidently thinks he is the only liberated and intelligent person alive. He is gradually closing himself in" (23). The reader discovers later, however, that Toppan had really written: "It's hard to say whether he knows his behaviour is odd or not. I give him credit for knowing that it is: Gerta says she isn't so sure, and particularly just in the last month or two. I could see she was dying to ask me whether I thought he was insane or not. . . . Personally, I don't think he is. I think it's all a belated sort of adolescent pose, the business of playing genius" (76-77). Thus, in two ways Ammen is freed from the suspicion of madness at the very beginning of the book. His own suggestion that he might be considered insane causes the reader immediately to discount the possibility. It is a cliché of psychoanalysis that whoever can detect the peculiarity of his own actions cannot actually be mad. The further testimony of the journal serves to characterize him as brilliant rather than insane. As Ammen moves more deeply into his psychosis, therefore, we are led to admire him more highly as a genius. Normal behavior, as it occasionally intrudes in Toppan's journal, comes to appear sometimes ridiculous, sometimes dangerous. The reader himself, who provides the only normal standard of judgment, is caught in a shifting of attitudes. He can never be quite certain about the appropriate perspective to adopt. For this reason, *King Coffin*, more than Aiken's previous novels, is purgative. At its conclusion the reader once more perceives what the normal really is. His understanding is deepened and redefined. Since Aiken manipulated his point of view in accordance with psychoanalytic prepossessions, it was important for the critics to emphasize Ammen's diseased mentality as the subject of *King Coffin*—to consider the novel as "the imaginative exercise of a dramatic possibility based upon the conventional melodrama of modern psychology, in short a . . . *tour de force*."[3]

If we consider *King Coffin* only as a *tour de force*, however, we must ignore the more basic, if less striking, aspects of the novel. In *King Coffin* Aiken accomplished a great deal more than formal neatness. The penultimate chapter, entitled "What It Is to Be a Stranger," is suggestive in elucidating the real discovery arising out of *King Coffin*. We may see the book most fruitfully as Ammen's attempt to recognize and resolve his own strangeness, to realize his ego completely by fully understanding its complexity. He is not only a stranger to everyone else but to himself as well. While psychologically, his decision to kill a stranger is indicative of his psychosis, symbolically it constitutes his attempt to eliminate the strangeness within himself. For in his megalomania, Ammen sees the universe as a projection of his own being. To kill the stranger—Jones, the universal, specimen man of "Gehenna"—is logically to illumine the dark corners of his own psyche. His King Coffin plan, then, is a distorted —because insane—version of Aiken's effort in *Osiris Jones* and the Preludes: the effort to bring the self wholly to consciousness, to leave no section of it unknown because unattended.

Ammen continually uses the devices common in Aiken's earlier poetry. On several occasions, for example, he uses the now familiar device of the ego confronting itself in a mirror. When this image first occurs, the self implicitly formulates the appropriate question of identity: "He went into the little bedroom, turned on the electric light, and looked at his face in the dressing-table mirror. . . . It was an intelligent face, and the eyes looked back at him steadily, but also with an unanswerable question. Yes, it was a noble face . . . the conscious end of the conscious world" (20). But as he comes to see, the question is not at all unanswerable. One can, he realizes, "gather one's past, one's collection of identities, in order to take the next forceful step forward into the future" (24). The King Coffin plan which he formulates is the way in which he seeks to be able to answer the question.

Ammen speaks of the problem in various ways—as an exercise in logic, in mathematics, and in purity. But primarily, his scheme involves a problem in aesthetics. Toppan had called him a pseudo-artist; but he has perverted the artist's instinct to create into the need to destroy. For him, destruction is the only means of self-creation. Early in his plan, however, he (like the protagonist of "No, No, Go Not to Lethe") had seen that above all he must stand aside, keep the problem "pure" by avoiding personal, emotional involvement. On this basis he had rejected a particular acquaintance as the victim; for to look at him "was to pity him and despise him" (100), and he saw clearly that "the stranger must be some one to whom one could be completely indifferent. He must be neither attractive nor unattractive, not to be loved or pitied, nor hated or feared, some one whose strangeness or anonymity (in the sense that one knew nothing about him and *felt* nothing) was pure" (100-101). That the arbitrarily selected stranger should turn out to be named Jones is consistent with the perfect logic.

But Aiken is arguing that in life as in art, logic, mathematics, and purity are not enough; they are not the means through which the individual can achieve his greatest degree of understanding. The dominant emotion of the book is pity, as its epigraph from Richard Middleton forcefully indicates:

> "I assure you that beyond administering the poison to his wretched body I have done nothing. Perhaps he is not dead. Can you hear his heart beating?"
>
> "I can hear the spoons of my children beating on their empty platters!"

"Is it like that with you? Poor devil! Oh, poor, poor devil! Philosophers should have no wives, no children, no homes, and no hearts." (vi)

Although Ammen can say with full conviction in the beginning of the book: "The essential thing in life is hate!" (85), by the end of the novel the reader knows that he is wrong, and that his real insanity is in believing this. As in *Crime and Punishment*, there is a contrast between the motives for action and the facts that prove these motives false. For instead of killing Jones simply, as he plans, after "a brief study of the man's daily habits, his goings and comings, the discovery of his name" (104), he becomes overwhelmed by a compulsive need to know the stranger; to observe him in the most intimate situations; to discover details about his home life—in short, to understand him completely. Contrary to killing his own strangeness "purely" and objectively, he wholly neglects to observe his own admonition of indifference; and, having failed to draw the line ("surely it was difficult to set any limit?" [141]) in learning about Jones, he penetrates his victim's consciousness so completely that he comes to identify himself with him.

Ammen's identification with Jones begins midway through the novel. Fittingly, it is evoked as Ammen again scrutinizes himself in the mirror: "Jones had joined him, had joined his life: it was almost, in fact, as if Jones had become a part of his own '*self*'" (194). As Ammen learns more about Jones, he thinks of him with progressive intimacy. He speaks of Jones several times as his shadow; of their relationship as a marriage; of their collaboration as parts of a single mechanism; of their alliance against society; and, finally, of "their queer relationship . . . hourly more obscure, and hourly more subtle in its underground ramifications" (280). He even reads books and takes notes on typography and advertising (since Jones runs an advertising agency); he sends Jones theatre tickets so that he can sit near him and observe his reactions.

At last the identification is complete. No longer is Ammen's own reflection so sharp and clear in the mirror as it was at the outset. What was formerly "the conscious end of the conscious world" is now "the obscure image which he saw coming forward to meet him there" (312). He has lost even that part of the self which he initially knew, and what emerges in the mirror is "not his own face, but the face of Jones" (312); for in knowing Jones so completely he has become him, even physically. He has become the stranger: "It was as if Jones, in that moment of vision, had said something, or been about to say something. . . . He had been about to say 'I am no stranger than you are'; or perhaps 'Aren't you really a stranger yourself? Have you thought of that?'; or else, simply, 'Now you know what it is to be a stranger'" (312-13). The cycle is complete, hatred has its revenge at last. By understanding, and so by loving, he has come to be the stranger; and in not recognizing this, he loses his own identity. He looks at his own reflection now with horror and hatred. With the reversal of roles, the logic entire, Ammen has no choice but to be his own King Coffin: to kill the stranger, he must kill himself. His position is the same as Raskolnikov's, who finally recognized his identity with his victim: "Did I murder the old woman? I murdered myself, not her! I crushed myself once for all, for ever."[4] He goes to St. Paul's and, reciting the rosary, performs the symbolic self-administration of his own last rites and funeral service; then, to Mt. Auburn cemetery, where it "occurred to him that it was a very neat and fitting opportunity for buying a grave—why not?" (328). The book ends with his suicide, performed, appropriately, with the indifference with which he had expected to murder Jones.

The importance of King Coffin, then, lies not in the "crisis-chart" presentation of a psychosis, but rather in Aiken's movement toward the new awareness that human relations are futile only if one lives impersonally. One must accept others, and profoundly. In his earlier work Aiken had assumed the classical dictum that except by analogy we can never know how someone else feels or what he thinks. According to this psychology, each man must remain enclosed within his individual ego. The deeper understanding that arises from *King Coffin* is that we *can* know someone else by participating emotionally and sympathetically in his experience. Perhaps (as a psychoanalyst does) we can know even better than that person how he feels and what he is. Ammen fails because in his disease he cannot account for the emotions which so profoundly affect him. The insight he achieves, therefore, leads him only into darkness, as his impersonality leads only to death.

In *King Coffin*, then, Aiken does not depart from his insistence in the Preludes upon the chaos and uncertainty inevitable in the human condition. But, he is now willing to declare, man achieves dignity in his defeat if he lives his life, and shapes his consciousness, lovingly. Aiken was to write of Noni in *A Heart for the Gods of Mexico*: "That a life should have been so beautiful, and so devoted to good and beautiful things, in the face of the uncompromising principles of impermanence and violence, came to him as a fierce renewal of his faith in the essential magnificence of man's everlasting defeat" (151). While Aiken still believed in the primacy of the imagination and the poet's responsibility in hastening the evolution of consciousness, he was now to see that in "charity: *caritas*, the love of loves" (Ush., 211), he might find the principle which would give his endeavor validity. He at last realized that love's "compelling elusiveness . . . was of course in oneself: and in this, the love was perhaps interchangeably identifiable with one's own consciousness, one's own being and becomingness: it was simply another disguise for the poetic and poietic psyche which is the very center of existence" (Ush., 315). To be conscious is not, as Cather thought, to suffer. It is to love.

155

Aiken's critical theory has always followed at a short but measurable distance upon his creative development. His theory derives from his poems, and not vice versa. "A Basis for Criticism," for instance, is the result and the summary in Aiken's criticism of his Divine Pilgrim poems. After *King Coffin* we can observe an accompanying shift in his point of view as a critic. He became less "scientific" and stressed the qualities in art which satisfy man's sense of his dignity rather than those which compensate for man's defeat. It is true that earlier, in 1915, Aiken could write that "if there is anything that is conspicuous in current American poetry, it is the lack of human warmth," adding that his contemporaries "are intellectualists: and that is a serious charge against any poet."[5] But in 1915 his criticism was governed by the early anti-intellectualist philosophy of *Earth Triumphant*—that all human life is earth's love-song. *Forslin* indicated a new direction in Aiken's poetry. His criticism, accordingly, began moving in the direction which was to culminate with "A Basis for Criticism" and "A Scientific Approach to Criticism," in which he predicted "the gradual decline of art" itself.

By 1940 Aiken's criticism reflected the new emphasis upon self-extension and *caritas* in his work. In such essays as "Poetry: 1940 Model" and "Back to Poetry," he condemned the tendency of modern poets to follow the tradition established by Pound and Eliot. Contending that "it is in the nature of English poetry to be romantic . . . so let us again have it romantic" (ABC, 102), he criticized Auden, Spender, MacNeice, Day Lewis, Ransom, Warren, and Tate. Continuing the attack in 1941, he insisted upon the essential conjunction of poetry and emotion, defining poetry as "the very act of loving, the profoundest sort of acceptance. And the greater the love and the wider its range, the greater the poet." On the relation of thought to poetry he added:

The approach to poetry is not and cannot be intellectual: no amount of taking thought will do the would-be poet an atom of good: he may be both witty and wise and still not a poet. Love is not of the intellect, the birds do not, as far as one can tell, mate intellectually, nor does one admire the blossoming of the rose or peony primarily for its wit. . . . Poetry is an elemental: the feelings come first, the rationalization comes afterward. The poet may, and should, *think*—certainly. The richer his awareness, whether of the so-called outer world, which his sensorium reports to him, or of that other and no less objective world which he can intermittently observe within himself, and the subtler his understanding of the inviolable twinnedness of these two worlds, the richer and deeper of course will be his poetry. . . . But the thinking, the awareness, cannot produce the feeling—one cannot *think* a feeling into existence, least of all into poetic existence.[6]

Kostyleff had earlier convinced Aiken that the stimulus of an emotional shock stirs preformed cerebral mechanisms in the poet. Whereas he had then followed Kostyleff in emphasizing the importance of the chains of verbal reflexes in poetry, whether "controlled" or uncontrolled by the poet, he now came to emphasize, as Kostyleff would not have, the emotion which is capable of calling these reactions forth, and without which they cannot be made conscious. This is to say that although he re-employed Kostyleff's basic motives—the initial emotion and the poet's sensibility—he redefined their relations in an entirely new way. He now saw that the original emotion was not merely initial; it was initiating, and therefore fundamental; for the nature of this emotion would, to a large extent, determine the experience which could be made conscious. The more comprehensive the poet's emotion, the greater would be the range of awareness he might communicate.

His enriched sense of human dignity made him see all the more forcefully the necessary tragedy of human endeavor against an indifferent universe. For he remained convinced that "the contemplation of life as a whole, or the recognition of its items as merely minute sand-grains of that whole, or an occasional recollection of man's twinkling unimportance, or a fleeting glimpse of the cruel perfection of the order of things, are among the finest headlands from which the poet may seek an outlook" (Sc., 237). From such promontories he views the experience of A Heart for the Gods of Mexico. And yet the dominant emotion of the book is neither despair nor pity (as in King Coffin), but that kind of acceptance which ultimately converts the "cruel perfection" of things into their loving perfection.

Because Aiken failed to *form* adequately the experience which A Heart for the Gods of Mexico contains, this is his least successful novel. It is the only one of his books never published in the United States. Indeed, most critics not only ignore the book but seem unaware of its existence. In one of his letters, Blomberg (who is Aiken's alter ego in the novel) makes clear for us what probably caused Aiken's own difficulty in fully rendering and delineating the emotions and attitudes which the trip through Mexico represents. Blomberg writes: "You see me for once not *reading* novels for a publisher, but actually *in* one. It really *is* a novel" (97). For once Aiken forgot the warning which he himself had so ably illustrated—that life is not a short story, that experience cannot become fiction without transformation. In dealing with an experience that seemed so rich, he failed to perceive the need of a technique adequate to form it. He wrote in Ushant that composing the novel "looked almost disconcertingly easy: it looked like the ripe fruit ready to drop into one's receptive hand. It looked as if one would scarcely need to touch it. Wouldn't that scene . . . wouldn't that progress simply write itself—?" (343). Much of it, however, turns out to be mere local color, especially in Aiken's descriptions, midway through the book, of St. Louis ("Fantastic city, down-at-heel jumble of romantic past and shoddy present" [86]); and later, those of the torrid and torpid Mexicans—via D. H. Lawrence ("these sinister looking Indians, too, these lynx-eyed cutthroats . . . with that look that stripped a woman down to sex" [116]).

Yet, despite its defects, the novel has considerable importance in a study of Aiken's development; for it is the first book in which he attempts to register *directly* the emotion of a *caritas* completely understood and completely accepted. It is an account of an ego not only preparing the report by which it may be understood, but also projecting and thereby contemplating the emotion by which it may be forgiven. In consciousness of its own value, the ego provides the solution to solipsism, and assumes dominion over both the inner and outer worlds. The style of the book, where it succeeds, reflects this new movement. Whereas *Blue Voyage* and *Great Circle* were built generally upon the preconscious monologue, the flashback, and the overheard soliloquy, and *King Coffin* upon an interior point of view, *A Heart for the Gods of Mexico* indicates a movement outward to tangible reality. This does not mean that Aiken offers descriptions for their own sake; he continues to portray nature as the expression of states of mind, as in Chapter II of *Great Circle* and *Landscape West of Eden*. Yet, it is clear that he has become increasingly interested in confronting and absorbing material reality. A passage such as the following would have been distinctly incongruous in one of the earlier novels: "A starved dog with a broken back, the hind quarters twisted, dragged itself crookedly to the little parapet of flower-pots by the entrance, and lay there, mutely begging. No attention was paid to it. The eyes, tender and trusting, beseeching, were enough to break one's heart; and when at last it gave up hope, and began to drag itself away, it heaved such a sigh of pure and beaten despair as ought rightly to have ended the world" (137). Seldom in Aiken's earlier work—since his stories in the Harvard *Advocate*—is there such empathy with the external world. In such *Advocate* stories as "Rabbit" (1908), "The Wallet" (1908), and "The Murderer"

159

(1909) he used his protagonists as scapegoats for his own tensions, and thus lavished his sympathy upon the characters whose downfall he was preparing. Hereafter such understanding was not only to appear more frequently but also to widen immensely in range. In his next novel, *Conversation*, Aiken would deal centrally with the necessity of confronting and accepting sensuous reality. The most striking single example of empathy in Aiken's work is perhaps the short story "Hello, Tib." He records the life and death of a kitten in an attempt to define empathy: "Perceptiveness! Good heavens, yes—this was a case in point, it was indeed *the* case. It was the fundamental instance of the all-embracing, all-cherishing, all-sustaining power of perceptiveness (S.S., 194).

In *A Heart for the Gods of Mexico* such empathy is extended, for the most part, to the heroine, Noni. Like Demarest, Cather, and Mr. Arcularis, she is engaged on "the great circle to Mexico, taking her heart as an offering" (55). All are testimonies to the fruitfulness of Thoreau's insistence, in the conclusion of *Walden*, that "Our voyaging is only great-circle sailing"—we return always to our starting point, the self. In her journey Noni moves both outward and inward. She is attempting, in the last moments of her life, to give herself to the man she loves; on the other hand, "she was living her own death" (121). Aiken has progressed from the divine to the human pilgrimage. It is the way she lives her life, not what she discovers about her self, that is important. She lives her life lovingly. With an acceptance beyond mere understanding she incarnates *caritas*, "as if she and it were the same thing" (32). And in this way she transforms the terrors of reality—with all its implications, as expressed in the Darwinian phrase which Aiken borrowed from Tennyson, of "nature red in tooth and claw" (141)—into something incommunicably good: "How explain such cruelty away? It's enough to make you really hate the whole nature of existence: but then, the joke is, the existence of *Noni*, and the way *she* takes this business, makes me really believe in something *ex-*

traordinarily good—she's herself a sort of proof of the divine excellence of things. A very subtle reversal" (100). It is not, perhaps, a very subtle reversal. During the decade which *A Heart for the Gods of Mexico* culminates, Aiken had striven for a principle whereby he might succeed in transforming reality. He had sought it first in the word, the world, and the wound. And he came to discover it in the heart.

· I I I ·

A Heart for the Gods of Mexico served Aiken chiefly as his means of adjusting to a new vision of the role of love in human endeavor. Painful as this adjustment might have been, it provided a wider scope to his experience and emotional intensity for the work to come. The immediate result was *Conversation* (1940), which carries out the same program of *caritas*, but with more art and insight, and an infinitely richer texture.

In *Conversation* Aiken presents a complex society through which the protagonist can move, and from which he can learn. That is, unlike his former novels, the society here exists independently of the hero. He moves *in* it, rather than its moving *about him* and existing only as he calls it forth. In a sense, society (including the Cape Cod landscape) is the real hero of *Conversation*. The plot itself is simple. The marital difficulties of Timothy Kane and his wife, Enid, are complicated by the arrival of a group of Greenwich Village "bohemians," led by Jim Connor, a fur thief, whom Kane had known in New York. In their presence Enid sees danger to the socially "correct" kind of life which she envisions as her ideal, and a threat to the stability of her family. Kane, on the contrary, finds in them a means of escaping from an oppressive domesticity. He seeks to separate his life from his art, escaping from matter-of-fact reality both in the Utopian idealism of the "Robin-hood" thief and through the imagination of his daughter, Buzzer. Aiken analyzes the tension between Kane and Enid and the breach which

161

steadily grows between them. The book ends as both partners give up their selfish interests. Kane learns that only by accepting mundane reality can he be an artist. The novel ends with a rebirth of love, and, Aiken implies, an accompanying renewal of the artist's creativity. But such an outline of the plot cannot show the strength of the book. For Aiken succeeds not as he shows Kane's coming-to-consciousness—the subject of *Blue Voyage and Great Circle*—but as he creates the society through which his protagonist is enabled to make the roots of his problem conscious. His awareness comes both from within and without. And we understand him not as he projects himself into infinity, therefore, but through his relations with other people. Rather than centering upon the conflict between Kane and Enid, then, we might with more profit consider the total organization of the novel.

In *Conversation* Aiken sets forth a group of people who are divided by one standard: some are characterized by their ability to love, in whatever form; others by their obvious lack of human love and sympathy. Prominent in the latter class are the companions of Jim Connor, Bucholtz and Karl Roth. Both use Connor for their own purposes, as Kane says, "sponging on Jim . . . without even the redeeming virtue of believing in him" (136). They are cynical, but otherwise emotionless, concerned only "for their own selfish ends" (191). Roth exhibits his dominant self-interest not only in his relation to Connor, but also in his attitude toward his wife, Kitty. She complains that he hasn't lived with her, but *on* her:

> ". . . If I hadn't worked my eyes out as a stenographer to support you—"
>
> "You knew what to expect, didn't you? You haven't got any kick coming. You can quit any time, as far as I'm concerned. I got along all right without you, didn't I? . . . You knew what the chances were. Why don't you stick to your bargain?" (168-69)

Aiken counterpoises the situation between Kitty and Karl to the Kane-Enid dilemma. In the bitter and disillusioned arguments of the former we see what potentially may happen to the latter if they, too, lose their ability to love. The situations are exactly parallel. In the crisis of the book, Kane and Enid speak in much the same fashion as had Kitty and Karl:

> "What do *I* get out of it? . . . I'm being starved, I warn you, Timothy."
> "I see. So it's like that. You won't stick to your bargain."
> "There *was* no bargain."
> "There was an agreement." (231-32)

The destructive principle which the Karl-Kitty situation signifies has almost vitiated Kane's marriage. But more important in the scheme of the novel, it has prevented the man from understanding and loving others. As a person, Kane is preparing his own death—without the saving grace of Demarest's self-crucifixion.

Kane's disenchantment results from his inability to reconcile romantic illusion with material reality. He himself realizes this and understands that in his marriage "the poetry had been too pure a poetry, its further implications (of all that body, and passion, could exact, or time and diurnal intimacy dishevel and destroy) had been too little understood. . . . The realities had come too quickly and harshly. . . . [The] shock of that 'meaty and butcher-shop reality' had been too much for him" (119-20). Contrasted to those characters who lack love are those others who possess it in one of two ways—either in the romanticism of the child, or in the reality principle of the adult. It is necessary for Kane to understand, accept, and, accordingly, synthesize the two if he is to solve the conflict within himself.

Pre-eminent in the first group are Buzzer and Connor. For Buzzer, the whole world is "a mystery, a mystery, a mystery" (12)—in her favorite refrain. She has her magical pebbles, her "secret place" in the forest, and the imagination which can transform the dark borders around the rugs into oceans. Kane cannot achieve sustained entry into the imaginative world in his art or his relations with his wife, but only in the romanticism of his daughter. Connor's Utopian idealism epitomizes the adult version of her romanticism. As Kane says to him: "Sometimes I think you expect too much of human nature, Jim" (72). And he conceives of himself as a Robin Hood who, in an aesthetic-Marxist drama, steals from the rich (he specializes in department stores) in order to support artists. Buzzer and Connor are clearly identified as childhood and adult versions of the Utopia principle in Connor's bringing of gifts to her upon his departure. He brings her the "typical, the eternal, pink cart of childhood" (244). Kane can understand these characters, for he is one of their kind. Enid calls him "adolescent" on more than one occasion. His problem, if he is to succeed in life as well as in art, is to combine their imaginative re-creation of reality with a sense of what reality actually is.

In Aiken's work, Kane's dilemma can be traced back to that of Festus. We will recall that Festus despaired of finding beauty when he discovered an orchestra of butchers playing an ethereal music. *Conversation* seems almost to be a deliberate answer to *Festus* in the spiral of Aiken's development. One of its minor characters is Mr. Paradise—a butcher! Kane must learn how his name and his occupation are not incongruous—and that all reality combines—fruitfully—the spiritual and the physical. Aiken suggests such combination in many details in the book. At its beginning Kane plants a hundred lilacs near the former location of a pig-sty which had been infested with rats and "millions" of fleas. The image is further complicated by his addition of manure to the sandy soil about the plants. As Terence, who is himself apparently almost a part of the earth, says: "What's the good of feedin' a horse, if she don't give you manure?" (61). Aiken again draws the two principles together in Kane's observation that upon the former site of his outbuilding, magnificent plants had grown with "leaves the size of howdahs, or palanquins" (44). Again and again Aiken points up the false dilemma of Festus. Both the romanticism of the child and the reality principle of the adult may be combined—and admired.

Will Pepoon, although he appears in the novel only briefly, is Aiken's most persuasive comic character, and the one who in the novel best incarnates sensuous reality, the bloody roots of earth. He appears in the book out of nowhere, as if "the creature had come straight out of the ground, out of the earth, with the caked earth still on him" (103). He had come to clean Kane's outbuilding, but was disappointed, for—another irony—Kane had converted the shack into a pump-house:

> "I clean 'em out." he said.
> "What?"
> "Name's Pepoon, they all know me, I come to clean 'em out. Want yours cleaned? I live over the river, go round to all the houses regular, Bill Pepoon. . . . Want me to clean it? I got bags to take it away."
> "Oh, I see. But I haven't got one."
> "Y'ain't got one? What's *that*?" (103-104)

His is an animal nature as honest as Donatello's, with his rustic innocence turned to comic purposes: "He was all of a piece, an earth-god, and an earth-god of the very lowest—and best!—order" (105), Kane says. His odd wholesomeness serves as a force of reconciliation. Before this gnome's appearance, Kane had been repelled by the violence of the earth; but in approving Pepoon as an earth-god, Kane begins to grow. He can accept the earth—if only, at this point, imaginatively. Pepoon with his bags becomes a kind of purgative symbol in Kane's psychological regeneration; Kane admonishes those who lack love with the ritual telluric curse: "Go crawl into . . . one of Mr. Will Pepoon's bags!" (227). Except in Kane, of course, the realms of romantic and sensuous reality do not meet. Buzzer's reaction to Pepoon is: "He *wasn't* a god! *How* could he be a god! He was too dirty. . . . Did you see my pebbles? *This* is kingy, and *this* is queeny" (105). But it is necessary for Kane to bring them together—to accept, as he says, the "bloody roots" of romance. For what both Pepoon and Buzzer mean, though at different poles, is *love*. And in various encounters with love—through Pepoon and Buzzer, but most of all through Nora, he comes to learn its real meaning. Nora (the Eunice of "The Night Before Prohibition") most effectively encourages and vitalizes Kane's spiritual—or material!—regeneration.

The novel opens with Kane's and Nora's love affair all but concluded; the letter he receives midway in the book certifies its end. But the letter—allied to the "indiscreet" dream which, the night before, preceded it—ends with, "*I shall always be glad it happened, and grateful*" (112). There is no reproach, no burden of sorrow and pathos in the letter, as there *had* been in the dream. Rather, Nora epitomizes gratitude, unbounded *caritas*, the willing loss of self-interest. Kane correctly associates her with an all-giving Mother Nature. Like Noni, love for her is as simple as a process of nature; it exists with no motives beyond its own existence. Through her Kane comes fully to accept the "bloody roots" of romance, to realize that "they were oneself, one's hand, one's heart, one's god" (125). Roth had said early in the book: "Never lead with the heart!" (176) Through the transformative and restorative nature and society which surrounds him, Kane learns to "lead with the heart," to surrender self-interest. The book ends with a rebirth of love in a revitalization of his emotion—"being ridiculous isn't always such a bad thing to be" (256)—and, one suspects, in the consequent renascence of his art.

· I V ·

In the attempt to write genuine love poetry, the modern poet is, as has been abundantly pointed out, at a distinct disadvantage; for the nineteenth century generally sentimentalized the subject and almost destroyed its possibilities. Aiken himself realized this danger. He wrote in 1925 that "since the seventeenth century there *is* practically no first-rate love-poetry in English," because "the love lyric has been stifled with sentimentality."[7] In *Conversation* and *A Heart for the Gods of Mexico* Aiken prepared an intellectual substance through which he might renew this area of experience, too long sentimentalized. Insofar as he came to understand himself and the function of poetry more deeply through these works, they allowed him to return to his poetry. He came to see that the Preludes were the core—which he must develop—and not the conclusion of his work.

Yet, sentimentality may result from an inadequate form as well as from a poverty of experience. We may define sentimentality as the poet's betrayal of a more intense emotion than his form is capable of expressing or arousing in the reader. In his novels, of course, Aiken had not solved the problem of poetic form; he had simply clarified his vision. *And in the Human Heart* (1940) is composed of a sequence of forty-three related sonnets. That Aiken should have turned to the series form was perhaps inevitable. He had already observed its possibilities for a complexity of exploration and expression in the two volumes of Preludes as well as in the poems which had prepared the way for them. His decision to employ the sonnet form with its predictable movement (but a movement capable of modulation) was also, to some extent, the result of earlier experimentations. A series of nine sonnets published with *John Deth*, in 1930, constituted his one previous extended attempt to write love poetry. Aiken was probably also influenced in his choice of the sonnet sequence by the example of Meredith's *Modern Love*. He frequently praised *Modern Love* as the chief example of success in love poetry during the nineteenth century. Certainly in "Sonnets I-IX" Aiken offers a theme similar to Meredith's— the progress of a love affair from complete harmony in love ("Be it confessed: I am idolatrous" [470]) to various stages of doubt and, finally, disenchantment. In IV the poet questions whether his constant "angelic love" can remain pure from the doubts and alternations of his thought. In v he catalogues his failures, in a less fragmentary, but essentially similar fashion to that of *Osiris Jones*:

> IMPRIMIS: I forgot all day your face,
> Eyes, eyebrows, gentle mouth, and cheek, all faded;
> Nor could I, in the mind's dark forest, trace
> The haunted path whereby that dream evaded.
> Secundus: I forgot all night your laughter,
> In vain evoked it by strong charms of thought:
> Gone, like a cry that leaves no image after,
> Phoenix of sound which no hand ever caught.
> Tertius: my wanton mind and heart, together,
> Forgetting you, you absent, have delighted
> For no more cause than bright or stormy weather.
>
> (472)

In VII their estrangement becomes the subject. The protagonist's failures to express his love had been a testimony to its magnitude; but now he has been supplanted in her affection. He therefore speculates in VIII upon the paradox in nature, the lesson of *Conversation*, that all opposites are mixed. In a desperate effort to retain his illusions he concludes: "What's love, with doubt's slow venom mixed, unless / It be a most ecstatic hue of hate?" (473) With the ninth and final sonnet, he rids himself of illusions and admits: "You are not all I thought you might be; I / Am not the god my rival was" (474). Their love has completed its circle; and, just as in Meredith's sequence, it ends in hate and complete estrangement.

Despite the high quality of seven of the nine sonnets, this sequence was not as effective as it might have been. Aiken's development of the estrangement is too rapid, and prevents the delicate gradation and modulation which is essential in the psychological portrayal of estrangement in love. The forty-three sonnets which compose *And in the Human Heart*, however, allowed Aiken full scope for the variation and development which the series form predicates. More than in any of his earlier series poems, Aiken achieves unity of sequence in *And in the Human Heart*. He uses several means to do so. The device of companion poems, which Aiken employed in *Priapus* IV and VII and in *Preludes for Memnon* XLV and LVIII, also occurs in this sequence. Both XI and XXVIII are poems in which the whole of reality is consistently seen in terms of a color. The first of these moves from the line "Blue, blue, and blue again, and blue once more" to "blue, blue, and blue again, and bluer still" (763). The second poem reverses the grammatical sequence along with the color symbolism—from "Green, green and green again, and greener still," to "green, green, and green again, and green once more" (771). A similar device, the link, is used in XXIII and XXIV, in which the last line of the one begins the next poem. So also in XXXI, the poet begins: "These items in our chronicle therefore set" (773), and, in XXXII, continues: "These items, too, put down" (773). XII is tied to XI by Aiken's reiteration of rhythms.

Such repetitive devices combine with Aiken's use of metaphors to effect more than incidental unity. For he develops and interweaves metaphors from one sonnet to another. In VI, for example, the poet imagines his body as an altar upon which the self performs its own communion; in VII, he becomes a church "with golden rumor filled" (761). In XIV he asks, "how shall we praise this flower" (764) and, through memory, preserve it from death? In the next two poems he shows how it may be done. This theme, in free association, leads him into a consideration of his own death in XVII and the two following poems; and then, finally, back to the flower metaphor in XX and XXI. Likewise, in the thirtieth to the thirty-seventh sonnets, he discusses love in terms of the sun and moon rising. The same kind of interweaving is everywhere evident. One poem moves inevitably out of another. Even the themes and images of the first poem appear once more, developed and transmuted, in

169

the last. Aiken is attempting, of course, to transcend the traditional limits of the sonnet form and give his series the effect of a new kind of oneness. Like *Osiris Jones* and the Preludes, the series ceases to be a series and becomes simply one continuing and exfoliating effort toward a certain end.

Aiken derived the title for his sonnet sequence from a line in *Preludes for Memnon*, XLV: "Time in the rock and in the human heart" (551). In using this one line to provide the title for the Preludes to Definition and the sonnet sequence, Aiken stressed the affinity of all three volumes. In *And in the Human Heart* Aiken continued his exploration of consciousness. Like the earlier poems, this too is a prelude to death and the final extinction of consciousness. His dramatic frame, however, is not mythic, but completely human. Peter Jones, of course, is literally a man who has died undergoing an operation. But in terms of the universal myth which he can embody and symbolize, he is Osiris Jones accounting for his life. These sonnets are not written in imitation of Osiris or for Memnon, but by the poet himself. They are the series of letters which the anonymous hero of the sequence writes from his sickbed to his loved one during an illness which threatens to prove fatal.[8] He is no more —and no less—than a man writing at a critical juncture of his life. The new insights which Aiken had achieved in *A Heart for the Gods of Mexico* and *Conversation* freed him from reliance upon the materials of myth. In the Preludes Aiken had sought to transcend the terrors of reality by the act of knowing them. Now, in *And in the Human Heart*, he insists that man must not only be conscious, but consciously love and celebrate; for only love and acceptance can transmute the hate and impersonality of the world into something valuable and eternal. The poet weighs his grain of love against the vicissitudes of existence to "match with love that deathless hate" (XI, 763). He need not deny chaos, the alterations of time, or the infinity of space in order to triumph over them—he need only counterbalance them with the instant of love. And his poetry is his love-song. By its act, "lovelessness, translated, will be song; / hatred and ice will not escape that rhyme" (III, 759).

The subject of the poem is, therefore, the contrast between the impersonality of nature and the intensity of his love, between the infinitude and cold indifference of time and space and the flickering intensity of his passion. He conquers his dilemma as soon as he states it:

> Space has no shape, nor will your thinking shape it,
> space has no confines, and no borders time;
> and yet, to think the abyss is to escape it,
> or fix that horror's margin in a rhyme. (XXVI, 770)

Again and again, he stresses the ability of love and consciousness to transcend time and space, to achieve eternity through memory:

> these, the unnumbered, let us love and cherish;
> which, like ourselves, if not remembered, perish.
> (XXIV, 769)

In the most triumphant movement of the book, the poet opposes the metamorphic and regenerative forces of love to the destructive powers of time:

> Time will dismiss? But love dismisses time,
> and knots him tightly in this love-knot rhyme.
> (XIX, 767)

Each poem celebrates—not merely records—a fleeting moment of consciousness as the incandescent instant is consumed by time. Even in his meditation upon the bitterness of change, Aiken exhibits a constancy of devotion:

> The kiss tastes bitter best
> when it is solved, or partly, in despair:
> nowhere shall love's head rest upon love's breast
> so deeply, or so mercifully, as where

that agony of counting, lost in numbers,
worships, despairs, and kisses—and then slumbers.

(xxii, 768)

If there is a fault in the book, it is not, as Randall Jarrell complained,[9] that Aiken uses such words as "chaos," "infinity," "time," and "space" obsessively. Aiken's diction is not merely rhetorical, but is demanded by his subject. The fault, rather, is that since Aiken too casually dimisses time and space, love itself becomes easy—not, as in *Conversation*, difficult—to attain. Time and space, so easily triumphed over, lose their power to terrorize. Even so, Aiken is dealing with a love already attained and shows only how he may celebrate and commemorate it. Moreover, since the poet is speaking to his loved one, he feels he has no problem of communication. In the first poem he tells her that he will "speak without cunning, love, as without craft, / careless of answer, as of shame or blame" (758).

He speaks with the ease and clarity of a sage. The complexity of the texture and the seriousness of the metaphorical development give the sequence an intellectual rigor to accompany and reinforce the emotional triumph. In ix, for instance, Aiken controls the emotion in developing the paradox that the lovers are both victors over and victims of time and space. He furthers the paradox by asserting that the lovers "in a thought, deny [time and space] power to harass, / and, in a kiss, accept them" (762). As in *Osiris Jones*, Aiken opposes the integrity of the mind to the weakness of the body. The fact that they are the victims of time and space constitutes their victory; for they derive power from the powers that defeat them:

What unknown circles have they, or lost regions,
wideness, or emptiness, or desolation,
what zeros of despair, in which our legions
are not already camped, and keep their station?
Their strength is our strength—how can we be weak,
who the whole wildness of the world inherit? (762)

172

In the closing couplet, Aiken resolves the paradox emotionally—although not so radically that we doubt it: "Let us remember this, when we embrace: / in us are met the powers of time and space." We need not seek far for such emotional complexity. In the octave of xii, the poet considers the universal ravages of time as it dismisses all things. But in the sestet he reverses the process of development by finding himself and his loved one to be the very principles of time—and, therefore defeating its power:

> Yet in this wrist that I hold out is time;
> his murder here, as in your cheek; and you,
> alas, my love, embody too his crime,
> to whom alone you will at last be true.
> Father am I of all then—you the mother;
> for we embrace time who embrace each other. (763)

The whole sequence is constructed upon such triumphant reversals. The all-encompassing paradox is the traditional death-in-life, life-in-death theme: "Snowflake on asphodel, clear ice on rose, / frost over thistledown . . ." (xv, 765). Anticipated as early as 1925 in "Changing Mind," this phoenix love seeks its eternal salvation in its daily destruction. This is the definitive paradox of the prelude, which embraces destruction that it may endure.

· V ·

Several months after the publication of *And in the Human Heart*, Aiken wrote in criticism of Yvor Winters' "controlled" poetry: "The discipline, whether of form or idea . . . is good as far as it goes; at its best, it produces a sort of negative purity, a mild decorousness. . . . The trouble with it is that it cannot understand or accept exuberance, either in image or word, that it is mortally afraid of *sound* . . . and that above all it dares not try for intensity or simplicity because it imagines these to be sentimental" (ABC, 387-88). Aiken's criticism has always moved

in unfashionable directions. At the beginning of the poetic revolution, he held out against looseness in form; later, in the
thirties and forties, when care for form and technique triumphed over emotion, he called for experiment, the "return
of the gift of the gab" (ABC, 371). Likewise, in each of his
poems he has sought to provide his culture with what it would
otherwise lack. Appearing in 1941, *And in the Human Heart*
is a case in point. In this book, as in the earlier and greater Preludes, Aiken consciously worked with an area of experience
which had been sentimentalized and debased. Through emotional and rhythmical intensity and metaphorical complexity,
he attempted to renew our attitude toward love and raise the
subject once more to the level of poetry. In an age which has
demanded that everything in poetry be made New—which indeed, has seen newness as the only goal of poetry—it is difficult
to show that such a procedure as Aiken's has in the past produced, and will again produce, great poetry. Against Pound's
emphasis upon discovery—"The scientist does not expect to be
acclaimed . . . until he has *discovered* something"[10]—Aiken
sets rediscovery; against the new he sets the renewed. Blackmur
has correctly observed that Aiken writes "in the easiest language
and the easiest external forms of any modern poet of stature.
He sings by nature and training out of the general body of
poetry in English. He writes from the cumulus of cliché in the
language, always, for him, freshly felt. . . . Aiken depends on
the force of his own mind and the force of metrical form to
refresh his language. . . . In his language, but not in his conceptions, he depends more on convention than most poets do
in our time, almost as much as Dryden or Pope."[11] In order to
understand the sources of Aiken's particular method of re-creating rather than creating, we must refer again to his psychoanalytic theory of language.

This theory, as I have outlined it earlier, maintains that an
external stimulus sets off in the poet the automatic discharge
of verbal reflexes. After the original stimulus, these verbal re-

flexes unravel in chains of association on their own momentum. Aiken combined this theory of language with his belief that "there are certain constant common denominators of beauty in the phenomenal world which cannot be ignored, which are in themselves more emotionally suggestive than other things."[12] Since the poet's duty, according to Aiken, is to advance man's awareness, he would best fulfill his function by working in these particularly suggestive areas of experience. These areas are the most meaningful to begin with. They are, he argued later, "the areas of potential awareness," and the poet must choose between "making good his claim to those areas by making finer use of them than was made by his predecessor," or by developing new areas of his own.[13] Aiken chose to work in the areas of greatest awareness; rather than creating new experiences for his reader, he sought to re-create the old. In a letter to Selden Rodman dated November 8, 1931, Aiken wrote concerning the "current vogue for pretentious unintelligibility": "Mind you, I believe in the use of pure affect, or the more purely affective sorts of speech, for certain purposes, and that nothing whatever can take their place; but one must be wise in their use, not blindly and conceitedly idiosyncratic. . . . But the best poet is—isn't he?—the one who has learnt how to make his idiosyncrasies intelligible to others—he will calculate the precise weight of his idiosyncrasy and mix it properly with more assimilable elements." While poets like E. E. Cummings have stressed the idiosyncratic ad absurdum, Aiken takes an objective view of himself—he does not simply reflect or reproduce his personality, he transforms and translates it.

In 1919 he applied Kostyleff's theory of language to the poetry of John Gould Fletcher and argued that "in the case of Mr. Fletcher the striking feature has always been his habit of surrendering himself, almost completely, to the power of these automatically unravelling verbal reflexes" (Sc., 108). Aiken came to see that Fletcher's surrender to his verbal reflexes was an error; for Fletcher thereby abandoned his poetry to his own linguistic idiosyncrasies and so failed to extend the understanding of humanity. His art did not become artifact, but remained purely personal and subjective. Therefore, he failed his audience. Aiken argued that in another fashion Eliot made the same mistake. Since Eliot's allusive symbolism does not disclose itself, the poetry it produces is as subjective (though in an antithetical way) as Fletcher's: "There is," Aiken wrote, "a distinct weakness consequent on the use of allusions which may have both intellectual and emotional value for Mr. Eliot, but (even with the notes) none for us. The 'Waste Land' or the Grail Legend might be a good symbol, if it were something with which we were sufficiently familiar. But it can never, even when explained, be a good symbol, simply because it has no immediate associations for us" (ABC, 178). Aiken criticized even his own *Nocturne of Remembered Spring* volume on these grounds: "Mr. Aiken displays here a tendency to take refuge in . . . emotional symbols which are so idiosyncratic as to be almost meaningless." He had not discriminated between emotional symbols "which are merely peculiar to himself, and those which are common to mankind" (ABC, 121). Neither by the lack of control over associations of the one poet, nor in the intellectually constructed (pseudo-) associations of the other, Aiken argued, could awareness be extended.

In contrast to Fletcher and Eliot, Aiken imposes a minimum of control on his associations by intentionally committing himself to a language which (at its best) is most familiar, and by choosing subjects or themes which originate in the areas of greatest "potential awareness." In so doing he hopes to refresh both the language and emotional associations which are most important to man. He relies upon the originality of his ideas to raise the outworn areas of awareness above the commonplace and trivial. As a result, I should quickly add, Aiken's language is anything but stereotyped; it carries with it a wide penumbra of association, especially from philosophy, psychology, medicine, and myth. By reinvigorating experience he purifies his language.

Clifton Fadiman has said that "Aiken is without doubt one of the greatest punners alive. His books, as well as his talk, glitter with gems."[14] Aiken's language as a whole does have something of the movement of a serious and rich pun: each of his words carries with it a chain of conscious associations, personal and traditional, with other words and attitudes. Let us consider, for example, his use of the words "systole" and "diastole." Aiken has used this pair three times in his poetry—in *Preludes for Memnon*, LXIII:

> Thus systole addressed diastole,—
> The heart contracting, with its grief of burden,
> To the lax heart, with grief of burden gone. (572)

"The Improvisation":

> Now systole and diastole should be hushed
> mortally under snow, slowed to the rhythm
> of water under ice on a night of planets. (S.O., 23)

and in "Aubade":

> Six o'clock in the crystal instant the crystal second
> the crystal pause between systole and diastole. (S.H., 37)

I choose this pair of words because they are not so common that their meaning in any case would be ambiguous. Unlike, say, "star," or "wing" or "ice" (favorites of Aiken) they tend to be used univocally. Aiken uses them, however, to suggest several things. In the first place, of course, they refer to the expansion and contraction of the heart—to biological existence. They are medical terms and imply the impersonality of the physical universe as opposed to the heart as the (symbolic) seat of personal emotions. Aiken also uses the terms to suggest the work of the poet (e.g. "hushed," "rhythm") in shortening and lengthening his syllables for metrical convenience. In his very diction he implies, therefore, the oneness of language and the universe. Although Aiken begins in the commonplace, by

177

intellectual force and verbal magic he revitalizes his subject, reinvigorates his language. It follows, as Blackmur has observed of Aiken's language in comparison with Stevens', that "the dictionary and the general symbolism of language are much less help in explicating Mr. Aiken than Mr. Stevens."[15]

From the very beginning of his work, Aiken sought to renew the most meaningful areas of man's experience. By 1923 he had formulated the basis of his method of association: "The [emotional] connections which first wear out, the ones most overworked, are precisely the most important and most vital to [man], the ones at the very heart of his consciousness—the connections with such of his concepts as love, life, death, hope, faith, time, space; and . . . it is still to these concepts that he desires, above all, to respond" (ABC, 65). It becomes the function of the highest art, an aspect of its service of mankind, to discover the new linguistic connections for these concepts. We can see Aiken working on this level as early as *Turns and Movies*, in which he sought, by applying Freudian analysis to their lives, to increase our understanding of vaudeville performers as heightened representatives of the desire for wish-fulfillment in every man. The same is true of *Forslin* and *The House of Dust*, where he casts newspaper sensationalism into psychological patterns. In *Osiris Jones* and the Preludes he attempted to place his own self-exploration at the service of man, as a conscious parallel of the process through which each man must go.

Aiken wrote in *Time in the Rock*, LXXXI, that knowledge can come from "observation of what has been unobserved"—that is, from new areas of experience—but also:

> and this is best, from the renewed inspection
> of a known thing, and long loved; something small,
> something tiny, but loved. The pimpernel,
> hidden, with dusty petals, in deep grass,
> obscure but always remembered, clear and

178

delicate, but with something obtuse as well,
obtuse and infinitesimal—this is the sort
of well-loving, and well-knowing, that changes
Tuesday to Wednesday. (741)

It is in the area of "the renewed inspection / of a known thing" that Aiken characteristically works, knowing that "originality is comparatively a small part in the writing of good poetry—it is the seasoning of the dish, but not the dish itself" (Sc., 155). For as the prelude brings order and faith out of chaos and despair, so also out of the area of outworn associations proceeds the highest kind of originality, "the language never old and never new" (L.P., 18).

In *And in the Human Heart*, xxx-xxxvii, Aiken re-creates his love through the experience of wonderment in the sun's rising:

the leaves, and the strung sound of birdsong, stilled,
all the arched night turned back, and hushed, to listen;
and then the heartbeat, and the dream—and then
fanfare of cock-crow, and our sun again. (xxxi, 773)

These are the stock characters of the dawn, the bird, the cock. But the combination of details which translates the bird-song into the harp made by the rays of the sun and the fresh observation of the fact that at the moment preceding dawn the night seems to deepen—these give the observation a power which renews our old wonderment in the familiar experience. The same is true, at its best, of the whole sequence. "Love, death, hope, faith, time, and space"—the concepts which he described as primary—are indeed the concepts out of which *And in the Human Heart* grows. This volume is the most complete example in Aiken's work of his attempt to renew and revitalize the primary associations of mankind. It is at once a culmination—the last of the "series" poems Aiken was to write—and in its greater emphasis upon directing the reader's associations toward only the areas of his greatest potential awareness, a new movement forward.

179

At their best, the sonnets in *And in the Human Heart* gain
strength by finding the complex in the simple, or rather, discovering that the simple is always complex, "a mystery, confined in
little space: / the whole world's wonder in a single face" (vi, 760).
In the simple, the daily, the common, Aiken seeks out the eternal.
Perhaps even more successful than the *Human Heart* sonnets
in balancing the usual and the ultimate, and in revitalizing and
revising our outworn emotional responses, is "Blues for Ruby
Matrix." Although it was not published until 1942, in the
Brownstone Eclogues volume, "Ruby Matrix" is contemporaneous with the Preludes. Like them it arises from Aiken's discovery of the magical resemblance between "the word, the world,
the wound" (T.R., viii, 672)—between the individual and his
universe and the language through which he can understand
and express this relationship. Ruby Matrix is:

> woman who art not woman but a wound,
> wound who art not wound but indeed a word,
> word that art not word but truly a world. (612)

In her the poet finds the essence and purpose of the universe;
in her love, her unastonished humility, he sees the matrix of all
things. The world began with a word—and the word was *caritas*:

> What she had was something with no name,
> if she were dead I'd carve it on a stone,
> it was as right as rain as true as time,
> necessary as rhythm in a tune,
> what she had was only a word or two. (614)

In his subject and title Aiken, of course, is playing with the resemblance between *matrix* (which refers generally to the eternal
and indestructible originative form of all creation, and specifically to the womb) and the Latin word *meretrix*. And Ruby embodies both; in combining them Aiken can work in two direc-

tions—and thence to resolution in shimmering ambiguity—in showing the terrific in the commonplace, the holy in the corrupt, inextricably twinned and intermingled.

The measure of Aiken's growth between, for instance, *Forslin* and "Ruby Matrix," is clear. Aiken has steadily complicated his vision, and refined his means of expressing it, as he has been able to absorb more and more experience into an all-embracing consciousness. We need only compare the early poems with "Ruby"; "A Blue-Eyed Girl in Virgo" from *Forslin*:

> Her eyes were shallow and hard, her face was powdered,
> She spat between kisses . . . And soon as their love was over,
> She left him to walk the streets.
> And now the whole sick world in the nauseous darkness
> Sprawled like a harlot's body, diseased and old. (105-106)

—with Aiken's magnificent conclusion of his elegy for Ruby Matrix:

> your hand that murdered men or drew the morning
> out of the seventh vial, or rolled the mountains
> against the tombs of all the gods, or poured
> the zeros one on other and destroyed
> the indestructible to create the new—
>
> came like a flame from sand, reentered water,
> was braided like the ice, became a wall
> sang through the trumpet of eternity
> and now, descended, holds a greasy key
> and presses it against a greasy lock—
>
> Farewell Ruby, for this is where I leave you
> your hand releases me its filth is on me,
> the holy filth of long corruption comes
> coldly upon me as an absolution,
> sharply we flower in this foul farewell.

181

But God's terrific wing that day came down,
loud on the world as loud and white as snow
out of the blue the white and then the silence.
O Ruby, come again and turn the time.

Ruby, your name is matrix, rock of ages
cloven by lightning, smitten by thunder,
the surged upon deep shore interminable,
the long, the nebulous waves, the foam of time,

beating upon you, breaking upon you foaming,
the worldlong fruitfulness of assuaging sea,
hammers of foam, O Ruby come again
be broken for our simple coming forth—

let the rocks fall upon us with fearful sound,
the long bright glacier of the stars be broken,
the beginning and the final word be spoken,
come again, come again, and turn the world.

This world that is your turning and returning,
matrix mother mistress menstrual moon,
wafer of scarlet in the virgin void,
O come again and turn the world to thought.

But God's terrific wing that day came down
snow on the world, and Ruby you were snow,
deceitful whiteness and the blood concealed
so that the world might know how worlds will end. (619-21)

He can now see her in a double aspect—with "the purlieus and
the cats, / the filth put out the food received the money" (616),
but also as ineffably good, "who found the stepping stone and
brought it back, / gave it to me because I stood and loved you"
(612). The stepping stone is love, as in *Conversation*, an all-

giving love. And in his poem the poet writes his elegy in recompense for this gift of love. Through imagination and the glass of eternity he can see clearly that she "had known the ultimate and called it nothing / and you have sightseen God with tired eyes" (614). And he therefore fills her elegy with memorials from the images and icons of infinity. In this way he defines her not only by the "Big Rock Candy Mountains," but also by the "rock of ages"; not only by the "pleasure parks on Coney Isle / which Ikey Cohn decreed," but also by the celebration of the resurrection at Easter, by the nightingale and the phoenix; not only by her body, but also by

> those curves of hers that curve beyond
> geometry of hand or eye or mind
> into the bloodstream and above again (616);

not only by "smells of fecundity, the human spawn," but also by the thurible, the incense, and her "angelic heart"; not only by the hot dog stand, the poached eggs, the "cachinnations above the sauerkraut," and the morning toast, but also by the prayer for "daily bread." Thereby she is transformed from what she is to what she means; not what she made of her life, but what the poet can see in it is important. The poem which speaks of her love is itself an exhibition of her love—which accepts, wholly and profoundly. She has given the poet the understanding—and thus the language—whereby he can re-create her as she ideally is.

Sometimes in theme, and fundamentally in method, "Blues for Ruby Matrix" prefigures the poems in *Brownstone Eclogues* (1942). In these later poems, Aiken again moves—less successfully, I think—to reversals of the judgments of the world, to seeing the ultimate in the momentary, finding faith in the hopeless. "The Lady in Pink Pyjamas" and "Blind Date," for instance, derive almost directly from the "Ruby Matrix" vision:

No more the swanboat on the artificial lake
its paddled path through neon light shall take;
the stars are turned out on the immortal ferris wheel,
dark and still are the cars of the Virginia Reel.
Baby, it is the last of all blind dates,
and this we keep with the keeper of the golden gates. (809)

In "Sursum Corda" Aiken generalizes this scheme by seeing that in the Christian drama of salvation, savageness, fierce energy, is the only meekness, the only suffering. In *Brownstone Eclogues* as a whole he distills city life, in its multiform aspects, as a continuation of the effort to rejuvenate our outworn areas of awareness, to make us see our daily reality anew. Although he deals with the subject he had formerly employed for *The House of Dust*, the changes which occurred between the two volumes are everywhere apparent. Aiken is no longer interested in portraying the city through typical incidents, with a pretense—and an effect—of completeness; nor with presenting a movement, say, from the simple to the complex, from the external to the internal, throughout the poem. Rather, he depicts, in an arbitrary fashion, the defeated lives of the city: "the things that come to end, / the idle promise broken; / in every tenement, in every room, a betrayed friend, / the deadly sentence spoken" ("St. Ambrose; Early Morning," 781). When the poems succeed, as, for instance, in "Dear Uncle Stranger," the poetry transcends such defeat through its all-embracing love. When they fail, it is because they do not maintain the necessary emotional intensity either in tone or metaphor. Love becomes merely pity. And the poet's pity turns what is meant to be a prayer of hope into despair:

> who doubts but they will find an end to illness—
> summer, and the long lost ships?
>
> .   .   .   .   .
>
> But no. In darkness, behind the shaken church,
> ribbed like the hurricane,

184

roars past the apse, while walls and windows lurch,
the first suburban train. (782)

Another way of putting this is to say that the too frequent
irony of the tone combats and defeats the sincerity of the emotion. The lives and hopes which are defeated by the city may
be an area of awareness to which the reader requires a fresh
response. But in *Brownstone Eclogues* the response is too often
willed, instead of imagined, by the poet. The compulsion to
write many of the poems came, one suspects, from an "intellectual" desire to renew the area of awareness rather than an
imaginative need to do so. In "The Lovers," for example, Aiken
compares a funeral parlor and a florist's, the coffins and the
flower-baskets, to two lovers. The poem strikes the reader as
basically witty, the product of thought. Here, as elsewhere,
Aiken falls prey to the fault for which he criticized the poet of
"The Habeas Corpus Blues":

> The poet prefers the black keys to the white,
> he weaves himself a shroud of simple harmonics;
> across the street a house burns, in its light
> he skeins more skillfully his bland ironics. (790)

In his preference for "bland ironics" the poet ignores the fundamental poetry of life as much as do the "teamsters . . . drinking
booze" or the acolytes praying in the cathedral. Each in his own
way avoids reality—the poet in intellect, the teamsters in unconsciousness, and the acolytes in mysticism.

The best poems in this volume are those which have distant
(but clear) affiliations with Aiken's earlier poetry. Such poems
possess an intellectual and emotional substance which supports
their sincerity. Some—"The Census-Takers," for example—
carry out, in human terms, Aiken's emphasis upon self-knowledge. "The Census-Takers" begins with an image of the usual,
anonymous census-takers asking their interminable questions, as
if at random. But almost from the very beginning the questions
assume a personal aspect, a dithering in certain peculiar direc-

tions. They ask questions about death ("Did you hear of the murder?"; "Will you visit the Funeral Home, and alone, when you die?") in immediate contrast to questions about life ("Stranger, did you ever play ball in a vacant lot?"). Then, with the question, "And where is the ferry, that meets you at half-past six?" the metaphor expands. The ferry becomes Charon's ferry for dead souls; the river, the river Styx; and the census-takers become the judges of life and death, calling forth the testimony of consciousness, asking "What time is it now by the heart?":

The questions that later tonight will take you to task,
When you sit down alone, to think, in a lonely place.

> .   .   .   .   .

Stranger, whose heart did you break? and what else did you do?—
The census-takers are coming to ask you tonight;
The truth will be hurrying home, and it's time you knew. (802)

Here the unimportant detail assumes ultimate significance, with the accompanying emotional shock; the casual suddenly becomes the intense.

Aiken took a sentence from Jean de Ruysbroeck for the epigraph to *Brownstone Eclogues*: "Needs must I rejoice beyond the age, though the world have horror of my joy." The volume seeks to illustrate the means of finding joy in the midst of horror. In poems such as "Shaemus" Aiken uses the city to symbolize the impersonal cosmos against which love and awareness are pitted. The success of the protagonist emphasizes the victory of *caritas* over the vicissitudes of space and time.[16] "Shaemus" leads to the same finality of poetic understanding as "The Census-Takers"—not in surprise but in the vision of a

> memory, that flew back years to find a name,
> found it, and fetched it up,
>
> .   .   .   .   .
>
> —and still the traces!—

186

Yes, still the traces of that love he loved,
and re-examined, but as if unmoved;
the names fished up from time, or Singapore,
joined and repeated on his bar once more;

as if no let or hindrance were permitted;
as if both time and space could be outwitted. (805)

Like his heroes, the poet derives his power from the power of
memory—what Berdyaev called "man's most profound ontological principle, the one that cements and preserves the unity
of his personality." What he can hold together through memory, this is what he can be: by remembering his past he sings
it into existence. Such poems as these constitute the end of
Aiken's long journey toward self-awareness. And he finds that in
understanding his own ego, he moves inevitably to a commemoration of other egos. In the shared revelation, the shared
love, he discovers the principle of man's continuance, his victory over chaos:

Dear Uncle stranger, Cousin known too late,
sweet wife unkissed, come, we will celebrate
in this thronged mirror the uncelebrated dead,
good men and women gone too soon to bed. (811)

187

REVIEWING St. John Perse's *Pluies*, Aiken wrote that there are two methods available to the poet. The first of these is the procedure in which the poet writes through what Aiken called *whole meaning*. Working in this fashion, the poet finds "his beginning in his end," his theme complete before he puts a word on paper. *Pluies*, Aiken argued, is such a poem; for it characterizes "the history of man in terms of rain, or the interpretation of him in terms of rain—rain as the fertilizer, rain as the purifier, even as the principle itself of life and change" (ABC, 321-22). Aiken's *The Soldier* (1944) and *The Kid* (1947) also work through such *whole meaning*. Both have a centripetal design, their method being the reverse of the Preludes and Aiken's other series poems. The Preludes develop extemporaneously, as it were; the reader is interested chiefly in the associational movement outward from the starting point, and only secondarily in the way in which Aiken has shaped the poems into a unified sequence. The same is true of an early poem on war, "1915: The Trenches," in which Aiken tried to present the psychological impact of war through the kind of symphonic variations made familiar in the Divine Pilgrim poems —particularly by ironically evoking the fragmentary details which the soldier's mind in fear, terror, and boredom calls forth. In *The Soldier* and *The Kid*, however, the reader is primarily interested in the development of the thesis toward a single end, and secondarily in the incidental "improvisation" which accompanies this progress. The difference in emphasis results in different kinds of poems, and *The Soldier* and *The Kid* indicate a new departure in Aiken's work.

The *whole meaning* of *The Soldier* issues from the claim that "the history of war / is the history of mankind" (823). Aiken portrays history in terms of a series of heroic struggles. But while he derives a new unity from the design he perceives in history, his fundamental purposes remained unchanged. In *The Soldier* he insists as much as ever upon the importance of advancing man's consciousness and *caritas*. Now he discovers their presence and progress in the history of man's wars—the wars that rage both externally and internally: the wars of the flesh and the wars of the spirit. Again he presents the great circle journey in which man moves at once outward and inward, and finds that both directions are the same. In the figure of the Old English Widsith both directions are crystallized; for he is "the Far-traveller, the tale-bearer" (815)—both the soldier and the poet. Several years before he wrote *The Soldier*, Aiken described the traveller as the prototype of the poet: "Authors have always been wanderers, pursuers of nostalgias to strange places; if they are voyagers in the human soul, they are also crossers of seas and explorers of far countries."[1] Like the later "Kid," Widsith is a shape-shifter whom Aiken identifies "with the wind, and then with the principle itself of change and exchange, whether in trade, travel, migration, or even finally in war, which of course must be accepted in the history of man as a true culture-bearer" (878-79). Widsith is the bringer of new ideas; he evokes the spirit which in different guises and disguises transforms and creates culture:

> Widsith, the Far-traveller,
> descends from air with a headful of notions; Marco Polo
> ribboned from Cathay; and the travelling salesman
> home from Memphis with a new line of fancies. (820-21)

But if he represents change, in his alternate role as poet he also embodies "the spirit [that] admits no seasons" (817). Like that of the heroes of Aiken's Divine Pilgrim poems, Widsith's wandering symbolizes mankind's evolution toward self-knowledge—that superhuman consciousness which "changes its name: / yet, moving with the moving seasons, is always the same" (817).

Aiken begins by analyzing the external, cultural effect of warfare. The necessity of geographical migration, he says, leads to war and, consequently, to a mixture of races and their customs, whereby new, more advanced cultures come into being. In war he finds the origin of art and government. Man invented music "to sound the note and accent / which the brave man utters in the hour of danger" (819). And "Law sets the boundary of war, and war of law" (819). In his central dialogic section, "The Wars," Aiken selectively reconstructs the total history of mankind in terms of its successive heroic battles.

Not until the final section, "The Unknown Soldier," do the implications of the accompanying theme, man as a soldier of the spirit ("man the unconquerable: you yourself: man the soldier" [818, 840]) fully emerge. After mentioning the tombs dedicated to unknown soldiers in Washington, London, and Paris, Aiken asserts paradoxically that in the war of the spirit there is no unknown soldier:

> The soldier is crystal:
> crystal of man: clear heart, clear duty, clear purpose.
> No soldier can be unknown. Only he is unknown
> who is unknown to himself. (839)

In the inner struggle, consciousness and love provide the means by which the self may endure. Widsith therefore becomes Socrates and Keats, who in their heroic struggles represent together the inner and outer conflicts. For Socrates was a soldier:

> 'How strange, men of Athens,
> my conduct would be, if I, who obeyed the command
> at Delium and Potidea, and stood at my post
> no less than my fellows, if now, when I hear
> this summons, to search in myself and others for knowledge,
> I forsook my post, fearing death.' (841)

And Keats faced certain death with the remark that he felt like "a soldier / marching against a battery" (842). The two worlds, inner and outer, are intertwined; in both, Aiken works toward the goal which he postulated as early as "Changing Mind"— the evolution of man's consciousness, the intensification of his awareness of what it means to be a man:

In the last war of all
we conquer ourselves. Look home from the desert, soldier:
to the regenerate desert of the heart come home:
and know that this too needs heroes, and endurance, and
ardour. (843)

In its method—the interpretation of all culture in terms of a single image—but not in its substance, *The Soldier* prepared the way for *The Kid*. Aiken had outlined the substance which was to inform *The Kid* in the much earlier essay, "Literature in Massachusetts" (1937), and in one of the narrative themes of *A Heart for the Gods of Mexico*. The subject which he developed in these works needed only his discovery of the method of *whole meaning* in *The Soldier* to bring them forth in *The Kid*. His essay on Massachusetts literature was a brief attempt, for the WPA guidebook project, to find a single principle whereby New England's literature might be defined. His discovery in 1920 of William Blackstone in the *Memorial History of Boston* had earlier provided him with a figure whom he saw as prototypic of the later and greater figures of American literature. Aiken saw Blackstone as the "predecessor and anticipator of the half-wild individualism that was to be so characteristic . . . of all that was most integral in America" (Ush., 288). In moving from the site of Boston to Rhode Island when the Puritans arrived, Blackstone symbolized, for Aiken, the individualistic demand for freedom of self and conscience which came to characterize American literature: "One cannot think of his perpetual centrifugal retreat from civilization . . . without visualizing him as a symbol, or a charming figurehead, of the individualism which was to be so striking a characteristic of New England" (ABC, 83). Given this centripetal figure, Aiken traced his spirit

through American history, arguing for a continuity in its literature: "It might be fruitful to consider whether in point of fact
the New England individualist was not just our old friend the
Puritan writ large; and conversely, whether also the Puritan was
not a good deal of an individualist" (84). In the Puritan's
emphasis upon the sanctity of his own choice, Aiken argued,
American literature began. The Puritan became the Unitarian,
who in turn became the Transcendentalist. And finally, in the
last stage, the American writer denied all external authority in
asserting the complete autonomy of the individual soul. The
soul turned and looked steadily into itself, "where the individual,
like a diver, plunges into his own depths to sound them, and in
so doing believes himself effectually to have sounded the world"
(88). For all this, of course, Blackstone (who had also written,
perhaps, the first American book) was an effective symbol, and
as early as 1920 Aiken envisioned using him as "the spiritual key,
or center, of a book on American individualism." He thought of
this, until about 1929, as a critical study defining the American
character, its origin and continuity. By the thirties, however, the
vision seemed to be shaping itself into a poem, one which would
both define and celebrate American individualism. Such a book
would proceed inward and outward "to the variations on the
theme, the essays on his grandchildren and great-grandchildren"
(Ush., 290).

In 1941, for a brief moment, his vision seemed to coalesce
and he was able to set down what was to become the climactic
moment of the poem—Melville's confrontation of the "all-hat-
ing and all-loving, all creating and all destroying implacable
god" (ABC, 91). Apparently prompted by a revitalized sense of
the interconnectedness of the American experience, Aiken wrote
on the fly leaf of his copy of Stanley Vestal's biography, *Kit
Carson*:

> He changed his name: Ahab became:
> Ahab and Ishmael, but the Kid just the same:

His father's god in a fury forswore,
for a god more evil, but to worship more:
the god of hatred, of blind white evil,
god incarnate as a bland white devil:
the hurricane's power, of capricious rage,
to spare a   or a printed page
and then laugh   to lay waste an age.
From the west, returning, and the axe let be,
turned, returning, to his mother, the sea:
island, the foreshore, southwest in the Sound,
packets and whalers to the eastward bound:
Acushnet's tide, and the Twin isles blest
where Coffin and Daggett   rest:
the slate stones facing, like the willows, the west.

John & Lydia, that lovely pair,
a whale killed him, *her* body lies here![2]

Vestal wrote that "Kit Carson has become a symbol of the American frontier . . . and it is important that we understand and love the thing he represents, that Frontier which made these States a Nation."[3] In this same sense Carson would have importance for Aiken as one more manifestation of the Kid. In Vestal's book is inserted a scrap of paper upon which Aiken noted two books for further research—"Authentic Life of Billy the Kid by Garrett; edited by M. Fuller, N.Y. 1927" and "Johnny Appleseed—by J. L. Himrod. Chicago. 1926." Another early fragment was pencilled inside the cover of Constance Rourke's *American Humor*. Aiken was consciously trying to be true—factually as well as imaginatively—to his sense of the American past. But in 1941 he could write no more than these eighteen lines. And for various reasons—mainly, as I think, because he had not yet hit upon a form adequate to sustain this inward-outward movement—he delayed writing the poem.

In A *Heart for the Gods of Mexico*, however, Aiken did employ this theme in a general fashion, although he did not use the figure of Blackstone himself. The train ride from Boston across America in A *Heart for the Gods of Mexico* was meant to suggest the archetypal American journey west and south. It culminates first in the serene baptism by immersion in the waters of the Mississippi and, finally, in the savage baptism by blood in Mexico. As a counterpoint to the actual train-ride, therefore, Aiken reconstructs the stages of the American conquest of the West. As Blomberg's mind hovers between waking and sleeping, he perceives the symbolic significance of the journey. Speeding from Boston, he thinks: "the Berkshires might still be there, and the Puritans who had conquered the Indians, and the wilderness which had conquered the Puritans" (50). The journey of the three people parallels the westward progress of the American frontier. They renew it in themselves and make it an ever-present progress: the former geographical becomes their present spiritual movement. It is the movement from innocence to experience or consciousness, from the bud to the bloom—to use Aiken's pun—from Billy Budd to Blomberg. Passing beyond New England to the midwestern states, Blomberg suddenly thinks: "even now the pioneers were crossing these in their covered wagons, building their homesteads, their snake-fences against the snow, laying the broad-axe to the foot of the tree, felling the savage forests" (59). After dipping her hands into the Mississippi, Noni declares: " 'Now I'm baptized, Blom, in this continent. Now I've got Indian blood' " (89). When at last they arrive in Mexico, they complete not only Noni's great circle in her death, but also the great circle of the symbolic American journey in their discovery that the end is identical with the beginning—for "here, by the tracks, grew goldenrod, already in bloom, strayed all the way from New England" (127). To treat A *Heart for the Gods of Mexico* in this fashion is perhaps to distort its real emphasis upon the figure of Noni; yet the theme of the American progress is important to the novel, and was derived in a large part, one supposes, from Aiken's discovery of William Blackstone.

194

The Kid is the only one of his poems which Aiken discusses more than briefly in *Ushant*. In that book, D. has not yet composed, but is planning, a poem upon Blackstone's America. There he mentions the fact that he had talked to "Hambo" about the Blackstone theme and that "at once, and without so much as a by-your-leave, [Hambo had] taken over the Blackstone idea as his own" (294). "Hambo" can be easily identified as Malcolm Lowry, the author of *Under the Volcano*. He had studied with Aiken, and appears as a character in *A Heart for the Gods of Mexico*, where he is also called Hambo. In *Under the Volcano* Lowry uses the Blackstone theme in much the same general way as Aiken had in *A Heart for the Gods of Mexico*. But he centers his interest upon the figure of Blackstone himself, not the progress which he symbolizes. The protagonist of Lowry's book sees that Blackstone's life with the Indians of New England was the archetype for his own life among the Indians of Mexico. Accordingly, he identifies himself with the mythical figure, commenting, "personally, I'd like to be buried next to William Blackstone." The consul realizes too what Aiken had emphasized all along in his poems—the overriding importance of full and intense consciousness of self; and he makes it clear that in his outward search for seclusion Blackstone represents man's inner search for awareness. At the moment of his greatest self-awareness, the consul again recalls the Blackstone theme:

> "Anyway, one day [Blackstone] arrived in what is now, I believe—no matter—somewhere in Massachusetts. And lived there quietly among the Indians. After a while the Puritans settled on the other side of the river. They invited him over; they said it was healthier on that side, you see. Ah, these people, these fellows with ideas," he told the cat, "old William didn't like them—no he didn't—so he went back to live among the Indians, so he did. But the Puritans found him out. . . . Then he disappeared altogether—God knows where.

195

... *Now*, little cat," the Consul tapped his chest indicatively
... "the Indians are in here. . . . Not real Indians . . . but in
here." He tapped his chest again. "Yes, just the final frontier
of consciousness, that's all."[4]

Aiken's essay on "Literature in Massachusetts," in which he first
formulated the symbolic uses of Blackstone in defining the
American spirit, his *Heart for the Gods of Mexico*, and Lowry's
Under the Volcano—all these were earlier and lesser versions of
the vision which Aiken would crystallize as *The Kid*.

To these we might also add the lesson of John Gould Fletcher's *Breakers and Granite*, which included poems on America—
on Lincoln, the Mississippi, and the Mexican Quarter. Although
Aiken had criticized the way in which realists like Sandburg and
Masters portrayed the American scene, he realized early that
"Fletcher's attempt to summarize America, past and present
. . . lends a solidity and a fragmentary grandeur to this book
which one cannot find in his others" (ABC, 213). Both Crane's
Bridge, although Aiken considered this unsuccessful, and Williams' *In the American Grain* and *The Wanderer* might also
have exerted some influence upon Aiken. And, certainly, between
1941 and 1946 Aiken had thought deeply about the poem and
had consciously tried to formulate the appropriate scheme
whereby to trace out the history of Blackstone's spiritual descendants.

Finally, in Aiken's development, it was the experience which
he was able to make articulate in "Mayflower" (1945) which
allowed him to write *The Kid*. In the same way that *The Soldier* gave him a method, "Mayflower" embodies a primary,
deeply felt acceptance of America as a subject for his poetry.
As he had created a myth out of his English experience in *John
Deth*, so here he finds his myth in America's and his own history. In "Mayflower" Aiken deals with what was to become the
"Ariel's Island" theme of *Ushant*—the contrast between England and America. "Mayflower" constitutes a reconciliation of

his attachments to the two countries. Because of the resolution Aiken made in this poem, he would be able to see the one country in the other when he came to write *Ushant*. The method of the poem is a continuation and adaption of that of *The Soldier*. Aiken employs a central symbol—a "crystal"—through which he can consider the history of man as well as the history of his own ego. In *The Soldier* he had simply emphasized the importance of the past in creating the present. But in "Mayflower" the past is not merely contained in the present—the two are actually made co-extensive, equally present at each moment; reality becomes, therefore, not three-, but six-dimensional. This attitude and method has come to dominate Aiken's important poems since "Mayflower," as it is also, obviously, the method of *Ushant*, in which the present (the actual written novel) *is* the past.

As the focal symbol, the Mayflower suggests both the ship upon which the Pilgrims sailed to America and the flower "to which, he had always liked to believe, the Plymouth fathers had given its name" (Ush., 336). At the center of the poem, therefore, are the Pilgrims, who made New England out of England—the reconciliation which Aiken seeks in the poem. He evokes their presence and gives them reality by the simple device of quoting their words—drawn from *Mourt's Relation*, which he also used in *Conversation*—whenever he imagines them to be speaking; for instance:

> 'by break of day espied
> land, which we deemed to be Cape Cod.'
>
> .   .   .   .   .
>
> the pleasant bay, wooded on every side
> with 'oaks, pines, juniper, sassafras,' and
>   the wild fowl rising
> in clouds and numbers past surmising. (S.O., 5)

In this way we observe the Pilgrims creating the language—as they created the name for the mayflower—which the poet is

197

still using to talk about them, the language which they, in turn, brought to America as part of their heritage from the great Elizabethans, "Will and Ben." England and America, therefore, are reconciled by the language they share as well as by the migration of the Pilgrims from one country to the other. The common language provides the continuity between the Plymouth fathers and the poet, and thus the deeper continuity between the poet and Shakespeare or Jonson. As in *Ushant*, the protagonist is thereby revealed both as man and as writer. In his realization of physical and spiritual continuity, the past becomes the present. Rufus and Amanda Clark, the original owners of Aiken's "ancient farmhouse," on Cape Cod in Brewster, Massachusetts, "gaily now step down the road past Stony Brook, / call from the pasture as from the pages of a book" (7). Time becomes timelessness; three centuries are concentrated into a single co-extensive season. And, through the benediction of their language, Will and Ben become the poet's godfathers, for:

> we hear ourselves still saying
> the living words which they said then—
> words for haying, words for maying,
> love of earth, love of love, love of God. (9)

In its abrupt revelation on two levels of the continuity between England and America, past and present, the poem released Aiken for the work which was to come. It gave him "the freedom one discovers in the delighted acknowledgment of one's debts, one's ties, one's roots, one's belongingness" (Ush., 337). And, with this feeling of belonging to America, understanding its experience, its myth, he could make America belong to him in *The Kid*.

Certainly in his development Aiken progressed steadily toward such a poem as *The Kid*. He has moved from the purely lyrical creation of an ego in *Senlin*; to exploitation and definition of the individual ego in *Blue Voyage* and the Preludes; then to an outward-going concern with the reciprocal effect of the ego and other selves in *Conversation* and *And in the Human Heart*; and, finally, he attempted in *The Soldier* to understand a whole culture in terms of man's evolution toward *caritas* and full consciousness. In "Mayflower" he found the means of absorbing America into the experience which he could make available for his poetry. In this sense, *The Kid* represents the culmination of Aiken's development. The books that follow it, though often, perhaps, greater, are variations upon the progress which this poem completes.

Properly, then, in *The Kid* Aiken finally synthesized the lyrical and dramatic themes and methods whose separation characterized his early poetry. The theme of *The Kid* is that there are two realms, uninvestigated, as yet uncharted—the "virgin land" of America and the immense regions of the spirit —and that the American genius has explored both. The "Kid," of course, combines both, since he wanders in both. When Aiken returned to the poem in 1946, he set down a list of the heroes who might serve to embody these two aspects of the American genius:

Blaxton	
Boone	Melville
Appleseed	Jackson?
Crockett	Dickinson
Girard?	Hawthorne
Carson	Gibbs
Billy the Kid	Twain
Jumpers Casey Jones	Edison
Bunyan	Whitman

Custer-Cody-*surveyors*

He drew an arrow from Blaxton [Blackstone] to Johnny Appleseed, and wrote "apple trees" next to it, indicating a principle of continuity between them. He also considered using John Eliot and Roger Williams. And above the whole list, emphatically, he wrote: "to keep *continuity* as of one person—!!!"

Although Aiken was to omit some of these and add others as the heroes of his poem, its ultimate structure is clear in this first outline. The Kid has two aspects. The first of these is dramatic, the second introspective or lyric. Aiken parallels these two areas of experience by the way he manipulates the language and rhythms in the poem. Basically, three kinds of language appear in *The Kid*[5]—an adaptation of Puritan speech, "normal" English, and the language characteristic of American ballads. With each kind of language is associated a particular rhythm or music.

Aiken uses a modified imitation of seventeenth-century speech whenever he imagines himself listening to the thoughts of Blackstone:

> Morning and evening, Lord, I beseech Thee,
> suffer my cry from this woode to reach Thee,
> these are Thy presents, Thy heart I find
> in the dark forest in sleet and winde. (851)

Such language as this is used, in an altered form, but with the same music, in the speech of the descendants of the original Kid, when they speak toward the end of the poem. Whereas Blackstone uses language to meditate on the magnificence and goodness of the divinity, the later manifestations of the Kid culminate in Melville's meditation upon the "god of hatred, of bland white evil" (860), the "crystal" section of the poem which Aiken composed in 1941. While in Aiken's paraphrase of Ahab's last defiant speech, the tone changes from love to hate, the rhythms, the fundamental spiritual continuity, remain the same:

> *Morning and evening, Lord, I reject Thee.*
> *In fraud and fury, as in fire, I detect Thee.*
> *In lust and in death I take and forsake Thee.*
> *In breath and corruption I make Thee and break Thee.*
>
> (861)

This kind of language and rhythm is Aiken's principal means of expressing the lyric, introspective theme of the poem through the interior visions he gives to Melville, Willard Gibbs, Henry and Brooks Adams, Whitman, and Emily Dickinson—all New Englanders and so heirs of Blackstone's sensibility. Both the diction and the rhythm are easily modulated and often are moved into a form somewhere between this and a second kind of language, as for instance, "eyes to the self's black sea-heart turned, / the fouled line followed, the labyrinth learned" (861).

This second type of language in *The Kid* is the "normal" English which any poet, writing as Everyman, would use. As it must, this type provides the *cantus firmus* from which the other types can vary and embodies the main narrative movement of the poem. Aiken stresses, of course, the specifically American experience in this language. Especially in section 1, words like "pinto," "chickadee," "katydid," "sunup," "lariat," "'possum," "moosewood tree," "chinquapins," "longhorn," and so on, assume particular importance, and lead to the third type of distinctive language in *The Kid*. The first type of language is allied to the lyric theme; the third is associated with the narrative-dramatic. It is ballad-like and open, and appears whenever the poem deals with the pioneer as he moves west across the continent:

> *I'm away, I'm away, I'm away to the west,*
> *I'll stay no more on my mother's breast,*
>
> .   .   .   .   .
>
> *I come from heaven and to heaven I'll go,*
> *but what's in between I'm a-wantin' to know!* (847)

In the third and fourth sections, Blackstone and Anne Bradstreet ask the primary questions regarding the American quest: "Was freedom of the heart? or hand? / of secret soul? or the wide land?"; and again: "which wilderness were best, / that of the world, or of the breast?" (853). With the persecution and martyrdom of the Quaker Southwick family at the hands of the

Puritans (section v), the Kid begins his movement west in search of physical and spiritual freedom. As he moves west, he more and more becomes solely the pioneer conquering the physical wilderness; the spirit is handed on from Audubon to John Chapman to Kit Carson and Billy the Kid. Aiken modulates his three types of language in accordance with the movement of the poem, until the ballad language dominates in the middle of the sixth section. Then, man's physical conquest of America completed, the Kid once more returns to the east, to begin the journey into the "self's own mid-night, the seeking ghost" (859). And in that return, the ballad music reappears for the last time:

> Said Railway Willy, O carry me back
> on the golden engine and the silver track,
> carry back east in a tall caboose
> this broken-down body that's no more use. (859)

It melts into the "normal" narrative music—then, finally, into the readaption of the Blackstone language as the Kid begins once again the journey westward (as in *Landscape West of Eden*) to consciousness. The body has no more use, it has done its job; and the ego takes its place at the center of the American quest.

There is a constant shifting in the direction of the journey. The Kid travels west and east, inward and outward, and vice versa. So also the music of the poem is usually, except in its extremes, ambiguous, as the ballad and introspective materials merge and change one another when the themes which they represent meet. For instance, the last lines of the poem are:

> Free flew the ghost: from the blood, from the land!
> Hymned with the sea-voice on Paumanok sand!
> Broke like a billow, skimmed like a bird,
> a rainbow on Greylock, by Walden a word!
> And sleeps in the churchyard, unlaureled the stone,
> where lies the intrinsic, unknown, and alone. (862)

202

These lines—like much else in this poem—achieve their dignity through the combination of the lyric and dramatic music, as they represent a fusion of the two themes. More precisely, they result from Aiken's combination of the measured poetry of journey with the pure lyrical meditation of the spirit. This can be clearly demonstrated, for instance, in the last two lines; we can even identify the lyric which is their basis—Emily Dickinson's "Laurel," placed last by Aiken in the selection which he made from her poems in 1924:

> Lay this laurel on the one,
> Too intrinsic for renown.
> Laurel! veil your deathless tree—
> Him you chasten, that is he!

Blackmur wrote that in *The Kid* "there is a music to the drama giving the inward, meditative form."[6] We may put this in another way. In the combination of his two themes, Aiken widens a perceptibly lyric movement by fusing it with an outward, dramatic form. This results in what we might call a "double metre" which reflects Aiken's double theme. There is the one metre of the narrative line and the other of the lyric which is its basis. Aiken's ability to write at this level, "at a level that few of our poets have even dreamed of," justifies Dudley Fitts's praise of his skill: "He is one of the supreme technicians of modern English poetry. There are few writers, either in prose or in verse, who can challenge his mastery of language, who give us anything comparable to his assurance in controlling the most powerful and varied and nervous resources of expression. His writing has the inevitability of the highest art."[7]

· II ·

Aiken's development, as we can now see, has been governed by his continuing conception of his function as a poet. Basic to all his work is his insistence—in a critical essay of 1923— that "art exists primarily for the fulfillment of an important social function" (ABC, 67). By putting his increased awareness at the service of his society, the poet fulfills his obligation to man and to himself. In *Forslin*, he exhibits the ego confronting itself in various guises. In *The House of Dust* he considers the possibilities of investigating personal identity. After his experiment in fiction the emphasis in his poetry shifts from the demonstration of universal principles to, as Aiken wrote, self-definition: "consciously or unconsciously to give the lowdown on himself, and through himself on humanity" (Wake, 29). The object, in either case, is the same; he investigates himself so that he may know man; he widens and subtilizes his awareness so that he may deepen humanity's. For this reason, in Aiken's work "confession" is never present for its own sake—but is the material out of which he constructs the artifact which, he hopes, will benefit humanity. His poetry, and the experience which is its subject, is both personal and impersonal; it issues from an "intimate and instinctive and curiously (in a sense) impersonal voice, which speaks not so much out of one's specific heart as out of one's generic."[8] His effort in the Preludes to resolve and so remove the problems of communication was governed by his sense that in this age the poet can only increase awareness if he can make his audience understand him. In the novels and poems which followed the Preludes, Aiken came to realize even more clearly that he might most fruitfully aid man by revitalizing the modes of his experience which, because they are the most important to him, have become stereotyped. In his concept of *caritas* he discovered and showed at work the principle by which man may achieve dignity. Finally, in *The Soldier* and *The Kid* he defined and made real the beliefs which give meaning to a culture. Briefly, Aiken has moved from the ego to culture; from the individual talent to tradition. But "tradition" does not mean the same thing to Aiken as it does, for instance, to Eliot. Aiken values tradition not for the restrictions it imposes but for the freedom it offers. Only when the artist understands the continuity of a culture can he take

the next forceful step into the future. Again, Aiken emphasizes the evolution of man's self- and social-consciousness. He
accused Eliot, therefore, of seeking an escape from the "psychological chaos of the 'I' and the 'now,'" in "a world of canons, forms, and rituals"; and added, in the most caustic comment he has made on what he takes to be Eliot's failure: "It
is a world to be explored, and there are still intrepid explorers.
Mr. Eliot might have been one of these—as indeed in his verse
at times he *has* been—and, but for the Grace of God, he might
be yet" (ABC, 185, 186).

Aiken explores the world of the "I" and the "now." Beyond
this he knows nothing, and has nothing to say. Yet, in the instant of awareness he seeks always to imply the universal; infinity is the moment magnified; humanity is the mirror of each
individual. The poet, the *primum mobile* of civilization, does
not generalize, but simplifies himself, therefore, in order to
become all men: the poet is essential man:

> Was this the poet? It is man.
> The poet is but man made plain,
> A glass-cased watch through which you scan
> The multitudinous beat-and-pain,
> The feverish fine small mechanism,
> And hear it ticking while it sings.[9]

During his early work in autobiographical fiction, he declared
that no work of art can be anything but the artist's self-portrait.
But even here he insists upon distinguishing the "objective"
from the "subjective" artist. The "objective" artist, he argues,
is one who, because he understands the needs of mankind, "employs affective terms—symbolisms of theme and form—which
are universally significant and intelligible," or which he can
make intelligible. The "subjective" artist, to the contrary, uses
art to assuage his own particular psychosis, and so "disregards
and scorns his audience, and considers himself a god, the only
true source of wisdom, the only true center of awareness" (ABC,

258). Aiken, of course, has attempted to be (in his sense) the "objective" kind of poet. Thirty years after he wrote this essay on "Disintegration in Modern Poetry" he still contended that literature should benefit society, not the individual (or not only the individual) who writes it. He defined poetry as "a portrait of *homo incipiens*: man, with the sweat on his brow, the blood on his hands, the agony in his heart: with his gayeties, his obscenities, his absurdities: his beliefs, and, perhaps, his doubts."[10] In short, although the artist investigates his own ego, his purpose must be more than egocentric. He must transcend the ego and transform his confession into an "artifact" which does not depend for its interest upon self-revelation but is universally affective and intelligible. In *Ushant*, which I shall consider shortly, Aiken illustrates precisely how the artist accomplishes this—for in *Ushant* he makes an artifact of his life.

Aiken has not, of course, always been completely successful in this transformation of the singular to the universal. He himself wrote of his poem "Mayflower" that "the predicament out of which the poem arose was perhaps too personal, too close, to become the basis for a construct of anything even remotely resembling universals, involving, as it did, that extraordinary childhood fixation on Ariel's Island, and the poet of White Horse Vale" (Ush., 336). One suspects that Aiken's intention here is not as derogatory as it seems; and certainly, this is less true of "Mayflower" than of other poems. Both *The Charnel Rose* and the poems in *Nocturne of Remembered Spring* rely upon personal associations. "Changing Mind" is so personal that it is painful to read the poem; it is perhaps the one poem, however, in which Aiken deliberately set out to explore and define *only* his own ego. *Osiris Jones* is not free from fault in this regard; only Aiken's own personality often holds the otherwise unrelated details together. Many of his short-stories—but not his novels—are inconclusive because his characters cannot relate their personal experience to the daily life of man.

This is not to imply that these works fail aesthetically—they are often admirable in form, striking in image, and emotionally intense—but only that they remain imbedded in the personal situation out of which they arise. On the other hand, Aiken has also erred, I would say more seriously, in attempting to write "public" poems when his own experience and emotional responses have not been fully formed. This is true, for instance, of "Everlasting." In dealing with the atomic bomb tests at Bikini, Aiken uses "Kilroy" in the same way he had used the figure of the Kid—as the eternal spirit of "the regicide, the Kilroy, always there: / ourselves—we know!—the god-destroyers and god-makers" (S.O., 45). But Kilroy did not have the same emotive significance for Aiken as Blackstone had. For once in his career, Aiken seems to have based his poem upon facts without strongly responding to them. The poem is based on Dr. Richard Sterba's discussion of collective myth, "Kilroy Was Here,"[11] but does not sufficiently dramatize the myth which Sterba explains. Thus the poem dwindles down to verbal proliferation:

> Sadeyes under Skylight One, waiting
> indifferent, unloving, and unhating,
> for the always unknown, always new,
> or partly known and partly new
>
> .   .   .   .   .
>
> towards the true or partly true,
> pacific or unpacific,
> specific or unspecific. (43)

But after Aiken's partial failures have been pointed out and granted, there remains an abundant body of work in which he has actually compounded the ego with the world. He has been pre-eminently successful in his most recent poems—in "A Letter from Li Po" and "The Crystal." In these and other recent poems, Aiken seeks his place in the history of consciousness and out of this history records the minds of all men:

207

Did you love? did you hate?
did you murder, or refrain from murder, on an afternoon
of innocent cirrus in April? It is all recorded
(and with it man's history also)
in the garden syllables of dust and dew.
                              ("A Walk in the Garden," L.P., 65)

Asking himself these questions, he hears the answers of the world. At its best, Aiken's poetry exfoliates in this fashion. It most succeeds when he does not write about what he has done in history, but about what history has done in him. As Emerson observed of Goethe's autobiography, it "is the expression of the idea . . . that a man exists for culture; not for what he can accomplish, but for what can be accomplished in him."[12] This is equally as true of *Ushant* as of *Dichtung und Wahrheit*; the movement in Aiken's work is ever from the ego outward, to man or culture—and finally, to man in culture.

A comparison of Aiken to Emerson's description of Goethe is apt; for it seems to me that Aiken has consistently developed toward the image of the Poet and the Writer as Emerson characterized them in *Representative Men*. And he has attempted to fuse both roles in his own career. I do not mean to imply that Aiken has deliberately or consciously imitated Emerson's sense of Goethe and Shakespeare, but by temperament and education he naturally followed in the tradition of the nineteenth-century sage, epitomized in Emerson's book, and recently discussed in John Holloway's *The Victorian Sage*. Sometimes Aiken's work so closely parallels Emerson's descriptions that his poetic activity seems almost to be a comment on them. Emerson wrote, for instance: "The Greeks said that Alexander went as far as Chaos; Goethe went, only the other day, as far; and one step farther he hazarded, and brought himself safe back" (273). *Preludes for Memnon*, xiv, begins: "You went to the verge, you say, and came back safely?" and ends with the lesson of Chaos, the "answer that no question asked"—beyond Chaos:

208

—And this alone awaits you, when you dare
To that sheer verge where horror hangs . . . .

.   .   .   .   .

It is to self you come,—
And that is God. It is the seed of seeds. (514-15)

Emerson said of the writer that "by acting rashly, he buys the power of talking wisely," for, "his failures are the preparation of his victories" (263). Such a philosophy as this is at the basis of the Preludes and *Osiris Jones*: "I was a rash man in my time" (P.M., LXII, 572), is the burden of both. By realizing their rashness and its consequent failures, the protagonists of Aiken's poems achieve their success. Moreover, Emerson's theory of the rotation of nature in the production of great men is implicit in some of Aiken's poems. Emerson observed that "When nature removes a great man, people explore the horizon for a successor; but none comes, and none will. His class is extinguished with him. In some other and quite different field the next man will appear; not Jefferson, not Franklin, but now a great salesman, then a road-contractor, then a student of fishes, then a buffalo-hunting explorer, or a semi-savage Western general."[13] Such a theory is clearly at the basis of Aiken's characterization of a culture in terms of its great men in both *The Soldier* and *The Kid*. In *The Soldier*, for instance, there is the progression from Widsith to Marco Polo to "the travelling salesman / home from Memphis" (821). Even more emphatically, in *The Kid* he traces the American progress through such figures as the Southwick family, Paul Revere, Audubon, John Chapman, Kit Carson, and Billy the Kid, as well as those who are more strictly literary descendants of Blackstone.

Far from suggesting that Aiken consciously commented on these passages in Emerson—which would be rather unlikely—such resemblances serve to illustrate further his close relation to Emersonian transcendentalism. Aiken inherited this philosophy more directly than almost any other modern poet. His grandfather, William James Potter, was minister of the First Congregational Society in New Bedford. He was the leading force of the Free Religion Association and a friend of Emerson. As did Emerson, Potter rebelled against what he considered Unitarian narrowness and separated himself from the parent body; unlike Emerson, he could take his New Bedford parish with him. Having resolved, as he wrote in his journal, "to submit everything of a religious nature, or otherwise, to the test of reason, being satisfied that Christianity is a rational religion, and capable of withstanding the search and the criticism of the keenest intellect," he studied in Berlin, Tübingen, and Heidelberg. Potter's liberalism easily accommodated Darwin's theories—he had also gone to visit Baron Alexander von Humboldt, just then completing his *Cosmos*—which, in his time, were emptying the churches and filling the lecture halls. In a sermon confronting Darwinism, Potter informed his congregation that he "was not long in reaching a new position, nor was there any serious conflict in my mind between the old and the new. Rather . . . there was opened to me a new earth and a new heaven, and planted in my thoughts the seeds of a grander and more fruitful conception of Deity than of any which I had found in the old theologies." Aiken would not have heard this sermon; his grandfather died in 1893. But in *Ushant* Aiken considers his own quest to increase consciousness as the fulfillment of his grandfather's religious liberalism. Although it is incalculable, of course, his grandfather's influence, and through him, the influence of transcendental theology, upon Aiken's thought was apparently profound.

Aiken himself has perhaps become aware of his place in the tradition of the sage. He seemed deliberately to claim this role for himself in an essay written in 1942: "Heir to all that is best in the history of mankind, let us hope that we can use our inheritance wisely, and that it can be said of us, as Sainte-Beuve said of Goethe, that he 'assimilated not merely tradition, but all traditions, and that without ceasing to be a modern of moderns; he keeps watch for every new sail on the horizon, but from the height of a Sunium. He would use the larger background and perspective to round out and support his individual insight, and so make of the present what it should be—not a servile imitation, nor yet a blank denial, of the past, but its creative continuation. To the errors and aberrations of the hour . . . we must oppose the masses of universal history' " (ABC, 111). Perhaps at first unconsciously, then, at last, with full responsibility, Aiken has chosen to play such a role.

The first and perhaps, in our time, the most serious problem which the activity of the sage raises is that of originality. I have already shown at length that in his language Aiken usually (though not always) works with the cumulus of cliché, our daily speech, rather than with the linguistic shock of new idioms. He makes our familiar world new by perceiving it in original ways. The ability to reinvigorate speech may indeed require the deepest kind of wisdom and verbal brilliance. But the strikingly idiosyncratic voices of Eliot ("short square fingers stuffing pipes"); Pound ("m Episcopus, waving a condum full of black-beetles"); or Cummings ("as freedom is a breakfastfood")—these have tended to obscure, by confusing idiosyncrasy with originality, the individuality of Aiken's work. The sage is not chiefly interested in striking originality of expression. He sees the culmination of culture in himself, and so takes what is most useful and best from that culture. He knows that "We were born / With words, but they were not our words, but others' " (P.M., xxxvii, 541). What words—and even what phrases and sentences—the sage finds useful he will appropriate in order to communicate his particular message. Aiken has even been willing at times to argue that "a poet [may] be great even if there be nothing remarkably original or bizarre about his work with respect to language or style—great by reason of the poetic content or thought, rather than for verbal or prosodic brilliance" (ABC, 40). Yet, Aiken has often been praised—deservedly so—for his prosodic brilliance, and criticized for a deficiency in ideas; for he has not endeavored to develop a philosophy beyond his interest in extending and ac-

211

celerating man's awareness. He has been content to redefine and so renew man's feelings toward the areas of experience most important to him. In one of his recent poems Aiken insists upon the necessity of such continuous wonderment in the familiar. He begins:

> when you are no longer surprised
> by the quiet or fury of daybreak
> the stormy uprush of the sun's rage
> over the edges of torn trees
> torrents of living and dying flung
> upward and outward inward and downward to space

and ends:

> then welcome death
> and be by death benignly welcomed
> and join again in the ceaseless know-nothing
> from which you awoke to the first surprise. (S.H., 48-49)

John Holloway has written that the chief characteristic of the sage is precisely this emphasis upon perpetual re-examination of common experience. He writes that "all of these authors insist on how acquiring wisdom is somehow an opening of the eyes, making us see in our experience what we failed to see before. . . . It is not of some quite new reality; it is seeing old things in a new way." Elsewhere, Holloway again insists that the sage's "aim is to make his readers see life and the world over again, see it with a more searching, or perhaps a more subtle and sensitive gaze." For the nineteenth-century sage, as for Aiken, only the renewal of awareness is important, not the arrival at wholly new knowledge: it is "a task often of awakening or reawakening something, not of transmitting information."[14] It is understandable that the sage's "message" should be regarded as commonplace a century later, for he provides his race with the means of transcending his own works. This is what makes him valuable, even indispensable, to us.

But the more serious charge of a deficiency in poetic originality has been directed against Aiken. He has been accused of
imitating (at a conservative estimate) several dozen other writers. In a satirical dream-dialogue which he wrote in 1918, Aiken
expressed his reaction to this criticism:

BODENHEIM: . . . Has Aiken any individuality? Does he
exist?

MISS MONROE: He is an echo of Masefield and of Gibson.
The *Jig of Forslin* is like Owen Meredith's *Lucile. Turns and
Movies* is like *Hiawatha. The Charnel Rose* is like *The Old
Oaken Bucket.*

POUND (*wearily*): Swinburne plus Fletcher minus Aiken
equals Aiken.

UNTERMEYER: Eliot plus Masters minus Aiken equals Aiken.

HERVEY: Baudelaire plus Evans plus De Nerval plus Verlaine plus Mallarmé plus Rimbaud minus Aiken equals Aiken.

KREYMBORG: Didn't you leave out somebody?

As might be obvious, the "personages of my dream were in many
cases making remarks which I know them actually to have made
in real life." Since Aiken had been accused so frequently of
chameleonism by 1918, it is not surprising that his successive
volumes have been criticized on these grounds. Aiken himself
appears in his dream, and replies to his critics:

AIKEN: . . . I will tell you my secret.

ALL: A secret!

AIKEN: Yes—you have been wiser than you knew. For I am
not really a poet at all. I am a mathematician. I have discovered that poetry can be written by calculus—

ALL: (*delighted*): Ah, that explains it!

AIKEN: And I have found a little machine which, if fed
words from a dictionary at one end, turns out the finest metrical verse at the other, quite indistinguishable from the genuine article. Now, in *The Charnel Rose*—

ALL: Yes?

213

AIKEN: It simply happened by mistake this little engine was fed a volume of Havelock Ellis—

BODENHEIM: Or Freud!

AIKEN: And in *Senlin*—

ALL: Yes! Yes!

AIKEN: (*bursting into tears*): I am ashamed to admit it—it was *Alice in Wonderland*. (ABC, 122-26)

Throughout Aiken's career, critics have felt that they must find an influence upon each of his volumes—and have proceeded to do so. His novels have been accused of indebtedness especially to Huxley, James, and Joyce.[15]

Despite Yvor Winters' warning that "Mr. Aiken's debt to Mr. Eliot has been over-estimated; it really amounts to little or nothing,"[16] Aiken has been most frequently accused of imitating Eliot.[17] Pound, Fletcher, Williams, Stevens—all have, at various times, been detected in Aiken's work. Because Aiken has become known as an imitative poet, critics have sometimes discovered "influences" where none have existed. Aiken has even been accused of imitating poets whom he was himself influencing. Surveying recent poetry, Hayden Carruth has written that Aiken's "influence—less than Eliot's in matters of taste, less than Pound's in matters of conscience, probably less than Wallace Stevens's or Marianne Moore's in matters of the procedural imagination—has nevertheless exceeded all of these in determining, almost while no one was aware of it, the look and sound of the poetry written in our age."[18] Could we now untangle the subtle network of influence—in tone or image, in irony or music—during the last four decades, we might well find Conrad Aiken at the center of the poetry of his age. In his honesty as a critic, his precision as a writer of fiction, and by the sheer talent of his poetry, he has helped to shape, even to make, the attitudes and timbre of his era. Other poets, achieving critical recognition sooner, have overshadowed the originality of his work. This is partly true concerning his supposed indebtedness to Eliot.

As Allen Tate said in citing Aiken for the Gold Medal of the National Institute of Arts and Letters: "[His] has been an influence so pervasive that we have not been entirely conscious of it." The problem of influence, of course, is a complicated one. While *Forslin* seems to borrow nuances from "Prufrock," *The Waste Land* seems to have close affiliations with Aiken's earlier symphonies. Eliot's "Gerontion" and Aiken's "Tetélestai," in which the critic might detect "influence" one way or another, were written at almost the same time; neither poet saw the other's poem. Moreover, some of the "influences" are in reality due to the fact that both Aiken and Eliot were influenced by similar interests in Elizabethan and Jacobean drama, in metaphysical poetry, and in some contemporary poets, like Jean de Bosschère, whom Eliot reviewed in the *Egoist* and whom both poets knew in England.

In short, Aiken was probably influenced most by the very poets whom he was himself influencing. The development of any great poet is an aspect of the development of poetry in his time. It is important to understand, however, that this is of little importance in the activity of the sage; that, for him, exotic originality matters less than the achievement of the poem. Toward his goal of answering ultimate questions, the sage seeks the best available means of communication; if he borrows his language from others, it is with a true gusto, not for Making It New, but for Making It His. And this transformation will constitute his true individuality.

Such is, we will recall, precisely the argument that Emerson used with regard to Shakespeare, the Poet of his *Representative Men*. He insists several times that "Great men are more distinguished by range and extent than by originality. If we require the originality which consists in weaving, like a spider, their web from their own bowels . . . no great men are original. . . . The greatest genius is the most indebted man." He could even go farther and entirely reverse the usual romantic emphasis on

215

originality: "Great genial power . . . consists in not being original at all; [but] in being altogether receptive." With these comments Aiken would be in almost entire agreement. Again, I should make it clear that neither Emerson's nor Aiken's emphasis upon receptivity implies an argument for the classical doctrine of imitation, which restricts the writer by imposing ancient models upon him. Rather, as Emerson maintains, while the great genius seems to be an original force, he cannot help man. Only when we perceive that he is an effect, not a cause, can we see him as the "exponent of a vaster mind and will"[19] in which we participate; only then can he lead us back to ourselves. Originality blinds us, receptivity liberates us. By its lack of originality true genius defends us from itself.

Aiken has spoken in much the same way of the relation between receptivity and originality in the activity of the poet. Whenever he has written on this matter, he has paralleled our own to the Elizabethan age, proposing that "in contemporary American poetry the Elizabethan vigor is being born again. . . . [It] is willing to take, no matter from what source, what is good."[20] As early as 1915 he firmly expressed his belief in the cyclical evolution of the arts, that "innovators in the arts are seldom successful, save for the moment: it is their successors who get the fruits." The job of the successors is selection rather than innovation—"discarding the ephemeral and valueless, singling out the enduring."[21] He has written, with some pride, that his own play, *Mr. Arcularis*, "is Elizabethan: it is a composite, a group collaboration, in which several hands beside my own are discernible" (A., ix). In his essays for *Poetry Journal*, he was allowed to comment editorially and was less limited than elsewhere by the need to review particular books. I would like to quote at length from one editorial in which he was wholly concerned with this subject of originality. The essay is not easily available, having been included in neither *Scepticisms* nor Aiken's recent volume of collected criticism. Its title is "The Impersonal Poet":

216

If we regard poetry as an instrument by which man seeks self-expression, an instrument which generation after generation of poets has perfected, each adding something,—some a new modulation, some a new harmony, some a new tone,—it appears only natural that any one poet should derive the fruits of the labor of those who preceded him. As a matter of fact, all poets have done this,—some more, some less. Roughly speaking we can divide them into two classes: those who contribute a definitely new note to the world's poetry (such as Marlowe, Villon, Ford, Heine, Verlaine, Poe, Byron), and those who are eclectic, who recombine and refine the known moods of poetry (such as Virgil, Dante, Shakespeare, Keats, Hugo, Goethe). Which class makes the more valuable contribution, it is impossible to say. We can only say that the two contributions, both necessary, are essentially different: that the contribution of what we might call the originative type of poet is chiefly a contribution of mood or attitude,— something unconscious, like the timbre of a voice, the expression of a face; whereas the contribution of the eclectic poet is chiefly an intellectual one—something conscious and schematic. The former is usually more subjective, more lyric,— the latter more objective, more analytic. For the purpose of explanation the cleavage has of course been made sharper than it really is. Every successful poet is both originative and eclectic.

In America to-day, as is perhaps natural, the emphasis is laid almost entirely on the originative type of work. The cry is for individualism at all costs. This has resulted in strainings after novelty, and in a too hasty condemnation of work which at first reading does not appear acidly original. A poet's voice has come to be considered more important than what he has to say: the interpretive, philosophic type of poet, who is preoccupied first of all with understanding and reinterpreting the phenomena of human experience, and only secondarily with questions of form and style, and who is therefore content to

217

accept hints of guidance in such matters from those who make a specialty of them, is found wanting, simply because his purpose, so different from that of most of his contemporaries, is not understood. We have become so accustomed to admiring poetry for one definite and perhaps idiosyncratic personality which shines through it, that an objective and impersonal poet, who endeavors to keep personality in the background, or to break up personality, for purposes of analysis, is often thought unoriginal. I believe that attitude is mistaken. I believe that just as art is becoming more and more international, or unnational, so, on another plane the poet may become less idiosyncratic, more impersonal. He will understand himself, discount himself: surround himself. If on one occasion he yields to the pleasure of creating pure illusion (a lyric type of work) he will on another occasion prove himself capable of riddling that illusion. If he indulges sometimes in experience for its own sake, he will also sometimes indulge in analysis of that experience. His point of view will not be single, or at rest, but multiple, and forever in motion. He will interpret things not merely as seen from one personal angle, but as seen, impersonally, in relation.

His method will be primarily eclectic: regarding the art of poetry as an instrument, each mood of which has been perfected by some poet, he will not be afraid to exhaust all its resources. What Shakespeare teaches him he will use, what Blake and Meredith teach him he will use, and if his contemporaries offer new emotional colors which seem to him of value, he will appropriate them as his own, add them to his gamut. This does not mean that he will be lacking in essential character. His originality will consist in his mental outlook, rather than in his speech: and in artistic virtuosity. Although he may invent no sharply new moods of his own, he must perfect the moods of others beyond the powers of those who themselves invented them. He must use them as parts of a larger scheme, he must not so entirely surrender to them, he must be capable of laughing at them. More than to most, values must appear relative to him.

All this may seem a trifle fantastic—it prefigures a type of work very different from that most generally admired to-day.[22]

Here, at the beginning of his career, Aiken outlined for himself and his public the beliefs that were to characterize and control his development during the next fifty years. As he developed, Aiken modified and complemented his notion of the poet's role, but the ideas he set forth in "The Impersonal Poet" remained the core of his philosophy.

While the poet whom he has always praised most highly is Shakespeare, Aiken shows in *Ushant* that he is most indebted to the nineteenth-century English poets. He writes here that he was at first influenced by Keats, Shelley, Coleridge, De Quincey, and Burns. The more lasting influence, however, came from Hawthorne, Browning, Whitman, Thompson (*Anthem of Earth*), Emerson, Hardy, and Arnold. In 1954 Aiken made up a "Personal Anthology" broadcast for the British Broadcasting Corporation. Interestingly, he chose only poets from the nineteenth century in an attempt to trace "some sort of emerging outline . . . of the note of modernity which was to become characteristic of the poetry of today." As his first poem he chose Coleridge's "Self-Knowledge," "for it is in this increasing tendency to self-examination, the fierce psychological probing which began with Shakespeare and Webster and Donne, that we will begin to see, I think, that emerging outline of the modern which we are looking for." To characterize and trace out the emerging modern, Aiken selects poems from Arnold, Browning, Meredith, Hardy, and Francis Thompson. Not in the *texture* of their poetry, but in their courageous self-examination in service of their culture, he sees these poets as his spiritual ancestors, and his own task as a culmination of theirs. Indeed, in his earliest poems, written for the Harvard *Advocate*, he had consciously modelled his own verse after nineteenth-century poets. In poems like "Francois Villon" (1908), "The Potter" (1908), "Polyphe-mus" (1910), and "To a Head in Marble" (1911), he recalls, respectively, Browning, Arnold, Tennyson, and Keats. From these writers Aiken unconsciously absorbed the distinctive atti-tudes of the tradition of the sage. With them, he was con-vinced that true originality consists in what Emerson called "the originality of all." He would also have found in Kostyleff's chap-ter on "Recherches Sur Le Méchanisme D'un Génie Poétique" an exhaustive survey of the ways in which such a poet as Hugo documented himself for literary creation. As Kostyleff shows, the poet's unique sensibility will keep his chains of verbal as-sociations personal as they proceed out of his indebtednesses. Again, he would have seen in the situation of contemporary psychoanalysis how one scientist might borrow fruitfully from another in pursuit of truth.

Since, for Aiken, then, originality results from the poet's ideas, experience, or sensibility, he has not felt it contradictory to criticize several contemporary poets for their lack of original-ity. He has written, for instance, that MacLeish's poetry is "a kind of ventriloquism; . . . he speaks now with one voice, now with another. . . . His voice is sometimes that of the Eliot of *Gerontion*—more often that of the Pound of the *Cantos* or of *Cathay*: a solution or dilution of these" (ABC, 284). He also criticized Pound for trying to make poetry an amalgam of the styles and attitudes of others, and giving nothing of himself. As a result, Aiken argues, Pound's work is "without a center. Who and what and where . . . is Mr. Pound? What is his identity? What is his own peculiar attitude towards this terrifying world? He seems, indeed, to have none; and one cannot help feeling that the lack is very serious" (ABC, 323). Aiken's objection to this kind of *cento* poetry is, in brief, that the poets color their experience in accordance with the speech they adopt instead of adopting speech in accordance with their experience. Their poems consist merely of an imitation of the language of other poets. Since they contribute no individual experience, they project no means to create their language anew. Aiken crudely expressed this attitude as early as 1914 in "Parasitics: To Certain Poets": "Know you these things? . . . Ah, you have read / In many a well-bound book instead" (E.T., 214). And, as I have shown, he turned to fiction in the twenties in order to discover and certify the primacy of his own experience. For, as he emphasizes in his criticism, it is in his individual life, his personal attitudes, and his answers to ultimate questions that the sage discovers the principle of his receptivity. He is not receptive to all, but only to that which he can make his own: "literature should be drawn from life, not from literature. . . . Experience first (and whole-heartedly . . .) and write afterward" (Sc., 183).

It is typical of the sage to emphasize the originality of the man behind the work, rather than the sheer creative force of the work itself. In effect, he thereby guarantees his personal integrity and consistency to his public. As Emerson wrote: "Talent alone can not make a writer. There must be a man behind the book; a personality which by birth and quality is pledged to the doctrines there set forth, and which exists to see and state things so, and not otherwise." His must be a constant devotion to a certain set of truths, which, as a sage, it is his duty to propound; for, as Emerson asks, how can he be honored if "he loses himself in a crowd; when he is no longer the lawgiver, but the sycophant, ducking to the giddy opinion of a reckless public; when he must sustain with shameless advocacy some bad government, or must bark all the year round in opposition."[23] On several occasions Aiken has likewise sought to warn the poet not to give up, in the interests of class or fashion, his personal identity and integrity. In an extended "Plea for Anonymity" he cautioned: "The good artist must now as always turn his back on any attempt to hoodwink him into being merely a tool for party or sect."[24] Elsewhere he attacked nearly all the modern poets who, following Eliot, delineated their society rather than the self, and thus surrendered "that passionate sense of identity which has always been the most preciously guarded possession of the poet. . . . For these poets no longer, alas, seem to have an 'I.' . . . It is no longer 'I, the person, did this, saw this, felt this, knew this'; it is now 'we the people'" (ABC, 98). This definition of the person wholly by his social identity is what Henry Adams called the "degradation of the democratic dogma." In his role as a sage, Aiken argued, the poet must stand clear of attempts to subsume his identity and integrity under a banner; he must go beyond the momentary aspects of movements and coteries to their deeper universals in order to be of value to his audience. Alone among modern poets Aiken has steadfastly held to the profession of writer; he has not taught, joined organizations, lectured or in any way attempted to further his reputation through group alliances. For him, the key is neither "I, the person" nor "we, the people"; but, in the articulation of his own private consciousness for the benefit of man, it is "I, the people."

Such a formula makes it clear, I think, that for Aiken the "sacred" personal identity of the poet is fundamental to his role as a sage. No matter how indebted he may be to others, no matter how much he seeks to move outward to aid and comfort man, he can only attain universal meaning by being wholly himself. He must lead, not follow, mankind. The poet is, after all, man "made plain," stripped to essentials. And mankind must follow him as its only means of evolving in awareness. Convinced of the social importance of art, however, Aiken early seemed to follow the "common denominator" notion of literature, best crystallized in extremis in Tolstoy's What Is Art? but also later given strong support by the various nationalistic literary movements—in, for instance, the prefaces and essays of Yeats and Synge. Because of Tolstoy's strong sense of the importance of a moral effect upon the audience, he sought to efface the individual artist for the sake of the "brotherly union of man," and, therefore, to derive the proper universal from the art which any peasant could grasp. Aiken made the same mistake early in his career in contending that the tastes of the

222

vulgar "give us, in clearest view, the common denominator of art" (ABC, 64). Since writing *Blue Voyage*, however, he has come to insist that the articulation of the sage's personal awareness is of primary importance. The public, even eventually the peasant, follows his example; he does not follow theirs. "Thus [as Aiken concluded] man gets his 'universal' in art . . . from the top, invariably, never from the bottom. . . . This vital competitive hierarchy in levels of consciousness is indispensable to the continuation of a healthy and normal renewal and growth in man's awareness" (ABC, 109). And it is the sage whose duty it is to provoke this renewal and growth. In being the master, he is the servant of culture. In this sense, Aiken's description of Chekhov may be the best definition we can give of the sage: "His sympathy, his pity, his tenderness, were inexhaustible. He lived, and thus permitted us to live, everywhere" (ABC, 153).

Associated with the sage's need to remain free of party faction is his insistence that his doctrine is not dogmatic or rational, but somehow beyond these. He emphasizes, Holloway says, "that his answers offer themselves to imagination rather than logic; that they are not recondite, for everyone can read them in his own heart."[25] His essential equipment is insight and imaginative penetration rather than a logical system. Now, Aiken has been frequently accused of adhering to, and offering wholly, the Freudian system. And it is certainly true that in his early poetry and much of his criticism he seems to consider Freud's hypotheses almost as *de rigueur* solutions for all of the problems which art raises. But after *Blue Voyage* his steadily increasing freedom in these matters is apparent. By 1928, Aiken had given up his efforts toward a "scientific" criticism built on a Freudian foundation. For the first time in his criticism, he was reticent about defining poetry. Other critics, he says, have seen the essence of poetry in "the unconscious," "the race," "god," "the over-soul," and so on. But, he adds, "whatever we call it, we know it when we hear it, and we insist that the finest poetry must have it. . . . [Even] its simplest statements and feelings should have the golden immediacy of word and rhythm which we can only satisfactorily compare with the golden immediacy of the yellow to the crocus. . . . And that is all we know."[26] And even before *Blue Voyage*, say as early as 1920, he could turn back upon his own Freudian arguments only to shatter them: "We do not pretend, as some seem to think we do, to have solved, with this simple hypothesis [of "sensibility"] —or even, for that matter, with the more fundamental Freudian hypothesis of which it is a corollary—the nature or limits of poetry. We make only a beginning: and one which shows in some regards singularly little advance from the Aristotelian doctrine of catharsis."[27] From the perspective of forty years, we can now even see, as Irving Howe has recently said, that from his earliest criticism Aiken "was not nearly so tempted by the coils of theory. . . . The relativism and skepticism which he everywhere detected were also present, often fruitfully, in his own reviewing."[28]

Surely since the thirties Aiken has constantly insisted upon the inadequacy of purely logical systems to answer human problems. He criticized Eliot, for instance, for resorting to established forms and rituals. In contrast to Eliot's practice, Aiken has asserted the necessity of an open-ended Emersonian individualism, and insisted that the great poet is one "whose range of reference is wider than any orthodoxy could endow, freer than it would permit: intellectual limitations . . . are crippling" (ABC, 363). Aiken has seen that the difficulty of the sage's role is multiplied by the self-imposed condition that he must never seek comfort in the security of forms from the ambiguity immanent in the grandeur of his message. In *Ushant* he urged that "the thing, of course, was not to retreat, never to retreat; never to avoid the full weight of awareness, and all that it brought, and above all never . . . to seek refuge from it in the comforting placebos of religious or mystical myth or dogma" (168). Unlike most modern poets, Aiken had no family tradition of orthodox

224

religious doctrine to which he was emotionally tied. Consequently, he was free to make the end of poetry—the acceleration of awareness—his only religion: to be "religious, without religion; skeptic, without dogma" (ABC, 82).

As Holloway has pointed out, in his *Grammar of Assent* Newman discussed and identified the basic kind of statement with which the sage works. Newman contrasted the assent given to the propositions of logic, science, or mathematics with the belief given to propositions concerning the nature of human life. In the former case, he said, assent is incomplete since the knowledge given is deliberately too restricted; assent to the second kind of proposition, or Real Assent, on the other hand, "is too rich to be sharply limited" to a minimum of meaning, although its knowledge is ultimately more useful.[29] In his movement from the certainty of orthodoxy to the rich indefiniteness of poetry, Aiken has made the same kind of distinction:

> Poetry, alas, is not science, it is not statistics, it is not algebra or geometry, it is not philosophy, it is not music. It may and should incorporate elements of these, but it can never attain to the cold, pure abstractness which is the principle they have in common. . . . After science, or statistics, or algebra, or geometry, even after philosophy and music, poetry has the last word. In poetry, could it not be maintained? always comes man's final statement, at whatever point in the evolution of his awareness. It is the whole speech of the whole man. (ABC, 168)

Dogma, certain knowledge, doctrine—these are not enough, Aiken has come more and more clearly to see. In his most recent critical statement, read on the occasion of receiving the National Book Award, he wholly concerned himself with a plea for "a maximum of freedom from orthodox, or merely inherited, dogma or belief."[30] Such fixed beliefs enslave; the sage seeks, above all, to liberate. Aiken best expressed his lifelong devotion, as he saw it, to intellectual freedom in *Preludes for Memnon*, L:

We have been round the Cape
With Freud, the sea-gull, Einstein, and the Bear;
Lived on the sea-moss of the absolute;
And died in wisdom, and been glad to die.

But let us die as gladly for such reasons
As have no reason: let us die as fools,
If so we will; explore the rash heart's folly;
The marshes of the Congo of the blood.
Here are such wisdoms—who knows?—as pure wisdom
Knows nothing of. Such birds of Paradise,—
Delusory,—as Euclid never knew. (558)

· III ·

In 1928 Aiken wrote of James Wood's *New World Vistas*:
"These studies are not exactly or purely reminiscences, nor are
they (strictly speaking) short stories, nor essays; it is a part of
their unique quality that they succeed in combining . . . the
virtues of all three of these forms. They have the exciting
revelatory or confessional quality of autobiography, the sharp
or leisurely critical detachment of the essay, the narrative un-
foldingness . . . of the story."[31] Whether or not he was influenced by Wood's example, Aiken gave *Ushant* precisely the
same qualities. The book is acknowledged to be autobiographical, and was generally received as such. But in most cases the
names of the people involved have been changed, and the
people treated symbolically, as they would be in a novel. Nor
does Aiken attempt to retell his whole life; rather, he selects
and magnifies certain aspects of it. The structure of the book,
too, is as complex and rich as any American novel since Henry
James'. Finally, *Ushant* has the analytic qualities of criticism,
and therefore Aiken appropriately gave it the subtitle "An Essay." Aiken's role in the tradition of the sage demanded this
kind of combination of forms. As sage, three kinds of activities
are demanded of the poet. First (the autobiography), he must

226

become ever more conscious of himself and the world about him. Second (the essay), he must remain, in a sense, impersonal, so that he can view himself and his activities objectively. Finally (the novel), from the awareness he achieves by the former two he must produce a new shape—an "artifact"—which will be useful to mankind, and not dependent for its interest upon the personal life of the artist who created it. Aiken points up this threefold intention near the end of *Ushant*. He maintains that the poet must put his increasing awareness "at the disposal of society—even, if necessary, on the chopping-block or the dissecting table. And in order to do this . . . the individual spokesman must himself remain completely neutral, the mere servant. The artificer, in the very act of deploying himself in the new shape of the artifact, must remain wholly neutral to that part of himself which is his subject. . . . [The] writer, if he were to do his duty, must discuss himself, *qua* material, as if this were merely an object to which as yet no name had been given" (305-306). Although Aiken, as we have seen, failed at times to translate his personal experience objectively into an artifact, his whole development issues from his need to find the means of success. By discussing his previous literary failures in *Ushant*, he hopes to discover the way to transcend them. In this sense, *Ushant* does not add a new theme to Aiken's art—it is a synthesis of the tendencies of his whole career. In another sense, to be sure, Aiken has created a wholly new form in *Ushant*, for he is able to unite, by interweaving, the confessional and aesthetic novels. At the same time that he reveals his life through art, he shows how the artist shapes art from life. Now, in his exploration, Aiken no longer needs a mythical framework (as in *Osiris Jones* and the Preludes); nor a dramatic situation (as in *And in the Human Heart*); nor a single meditative symbol to create history (as in *The Kid*). He celebrates the self for its own sake—which is to say, for the sake of mankind.

Although it was not published until 1952, Aiken began *Ushant* in 1933, when he first outlined its scheme, put down notes "about six inches thick," and wrote eight full pages.[32] During the twenty-year interval between the conception and actual composition of *Ushant*, Aiken planned his book. Not as a fact, but as an ideal, therefore, *Ushant* lay behind two decades of Aiken's work; the intentions which Aiken examined in *Ushant* governed his poetry and fiction from the early thirties. In this sense, *Ushant* is Aiken's attempt to bring his lifetime of work into the bright focus of consciousness. It is the apogee in Aiken's career of the ego realizing itself for the sake of its culture—the same intention which, Emerson claimed, underlay Goethe's autobiography: "This idea reigns in the *Dichtung und Wahrheit* and directs the selection of the incidents; and nowise the external importance of events, the rank of the personages, or the bulk of incomes. . . . [There are] few dates, no correspondence, no details of offices or employments, no light on his marriage; and a period of ten years . . . is sunk in silence. Meantime certain love affairs that came to nothing, as people say, have the strangest importance."[33] Neither in Goethe's nor Aiken's "autobiography" is the author concerned with his work, or even with his public career (both of which are products of his *achieved* consciousness), but only with the incidents of life which brought about a deepening of his awareness. We can be almost certain that Goethe did not influence Aiken. But the role of the sage has remained fundamentally the same since Goethe. He explores himself not as person, but as artifact. He dares to be a culture-hero. With both self-absorption and self-forgetfulness, he takes the ego as his only province—but from it creates a world.

Aiken has also seen that in his insistence upon consciousness, the poet (or, the poet as a sage) has a second, though no less important, obligation to his audience. Since his *raison d'être* is his being at every moment as conscious as possible, then he must at the same time be equally as conscious of his own creativity—of the sources and devices of his poetry and the compulsions which make it desirable, if not necessary, that he should have become a writer in the first place. He must simultaneously elucidate both his consciousness and the means by which he carries out his elucidation. Investigating the causes for the popularity of psychoanalytic biographies of authors, Aiken had written that it results from "a passionate desire to know and understand, through the unraveling of these lives, something of ourself. Here, fortunately for us, are these gifted folk who knew how to make their minds and hearts manifest; they tell us exactly how they thought and felt; and if, by comparing their own record of their lives with the reports of others, we can move a fraction of an inch further toward wisdom, we shall have performed . . . the true office of the critic."[34] One of the results of Aiken's working in criticism side by side with his poetry was that he finally absorbed this function of the critic into the framework of his verse. While revealing himself he tried at the same time to explain to the reader the means whereby he does so. We have observed such an effort throughout Aiken's development. In various ways he explained how his poetry might be understood, in order that his audience might understand his—and, hence, their—inner life more deeply. As might be expected, his criticism performed much of the task early in his career. The essays in *Scepticisms* deal nearly as much with an attempt to explicate his method as with its actual application. "Apologia Pro Specie Sua" and "The Mechanism of Poetic Inspiration," the first two essays in the book, investigate the methods of criticism and poetry. In the final two essays, "Magic or Legerdemain?" and "Appendix: A Note on Values," he returned once more to discussion of, respectively, poetry and criticism. Taken together, these four essays give *Scepticisms* a kind of spiral structure and an explicational frame defining and delimitating his critical practice. "Changing Mind" might be seen as falling into two parts. In the first three sections, Aiken endeavored to present the reader directly with the aspects of his life which have made him a writer. The fourth section is his illustration of a poem as it has grown out of that life. "Cliff

Meeting," as I have remarked, is constructed upon a similar plan. In lines 1 to 39 Aiken dramatizes an actual love affair; in the second half of the poem, he symbolizes the love affair in his dream of the blue cormorant. *Blue Voyage* was a more ambitious attempt at the dual revelation of his consciousness as a person and his consciousness (via "A Basis for Criticism") as a writer. The novel is the process whereby he can discover and discuss the elements which compelled him to write the book. And he casts his narrative in the third person so that he might discuss his compulsions more honestly, because more detachedly. In his emphasis upon language in the Preludes and his exhibition of the genesis of fiction in "Life Isn't a Short Story" and "Thistledown," he created literature by exemplifying its methods and mechanisms.

In *Blue Voyage*, Aiken's revelation of Demarest's artistic awareness was incidental, almost extraneous. There was little dramatic verisimilitude in Demarest's long discussion with Silberstein on the origin and function of art. But in *Ushant* his definition of D.'s artistic aims is implicit in the structure of the whole book. The reader cannot turn—as in *Blue Voyage* he could turn to Chapter v and the first two letters of Chapter vii—to any particular section of *Ushant* in order to understand D. Only as the narrative unfolds do we slowly discover D.'s motives and methods; and not until the book ends do we understand them completely.

The narrative in *Ushant* moves on three levels, with, as in *Landscape West of Eden,* each level shifting and moving into the other. The book begins with a fragment of the protagonist's dream of the sea and of the challenge and perils of Ushant; the dream is not explained or brought into focus until the end of the book; for the dream is interrupted, as in the Divine Pilgrim poems, by the intrusion of material reality. Bells strike on the converted troop-ship in which the protagonist is sailing to England two weeks after the end of World War II. Through D., the protagonist (who is Demarest trimmed down to essentials), we observe the other occupants of the cabin, and are given the details of their lives. D. speculates upon the compulsions that are driving each of these people back to England or Europe. The process of free association leads him to the same kind of speculation about his own compulsions to return. His descent into the self begins with random memories of England. He thinks particularly of his house in England, which, as he now sees, is "the *Doppelgänger* of something at Savannah" (23), the house of his childhood. As a result, he is led back to review his whole life in tracing out the mystic connection between the two (symbolically identical) houses. The narrative thereby produced forms the autobiographical aspect of *Ushant*, and gives the book a sustaining factual richness. On this narrative plane, D. is a dreamer, dreaming his own life in order to understand it. But he must, in consequence, also accept it with strict honesty. In "The Improvisation," published two years before he wrote *Ushant*, Aiken formulated his attitude and method:

> Let us not be afraid, for all is acceptable,
> unknown past and unknown future alike acceptable:
> the steppingstones of the known to the past,
> and the steppingstones of the known to the future,
> will lead us, item by sunlit item, till we drown in light.
> Dear stranger, in whom the strangeness becomes dear,
> and chaos familiar, what would I not know and love
> of all your world that whispers back in time,
> of all this time that images forth a world
> to call itself the temporal 'you'! (S.O., 25)

As I have said, the three levels of consciousness shift and intermingle, so that this autobiographical narrative does not proceed in a straightforward fashion to its completion. Aiken's early preoccupation with the musical analogy, though refined and subtilized, is still present. He introduces his second theme almost simultaneously with the first. On this narrative plane,

231

D. is presented in his role as a writer. We discover that he has a nebulous plan for a novel he wants to write. He has been thinking about the prospective book under the guise of several titles: *Rooms, Streets, and Houses; Twenty-Thousand Days: An Analytic Biography; Ariel's Island;* and most recently, *Reading a Book,* or *Ushant.* The last title, of course, partly explains the dream which opened the book. The novel is to be based on the original dream of Ushant, dreamed many years before on a ship that "was perhaps in difficulties as it turned north towards the dangerous shoals south of *Île d'Ouessant,* Ushant" (29). Just as on the autobiographical plane of consciousness D.'s present situation forces him to reconstruct his past, so also, as he now again sails toward the *Île d'Ouessant,* the fragment of his recurring dream of Ushant recalls that earlier dream. As he is led to investigate his life, so also he investigates the means by which he might succeed in shaping his dream into a novel. Much of the book on this level is a discussion of the novels which he has written: *Purple Passage (Blue Voyage), Dead Reckoning (Great Circle), A Heart for the Barranca (A Heart for the Gods of Mexico),* and *The Quarrel (Conversation).* In an attempt to learn what is necessary to write a begin-all, end-all novel, he mercilessly dissects his past efforts to write such a book. By so doing he hopes to attain success in his translation of, as he calls it, the noumenal into the phenomenal.

The original dream is, of course, central to the attempt. In its essential ambiguity lies its attraction. He dreamed of four people—D. recognizes himself as "The Narrator"—who are engaged in translating a German *novella,* but who can never agree precisely how much they have translated, or exactly where the story takes place, and even what language it is really in—German, Provençal, or Spanish. Moreover, it becomes increasingly clear that the four characters in the story are the same people who are translating it. "The little story was a progress; just as the reading of the book, and the translation of it, were a progress; and the four people were involved in the progress, but simultaneously, and in two dimensions. And beyond this, *any* step in *any* direction must be towards ambiguity. Seven types—? Child's play" (26). This then is the second level of meaning in *Ushant*. In brief, as D. on the factual, first level is the dreamer dreaming his life, so on the second level, D. is a writer engaged in dreaming of the book which will emerge from that life. In both cases Aiken contrasts his failures with his intentions. He opposes the life which failed in human kindness to the life which learned its lesson of love; the novels which never fully succeeded to the prospective success of the novel he is contemplating.

Although we only gradually realize it, the third narrative strain also begins with the first words of the book. This is Aiken's actual construction of the novel which arises out of D.'s dream of the translators. And the novel is *Ushant*, the book which we are reading, and into which, therefore, we are drawn. For as D.'s plan becomes reality, we see the book being written "as it were, before our eyes."[35] In the reader's realization that he is reading the book which D. projects, his awareness of the relation of art to life will be widened and deepened—so Aiken hopes. By reading *Ushant*, we not only learn of D.'s various schemes for his book but also observe how they are actually executed. D. characterizes his intention as "a breaking-down of reality into its so many and so deceptive levels, one under another, one behind another, as if one were peeling off the seven or eight layers of time, and language, and meaning" (322). Its design is to be "architected, with its own intrinsic and natural spiral of form, as a whole drama of the human soul, from the beginningless beginning to the endless end" (323). Of its rationale, he argues that such a pursuit of consciousness is "the most essential of dramas . . . since that pursuit is the central undeviating concern of every living individual human being" (323). These plans describe *Ushant* exactly. For instance, as D. conceives the book, so it is written: the first words in *Ushant* are "beginning without beginning," and the last, "can have no end." Aiken presents us with the notes which D. set down after the dream and throughout the following years— and even with an algebraic diagram of the structure and a fragment of a false beginning.

I may now complete my outline of the relationship between the three levels of meaning in *Ushant*. On the first level D. is a man dreaming his own life. On the second, he is portrayed as a writer who is planning a novel based on his ambiguous dream about the four translators. On the third, he finds that his novel as it is to exist is, in actuality, the curious story which they have been engaged in translating. If the language and landscape of that *novella* kept changing, it is because the *novella* is itself their lives. They are translating the myth of their lives. As The Narrator of the dream, D. must give it form in language, in order that it may be transformed (by being translated) into an artifact which may be put at the service of mankind's evolving awareness. The *novella* and *Ushant* are the same, in the same way that the "design and the designer are the same, / the namer is the name" (L.P., 76), if one, with constant devotion to honesty, can only find the right words.

The right word, of course, is "Ushant," the word which magically comprehends the whole, and on all three levels. On the first, the autobiographical, plane of meaning it signifies the actual *Île d'Ouessant*, lying off France at the head of the English Channel, whose lighthouse gives the shipboard traveller the first sign that he is approaching his destination. It is, therefore, the sign for which D., as actual traveller, looks to tell him he is approaching England. That it is near Sussex, where the house to which D. is returning is located, provides D. with the key by which he enters the dream of his life. The fact that it looks both east and west, toward England and toward America, sets the basic narrative pattern for that life, with its journeyings back and forth across the Atlantic. Its two directions likewise symbolize D.'s father and mother, the motherland (England) and the fatherland (America). The story of his life, in essence, is his progress toward acceptance of both mother and father, England and America. He realizes that he must accept the heritage of suffering and consciousness which, by their suicide, his parents imposed upon him—and that, in fact, "he was irrevocably dedicated to a lifelong—if need be—search for an equivalent to it all, in terms of his own life, or work; and an equivalent that those two angelic people would have thought acceptable" (303). In accepting them, he can make them (symbolically) accept him; the understanding and the forgiveness work both ways. And in the same sense, he learns to reconcile England and America: "he had gone to England merely that he might, in the end, hear [America] the more clearly, understand it the more profoundly" (335). East and west—he finds that both directions are the same: all directions are inward.

This points to the second level of symbolism of "Ushant." For the Greek mariners, the *Île d'Ouessant* was the western limit of the known and inhabitable world. Likewise, for D. as writer, planning a novel, "Ushant" signifies the farthest reaches of consciousness—which he must attain in order to write his book. It contains the dual possibility of "promise of landfall or menace of shipwreck" (327)—both the ideal attainment, "Ushant," and the frustration of attainment, "*You Shan't.*" For this reason D. reviews his former novels, his spiritual shipwrecks, in order that he may learn the perilous navigation of the soul and succeed in his prospective novel. By sifting out his failures, he hopes to achieve full honesty of consciousness. No longer can he be content with his ambition in *The House of Dust*—to deceive the reader only so much as he deceives himself. Now he must not deceive himself at all. "To approach [*Île d'Ouessant*] at all, in thick weather, was of extreme danger" (327)—to approach "Ushant," the ideal, with anything but full clarity of consciousness is disaster. Finally, on the inmost level of meaning, "Ushant" becomes the magically all-embracing word for the book as it actually exists, the one we are reading, produced by Aiken's (and D.'s) awareness of the first two levels, and composed of these.

The book as a whole, then, constitutes an experiment in creating a new kind of form in order to reflect and refract the self—both personal and impersonal—truly. Such an approach has its dangers. The reader may well be bewildered. Aiken, one thinks, depended on the sheer entertainment value of the book to keep the reader going. Immersed in the autobiographical narrative, the reader is interested in seeing how the author, as D., develops from the child to the man. Then too, Aiken's presentation of three decades of the literary scene in Boston and London provides the reader with an informal and revelatory background for the self-investigation. T. S. Eliot (the "Tsetse," his initials), Ezra Pound ("Rabbi Ben Ezra," a comment on his anti-semitism), John Gould Fletcher (the "farouche John"), and the other creators of the poetic renaissance populate the autobiography. Such autobiography has its own personal and political problems.

But a deeper problem lies in the fact that Aiken was, as he wrote to Henry A. Murray in 1951, "early convinced that I should have to plump for an all or nothing nebular and tensionless spiral. . . . [Ushant] will thus select the particular reader I want. . . . [The] whole effect will be there for him if he wants it." From this viewpoint, to give Ushant a thesis—as Henry Adams and Louis Sullivan gave to their autobiographies—would falsify the book, Aiken felt, because this would formulate what is not, except by the act of writing and completing the book, formulated. As Aiken said: "The formulation will have to come out of the whole thing. When at last it has come round on itself, if it ever does." In his awareness of the first two levels of meaning, the reader can formulate what in Ushant itself is only beginningless beginning and endless end.

The Ancients also believed (as Aiken points out) that the Island was the last resting place of the souls of the departed on their way to the West. In Landscape West of Eden Aiken used the West to symbolize the consummate stage of consciousness toward which man must aspire. *Ushant*, as it has been translated from life, represents the final step in Aiken's journey toward that "indecipherable land." And his whole career enabled him to take that step—with humility, but also with confidence.

· IV ·

Of the fifteen poems in Aiken's *Skylight One* (1949) volume, "Mayflower," "Hallowe'en" and, perhaps, "The Clover" indicate an advance over his earlier poems. In these poems Aiken achieved the understanding which he was to require for the composition of *Ushant*. The other poems in *Skylight One* generally are indebted for their method and substance to his earlier books of poetry—"Summer," for instance, to the themes of *Brownstone Eclogues*; "The Lovers" to *And in the Human Heart*; and "Everlasting" to *The Soldier*.

In Aiken's development, particularly with regard to his preparation for *Ushant*, "Hallowe'en" has much the same heuristic value as "Mayflower"—although it is certainly the finer poem of the two. In "Hallowe'en," written four years after "Mayflower" and two years after *The Kid*, Aiken profited from his former experiments in re-creating the past through a single iridescent symbol. He now was to see in his grandfather's liberalism the principle of his own career. In his earlier poems—in "Changing Mind" and *Osiris Jones*, for example—Aiken had considered his ancestral inheritance only in terms of his father and mother. "Hallowe'en" constitutes his recognition of his grandfather's importance. This allowed him to imagine in *Ushant* the implicit communion and exchange between him (as a child) and his Unitarian grandfather: "Had grandfather not been saying, the white beard saying, 'Thee must now—always remember this, little D.—thee must now and hereafter do *my* thinking for *me*, thee must be the continuance of me. . . .' Yes, this was true. Something like this had really hap-

237

pened" (Ush., 112). Through the power of this communion he comes to understand the influence of all his ancestors upon him. In *King Coffin*, Ammen said that the past should be "remembered not for its leaves but for its seeds" (4). So also in "Hallowe'en" and *Ushant*, Aiken's ancestors (and, consequently, all of culture) become important and memorable, not for what they accomplished, but for what of them is completed and perfected in *him*.

"Hallowe'en," as a result, deepens the traditional life-in-death, death-in-life theme. Although it may have been influenced by Yeats's "All Souls' Night," the "philosophy" of "Hallowe'en" is not spiritualistic, but psychological and biological. The poem seems to have distant affiliations with one that Aiken wrote in 1936 for a Harvard College Memorial Service of the class of 1911, titled "In Memoriam." It concludes:

> Not for our pity here, do their ghosts come,
> but for our love, who have ourselves become
> their house and home;
>
> And move within us, and within our love,
> as we ourselves shall later love and move
> in those who live.

Taking this as the basis of his poem, Aiken can, in his "crystal" vision, move back to recreate the racial and cultural past in terms of the Hallowe'en ritual.

Through the emphatic three-day commemoration of the dead, "All Saints', All Hallows', / All Souls', and Hallowe'en" (S.O., 34), the poet is led to speculate upon what the living mean to the dead. Aiken adopted Dr. Richard Sterba's socio-psychoanalytical comments on the American Hallowe'en ritual to his own purposes. Sterba writes: "They are just ordinary business days, and we have forgotten about our obligations to the dead. . . . Still the dead themselves have not forgotten it, as it were, and come to take revenge for our neglect. It is our children who

238

take upon themselves to be the executors of our conscience."[36]
Aiken generalizes this idea to include the relation between the
past and present in the history of consciousness. In the evolution of consciousness, the past makes the present possible. In
this sense of the transmigration of consciousness, the dead constantly return to life:

> And now you come back to complain and to haunt me,
> you, and my brother, and the others.
> Was your vision of god not enough, that you come
> for the vision of the not-yet-dead? (35)

The poet thus realizes that in not having understood the relation between past and present he has failed to understand the
nature of his consciousness. He has betrayed his memory; "for
the dead do not forget us, in our hearts / the dead never forget
us" (36). The theme is thereby reversed, and the poet realizes
the importance of the dead to the living. For each man contains both the past and the future in himself: and if he is false
to the past in neglecting the homage due to it for his inheritance, so he is therefore also false to the future, the children
who are his inheritors. He is, in every sense, false to himself:

> it is our ancestors and children who conspire against us
>
> .   .   .   .   .   .
>
> for we have neglected not only our death
> in forgetting our obligations to the dead
> we have neglected our living and our children's living
> in neglecting our love
> for the dead who would still live within us. (36)

The dead live in their seeds, what they make available for inheritance. And the poet will also live in what consciousness he
in turn can pass on, to his children, to his culture. The past
dwells "in ourselves, those who inherit"—so that, paradoxically,
the dead dwell in the living, the living dwell in the dead.
Aiken's grandfather, therefore, is his ancestor, who made cups

239

and saucers out of acorns for the boy's delight. But he is also the poet's child—the "dear pumpkin-head! / who masquerade now as my child" (38). In the poet's perception of his grandfather's importance, he is present both as past and future, dead and living. By understanding his spiritual continuity with his grandfather, the poet comes to understand himself, for he is the incarnation of his descent.

In "A Letter from Li Po" and "The Crystal," recent poems, Aiken brilliantly culminates his career. Formulated in "Mayflower" and "Hallowe'en," their method has been Aiken's most successful recent means of exploring his own and man's collective ego. In all of them, he endeavors to establish a realm in which the past, present, and the future, or the dead, the living, and the unborn are all one. For in this dimension self-investigation can move freely, even simultaneously, in several directions. Characteristically, these poems fasten upon *personae*—Rufus and Amanda Clark and "Will and Ben" in "Mayflower," William James Potter in "Hallowe'en," the eighth-century Chinese poet Li Po and the Quaker Abiel in "A Letter from Li Po," and Pythagoras in "The Crystal." Each *persona* acts as a "crystal" in which Aiken can read the history of man's mind by seeing his own ego as a product of the history which they made. The theory of the "crystal" moment, of course, supplied the title for the most recent of such poems; as Aiken said in a note to the poem, "both poem and title had been in my mind for several years" (S.H., 5). Indeed, he had used the concept and formulated his method as early as *The Soldier*: "The soldier is crystal: / crystal of man: clear heart, clear duty, clear purpose" (839). By considering the *historia* of the soldier we understand all men: thus, "man's mind / becomes crystal, man's heart becomes crystal, even as the soldier / is crystal, was always crystal" (842). His concept of the myriad-faceted "crystal" provided the means whereby Aiken could work upon several planes of meaning. *Landscape West of Eden*, as we have seen, prefigured the structure of these poems in its presentation of

240

three developing states of consciousness—say, *a*, *b*, and *c*, in which *a* is seen moving to *b*, *b* to *c*, and *c* to *d*. The poems which I am now considering, however, are not nearly so method- ically designed as *Landscape West of Eden*. In them Aiken ordinarily contrasts himself to his *personae*, and then impro- vises upon the similarities and the differences which arise from the contrast. Sidney Lanier had himself used a similar concept in his own poem titled "The Crystal." He dramatizes himself as sitting at midnight, the time "When far within the spirit's hearing rolls / The great soft rumble of the course of things,"[37] and calling upon the great poets and sages—Shakespeare, Homer, Socrates, and others. Only, finally, in the "Crystal Christ" does he find no defect. Aiken, too, seeks out the kind of perfection implied by the crystal.

In "The Crystal" (1958) Aiken immediately emphasizes the question of time, beginning, "What time is it now, brother Pythagoras, by the pale stone / set like a jewel in the brow of Sheepfold Hill?" (S.H., 11). And as the poem develops, we see that the poet and his *persona* are involved both in a particular time ("Six o'clock, here, in the western world" [13]), and in timelessness, the eternal flow of memory ("the center of your thought, which is timeless" [20]). While it is true that there is an actual past, as in section 1, where Pythagoras' journey is described as "long ago: far away" (12), and an actual present, set in the "ancient farmhouse" of "Mayflower," it is equally true that in a deeper sense, the past is the present and the present the past. The two are made one in Aiken's notion of the transmigration of consciousness—his extension of, and parallel to, Pythagoras' doctrine of the transmigration of souls. Beneath the locus of change, consciousness is constant:

> You taught the migration of souls: all things
> must continue, since numbers are deathless:
> the mind, like these migrants, crosses all seasons,
> and thought, like these cries, is immortal. (20)

241

The poet and his *persona* are engaged in a search for the principle of their continuity and continuance. Aiken finds this, of course, in the magical nature of the crystal, just as in *Ushant* he found it in the single, rich word, or in "Hallowe'en," in the ritual myth.

Aiken wrote that the poem was given its form by the figure of Pythagoras. In many ways, Pythagoras is the perfect *persona* whereby Aiken could make fully concrete his notion of the crystal moment of consciousness. He was the son of a gem-engraver named Mnesarchos, and for many years in Samos he himself followed his father's profession. Prompted by his observations of the crystals used by gem-cutters, he began the mathematical enquiries which resulted, finally, in his philosophy of form. Taking mathematical relationship as expressed in number—instead of matter—as the essence and highest reality of the universe, Pythagoras worked from principles which Aiken can expand to imply and include his own notions. Number is the principle of music, essential to poetry, and Pythagoras himself is said to have invented the lyre. Then too, number in all ancient societies was traditionally associated with words. For the Jewish and Christian Kabbalists, the Babylonians and the Gnostics, words have numerical equivalents. Each letter in the Arabic alphabet, for instance, has a fixed numerical value, and vice versa. *Alif*, the first letter, is also the first letter of the name of Allah; and in its numerical value, one, it represents Allah, the One God.[38] For all ancient people, in the Bible and in Plato, words—the active aspect of relation—created the universe. In the relation between numbers and words, Aiken finds his relation to Pythagoras. Ultimately, as he sees, they both are engaged in the same search for reality.

The search is given design by the definitive form of Aiken's thought—the monologue, the self-revelatory letter, the document in one's history, the parable, the self-composed obituary, the prelude. All have the same purpose: to fasten upon the one thing in life—an object, a relationship, an experience—which will best represent the whole, and thus assure the self of continuance. The particular form of "The Crystal" most resembles that of "Your Obituary, Well Written." The poet asks of Pythagoras: "what part of this ritual [of life] / would we choose for reenactment? What rite / single out to return for?" (15). Through the suggestion and rejection of various possibilities, he investigates Pythagoras' personality—and thus, in the "forever-together" (17), his own. In his enumeration of successive possibilities, Aiken exhibits the surest control of any of his poems over the richly detailed image. Considering that he might revisit his home after death, he writes:

> Easy enough, it would be, to find in the darkness
> the familiar roadside, the shape of a known tree,
> and then, how naturally, alas, the faded signpost
> stuck in the sand: and on it to make out with joy
> the names that point homeward,
>
> .   .   .   .   .
>
> And arrived there, to find the door open,
> the fire on the hearth, the pot on the trivet,
> the dish on the table—with a red rim—for grapes,
> and the ripe blue cluster; to feel with one's foot
> the slope of the floorboard, and on it the scars
> ridged by the adze.
>
> .   .   .   .   .
>
>   And then, to lift gently
> the one thing most loved: as if in this thing
> one could best hold them all. And thus, it might be
> a spoon from one's childhood: a shell of thin silver,
> a handle shaped like a tiny brick chimney,
> atop of it, perching, a dwarf with a horn,
> a curled horn tilted to heaven. (15-16)

But the poet rejects this as the one thing which might summarize his life. He and Pythagoras agree that both the heart and the mind must be satisfied by the choice. That is, the one

243

thing which would best symbolize a whole life must combine the concrete or actual (the heart) with the ideal (the mind). This is only possible in the completed artifact, the fully formed work of art which reaches beyond their individual selves. Such an artifact is the crystal—like the emerald signet ring which Theodoros carved in intaglio for the Samian tyrant Polycrates—whose facets suggest inner and outer complexity, the ambiguity and eternality of multiplicity:

> the emerald held in a vice, then the green
> ice of the clear stone gives up its goddess,
> the tiny wave bears up its Venus, green foam
> on the brow and the shoulder. The image?
> Of course! But beneath or behind it
> the knowledge, the craft: and the art, above all. (17)

In its perfection as an artifact, it not only re-encompasses their own individual selves, but is "the one / everlasting of experience, a pure delight" (19).

But Aiken's search for the crystalline moment of vision is itself an artifact and gives its own vision; his search for full consciousness of "the miracle of interconnectedness" (18) is an example of such interconnectedness. The completed poem grows out of the search for it. His poems ideally become more than poems, by doing what his *personae* are attempting to do. While the poet and Pythagoras, writer and geometer, join to create something new—"the song of the square / echoing the squares" (12)—the poem which Aiken has written seeks also to be the same kind of rediscovery of the eternal design in reality. It too satisfies both heart and mind. The crystal which they seize upon as its principle therefore becomes "The Crystal," the poem so written.

The Chinese poet who is the alter ego of "A Letter from Li Po" serves a purpose similar to Pythagoras. But Pythagoras' qualities of awareness lie chiefly in his mathematics and mysticism; for him, number or relation is the essense of reality. Correspondingly, for Aiken, the poet uses music—derived from number by Pythagoras—in order to define reality correctly, to say the things which prose cannot. In choosing such a figure as Li Po for his protagonist, Aiken found the means to investigate the problems of the poet and of poetry itself. In this sense the two poems complement each other as summaries of Aiken's career: by his music and language both, the poet provides his audience with the insights whereby consciousness might evolve. He is able to insist in the *Li Po* poems, as he did in the Preludes, that in language we may read the design of the world. In "Overture to Today," for instance, he writes:

> The world as word
> this is the poem which the wise poet writes
> in us and through us and around us writes
> o and invites
> all things created, and all things to come,
> each to make tribute and contribution make. (81)

Such is the poem which Aiken writes in "Li Po." In it he brings together not only the self and the not-self, the present and the past, life and death, but also the language and the landscape and the poet who understands them both, all intertwined in what he calls elsewhere "the miracle of interconnectedness."

Aiken originally ended his poem as, contemplating the relationship between Li Po, Cousin Abiel, and himself, he wrote:

> The poems and the prophecies are ours,
> becoming self, becoming purer word;
> and these are with us as once more we write
> Li Po's unfinished letter to lost friends.

Abiel Aiken had himself written such a letter, and so is commemorated with Li Po in the Quaker graveyard where, under stones of equal size, farmer, fisherman, and poet lie side by side. By writing a poem—another such letter—arising from his response to his real and spiritual ancestors, by acknowledging his inheritance, Aiken renews the dignity of the present. In resuming their task he builds a myth of himself.

As part of his effort in the Preludes to mirror, in language, his drifting, random receptivity to experience, Aiken minimized the rhetorical aspects of poetry, sometimes dispensing with formal syntax and punctuation. He does this in order to illustrate the deeper and more basic syntax of the things themselves. Even the well-known prelude in which Verlaine insists to Rimbaud, "We must take rhetoric and wring its neck!" is, ironically, a formal organization in which each of its eight stanzas has one line less than the previous one.

So also in "A Letter from Li Po," Aiken writes with such ease—whether in rhymed alternate lines, in free verse, in lines loosely rhymed, in couplets, or even in triplets—that his own poem seems to rise spontaneously from the magic and myth he celebrates. To be sure, the art, as in most of Aiken's work, derives from the presumption of artlessness. Before the recent vogue for destroying the rhythmical character of poetry by organizing the verse-line telegrammatically, ignoring syntax, and juggling the printed appearance on the page, Yeats wrote in "Adam's Curse" of the poet's problem:

> 'A line will take us hours maybe;
> Yet if it does not seem a moment's thought,
> Our stitching and unstitching has been naught.'

Many poets in the twenties and thirties, to the contrary, tried to insist that their often awkward and hesitating verse was a consequence of the magnitude of the issues they were trying to face and solve. Aiken has even been condemned for his consistent ability to effect the apparent artlessness which Yeats describes—for having "a really expert facility which enables him to turn out verses satin-smooth or burlap-harsh at will."[39] The ease with which "Li Po" seems to be written, however, makes for its greatness. As each succeeding section explains, answers, or adds to earlier assertions or ambiguities, deepening and extending them, the poet, as it were, disappears: through its own flowing continuity the poem seems to come into existence already perfected. Its movement is as inevitable and predictable, or surprising and various, as that of life. Thus the reader experiences the life of the poem directly, without a poet's voice intervening, as if it *were* life itself that he is experiencing. As early as his 1917-1918 Preface to *The House of Dust*, Aiken had tried to convince his readers to regard his poems as "the adventure of life itself." "Li Po" meditates on the sum of man's experience, inner and outer:

> The peachtree in the poem is still here.
> The song is in the peachtree and the ear. (23)

It sings life into a reason for being.

"A Letter from Li Po," therefore, represents Aiken's synthesis of the tendencies of his whole career. With regard to language, he can fully surrender to the rich and glittering ambiguity of the interchangeability of the landscape and the language and the self:

> Which is which?
> The poem? Or the peachtree in the ditch?
> Or is all one? Yes, all is text, the immortal text,
> Sheepfold Hill the poem, the poem Sheepfold Hill,
> and we, Li Po, the man who sings, sings as he climbs,
> transposing rhymes to rocks and rocks to rhymes. (23)

Consciousness and language—consciousness *expressed*—build their ramparts against annihilation by time ("time becomes still . . . in rhyme" [21]) and so hold all history in one multiple, iridescent moment. The moment commemorated in Li Po's song of Lady Flying Swallow, for example, is forever crystallized: "Even the fountain's falling blade / hangs in the air unbroken, and says: Wait!" (21)

It is in the sage, who attempts to embody all culture, that the past is brought to bear fruitfully on the present. In "Li Po,"

247

consequently, Aiken most consciously comes to accept the functions and responsibilities of the sage. He seeks particularly to clarify the role of the poet in society. Poetry, as the sage contends, must move outward and benefit society—not inward to idio-therapy, benefiting only the poet. Aiken speaks, for instance, of the essence of poetry as love. But he quickly adds that he does not mean love "in the self's circle so embraced," for personal love is "too near, too dear, for pure assessment" (11). The love out of which true poetry arises, he insists, must possess that curious impersonality that allows it to be transformed into an artifact. Likewise, in "Li Po" Aiken treats the question of originality as opposed to tradition. Since the past is contained in the present and the present in the past (as he also contended in "Hallowe'en" and "The Crystal"), the act of writing presumes (and includes) all previous writing if the poet is, as he must be, fully conscious. To write poetry—

> is to assume
> Li Po himself: as he before assumed
> the poets and the sages who were his.
> Like him, we too have eaten of the word. (10)

Early in his career, commenting on the uses of the poet to his culture, Aiken had written: "Inheriting Shakespeare, for example, we inherit an added capacity for experience and an enriched ability to adjust ourselves to the singular world into which we are born. In this sense the poet is the brilliant father from whom we inherit a sharpened awareness, a deepened emotional nature, an enhanced predisposition to wisdom."[40] In short, the poet is a super-consciousness who makes the future evolution of mankind possible by embodying—as, without him, his audience cannot—an objective past. Aiken has consistently deepened his awareness of the past and has seen more clearly his responsibility to the future. What Henry Adams said in praise of another man is perhaps even more true of Aiken: "He betrayed the consciousness that he and his people had a past, if they dared but avow it, and might have a future, if they could but divine it."[41]

The last lines of "Li Po" are a compendium of all of Aiken's themes. In the "crystal" of the poem, Aiken associates his own Quaker ancestor, buried in South Yarmouth, with Li Po and emphasizes the power of love and language against time, the continuity of history, and the evolution of consciousness:

> In this small mute democracy of stones
> is it Abiel or Li Po who lies
> and lends us against death our speech?
> They are the same, and it is both who teach.
> The poets and the prophecies are ours:
> and these are with us as we turn, in turn,
> the leaves of love that fill the Book of Change.

It is this Book of Change whose leaves Aiken has been turning all along, from Senlin's identifications with "Nuns, murderers, and drunkards, saints and sinners, / Lover and dancing girl and sage and clown" (C.P., 205), to, nearly forty years later, Li Po's poem on Chouang's dream (based on a celebrated passage in Kwang-Tze), with its succession of changes in the "liquid 'I' ":

> the player queen, the lover, or the dunce,
> hero or poet, father or friend,
>
> .   .   .   .   .
>
> savants, or saints, or fly-by-nights,
> the novice in her cell, or wearing tights
> on the high wire above a hell of lights. (17-18)

It is almost as if Aiken were consciously recalling *Senlin* (perhaps he is) so that he may resolve the problems of his earlier poetry in his very progress toward resolution in "Li Po." For in *Senlin* he could end only by admitting the incommunicability, and thus the dissolution, of the self in the face of chaos. But the forty years have made a difference, and Aiken now knows that there is protection against chaos—in the moment of consciousness, the moment of love, the moment, above all, of creation and the poet who creates—

> the master of the cadence, who
> transforms all things to a hoop of flame, where through
> tigers of meaning leap. (18)

Such a master as Conrad Aiken.

NOTES

INTRODUCTION

1. "Mr. Aiken's Second Wind," *New Republic*, 89 (1937), 335.
2. "Merry-go-Round of Opinion," *New Rep.*, 108 (1943), 292.
3. "A Word in Praise," *Poetry*, 88 (1956), 179.
4. "Poet's Progress," *New Rep.*, 69 (1931), 23.
5. *Essays in the History of Ideas* (Baltimore, 1948), pp. xv-xvi.
6. To be sure, Aiken received some of the extravagant praise so common in the period. In writing of Aiken's poetry, Burton Rascoe, for instance, exceeded even his usual exuberance. He wrote: "Conrad Aiken's *Punch: The Immortal Liar* is, in my opinion, the finest poetical narrative with the exception of *The Waste Land* by T. S. Eliot ever written by an American." Later in the same article, he continued: "Aiken's *Senlin: A Biography* and *The Charnel Rose* contain what I am pleased to consider the finest individual passages of melody written by any poet since Poe." "Contemporary Reminiscences," *Arts and Decoration*, 20 (March 1924), 12.
7. Harriet Monroe, "Its Inner Meaning," *Poetry*, 6 (1915), 305.
8. Joseph Freeman, "Ivory Towers—White and Red," *New Masses*, 12 (Sept. 11, 1934), 22.
9. Aiken criticized Auden, C. Day Lewis, and MacNeice for being "off-hand and artless" and writing "shirtsleeve poetry" which dispenses with rhythm, rhyme, color, and modulation of tone. ("Poetry: 1940 Model," *New Rep.*, 102 [1940], 540-41.) See Selden Rodman, "Reply to Conrad Aiken," *ibid.*, 645: "It is true that MacNeice, in his ambitious and sometimes successful effort to come to grips with the major issues that trouble (some) poets, does not use a jeweler's tweezers. But I predict that *his* way is the way the significant poetry of the next ten years is going." Rodman, of course, was right: the mainstream of poetic activity went in quite different directions than the development of Conrad Aiken.
10. In Erich Posselt, ed., *On Parade: Caricatures by Eva Herrmann* (New York, 1929), p. 2.
11. *Man the Measure: A New Approach to History* (New York, 1956), p. 18.

12. "Conrad Aiken,"*New Rep.*, 61 (1930), 255.
13. "The Critical Years," *The Meridian*, 2 (1958), 1-2.

ONE: WORK IN PROGRESS

1. See Roy Harvey Pearce, "American Renaissance (1): The Poet As Simple, Separate Person," *The Continuity of American Poetry* (Princeton, 1961), pp. 137-91; and "The Old and the New," *ibid.*, pp. 286-92.
2. This poem was originally titled "Medusa" and was dated 1917 when it appeared in Aiken's *John Deth* (1930) volume.
3. Harriet Monroe, *A Poet's Life* (New York, 1938), pp. 307-308.
4. E.g. "Anthologies, Good and 'Bad,' " *New Rep.*, 62 (1930), 333-34.
5. "The New Elizabethans," *Yale Rev.*, 11 (1922), 634-35.
6. "What I Believe," *Nation*, 135 (1932), 80.
7. "Conrad Aiken: The Poet," *Atlantic*, 192 (Dec. 1953), 78.
8. "Imagism or Myopia," *Poetry Journal*, 3 (1915), 239.
9. Letter to author, January 2, 1960.
10. "What is Poetry?" N.Y. *Times*, Feb. 7, 1915, p. 45.
11. "Freud and the Layman," *New Rep.*, 2 (Apr. 17, 1915), Pt. II, 9-10.
12. Henry A. Murray, "Poet of Creative Dissolution," *Wake* 11, p. 102.
13. *New Verse*, 11 (Oct. 1934), 13.
14. Frederick J. Hoffman, *Freudianism and the Literary Mind* (Baton Rouge, 1957), 2nd ed., pp. 84, 274.
15. Aiken to Hoffman, Jan. 23, 1944, *Freudianism*, p. 275.
16. N.Y. *Times*, Feb. 7, 1915, p. 45.
17. The question arises of how far Aiken supposed these books would be available to a popular audience. He was certainly encouraged by the fact that "in 1916 . . . more volumes of poetry and drama were published than of any other class" (Sc., 55). In 1922 he criticized Van Wyck Brooks's skeptical essay on "Literary Life in America," and argued: "One wonders . . . whether America is not the best place on earth for the production of genius"; for the American audience has "a tradition of great men; [and is] . . . a self-perpetuating audience which, if slow to accept and understand, nevertheless does at last accept and understand, on

the grand scale, and with idolatry." ("A Letter from America," *London Mercury*, 5 [1922], 417, 418.) In both 1931 and 1954 he argued that there was a great audience waiting for the poet who could "embody the full consciousness of man." ("The Future of Poetry," *ABC*, pp. 78-82; "The Poets Are Awaiting," *Publishers' Weekly*, 165 [1954], 776-77.) Aiken would logically have had to assume that his books might circulate widely in order to maintain his central belief that the poet deepens the consciousness of mankind. Appropriately, then, he has complained bitterly in private of the poor sales of his best books. Replying to Malcolm Cowley's request in 1934 for a list of neglected books, Aiken wrote in postscript: "Might I also suggest for your list of Neglected Books a novel by c. aiken called Great Circle, of which the royalty report, to hand this morning, chronicles a sale of 26 copies in its second half year? and Preludes for Memnon, which I think is my best book, and which has sold about seven hundred copies in three years." (Wake, 30)

18. *Theatre Arts Monthly*, 16 (1932), 894.

19. Helen Hoyt, "A Symphonic Suite," *Poetry*, 10 (1917), 162. Earlier in the same year O. W. Firkins had delicately expressed his shock at Aiken's licentiousness: "As to 'This Dance of Life' . . . I prefer the stigma of prudery to the recreancy of leaving unreproved a quality in this poem which I can only designate as plashiness. Without the realist's excuse or the moralist's justification, Mr. Aiken has abused a privilege which an enlightened age concedes even to realism and morality [only] with a due measure of discretion and reserve." "Meteorites in Verse," *Nation*, 104 (1917), 45.

20. Quoted in *This Modern Poetry* (New York, 1935), p. 132.

21. "A Letter from America," *London Mercury*, 6 (1922), 196-97.

22. *Harper's Bazaar*, 93 (Jan. 1960), 114-15.

23. "The Music of the Unconscious," *New Rep.*, 26 (1921), 21.

24. "Narcissus as Narcissus," *The Man of Letters in the Modern World* (New York, 1955), p. 335.

25. Padraic Colum, "The Poetry of Mr. Conrad Aiken," *Freeman*, 3 (1921), 117.

26. John Gould Fletcher, "The Revival of Aestheticism," *Freeman*, 8 (1923), 356.

27. Conrad Aiken, "The Start Was Golden," N.Y. *Herald Tribune, Bk. Rev.*, Oct. 12, 1952, p. 26.

28. *Ibid.*, p. 26.

29. "Who's Who," *Chicago Tribune*, July 19, 1919, p. 9.

30. Amy Lowell, "Marionettes of Fate," *New Rep.*, 28 (1921), 139.

31. Murray, "Poet of Creative Dissolution," *Wake 11*, pp. 95-106; Houston Peterson, *Melody of Chaos* (New York, 1931), *passim.*

32. As does Eunice Tietjens, "Mr. Aiken's Bow to Punch," *Poetry*, 18 (1921), 161.

33. T. E. Hulme, "Romanticism and Classicism," *Speculations: Essays on Humanism and the Philosophy of Art*, Herbert Read, ed. (London, 1954), 2nd ed., pp. 116, 120.

34. "Industrial Poison Seen in Lyric Spring," N.Y. *Evening Post*, Feb. 23, 1929, p. M11.

35. Conrad Aiken, in a letter to Houston Peterson dated October 5, 1928. Quoted by Peterson in *Melody of Chaos*, p. 205.

36. George Santayana, "A Long Way Round to Nirvana," *Some Turns of Thought in Modern Philosophy* (New York, 1933).

37. Aiken, "Candidly Speaking," *New Rep.*, 51 (1927), 53.

TWO: THE USES OF THE FICTION

1. Trans. Arthur Mitchell (New York, 1944), p. 182.

2. I am indebted to Mark Schorer's treatment of this story in "The Life in the Fiction," *Wake 11*, pp. 57-60. This essay was extended and reprinted as an introduction to Aiken's *Collected Short Stories* (1960), pp. vii-xiv.

3. "Speak As You Must," *Dial*, 83 (1927), 63.

4. Yvor Winters, "Recent Verse," *Hound and Horn*, 3 (1930), 455.

5. "The Short Story as Confession," *New Rep.*, 35 (1923), 309.

6. "The Start Was Golden," N.Y. *Herald Trib. Bk. Rev.*, p. 26.

7. *The Crushed Flower and Other Stories*, trans. Herman Bernstein (New York, 1917), p. 275.

8. Letter to the author, October 15, 1961.

9. *Melody of Chaos*, p. 226.

10. "Disintegration in Modern Poetry," *Dial*, 76 (1924), 535-40.

11. He is "anonymous" chiefly because anonymity gives him the freedom he requires for objective self-analysis. This is the same method Aiken was to adopt in *Blue Voyage* and *Ushant.*

12. Interestingly enough, in *Blue Voyage* he inverts this device, as the rhymed poem "Goya" comes fully formed from the chaos of Demarest's preconscious meditations.

13. "The Whale Ship," *Dial*, 82 (1927), 461-69.

14. *Melody of Chaos*, p. 232.

15. Letter to Selden Rodman, November 8, 1931.

16. Desmond MacCarthy, "Books in General," *The New Statesman*, 29 (1927), 344.

17. R. P. Blackmur, "Scapegoat," *Hound and Horn*, 1 (1927), 163.

THREE: THE WORLD, THE WORD, THE WOUND

1. Conrad Aiken, "Note," in W. R. Benét and N. H. Pearson, eds., *Oxford Anthology of American Literature* (New York, 1938), p. 1333.

2. Aiken himself commented on this poem in a poem parallel to it in *Time in the Rock*: "Who would carve words must carve himself/first carve himself" (XLII, 707).

3. Aiken, "Note," *Ox. Anth. of Am. Lit.*, p. 1336.

4. *Melody of Chaos*, p. 220.

5. *The Closed Door*, trans. F. S. Flint (London and New York, 1917), p. 105.

6. New York, 1961, p. v.

7. Marianne Moore, "If a Man Die," *Wake* 11, p. 50.

8. John Holmes, "A Poet's Voluntary Resumptions," *Saturday Review*, 39 (Mar. 31, 1956), 18.

9. Harlan Hatcher, *Creating the Modern American Novel* (New York, 1935), p. 186.

10. Julian Symons, "The Poetry of Conrad Aiken," *Wake* 11, p. 112.

11. Cf. *Arcularis*, pp. 76-77.

12. C. G. Jung, *Psychology and Religion* (New Haven, 1938), p. 19.

13. Aiken, "Note," *Ox. Anth. of Am. Lit.*, p. 1339.

14. R. P. Blackmur, "The Day Before the Daybreak," *Poetry*, 40 (1932), 40.

15. Lippmann, *Public Opinion* (New York, 1922). Reprinted in C. Wright Mills, ed., *Images of Man: The Classic Tradition in Sociological Thinking* (New York, 1960), p. 28.

16. "Composition in Nine Poets: 1937," *The Expense of Greatness* (New York, 1940), p. 222.

17. I have quoted from *The Dialogues of Plato*, trans. B. Jowett (Oxford, 1953), 4th ed., III: *Cratylus*, pp. 41, 49, *Phaedrus*, p. 185.

18. Aiken, "Phases of English Poetry," *Bookman*, 69 (1929), 104.

19. "Imagism or Myopia," *Poetry Journal* (1915), p. 239.

20. "Illusory Freedom in Poetry," *Poetry Journal*, 5 (1916), 190-91.

21. Nicolas Kostyleff, *Le Mécanisme Cérébral de la Pensée* (Paris, 1914), pp. 195-96. Italics his.

FOUR: CARITAS—

1. Vincent McHugh, "The Monstrous Tree," *New Rep.*, 85 (1935), 109.

2. Clayton Hoagland, "Explorer of the Ego: The Fiction of Conrad Aiken," *Southern Literary Messenger*, 2 (1940), 262.

3. R. P. Blackmur, "Notes on The Novel: 1936," *The Expense of Greatness*, p. 189.

4. Fydor Dostoevsky, *Crime and Punishment*, trans. Constance Garnett (New York, 1951), p. 425.

5. "Poets and Poets: Contemporary Verse Writers and Tennyson, Longfellow, Whittier," *N.Y. Times*, Jan. 17, 1915, p. 19.

6. "Poetry: What Direction?" *New Rep.*, 104 (1941), 670.

7. " 'It is in Truth a Pretty Toy,' " *Dial*, 78 (1925), 107, 109.

8. In "Poets as Reviewers," *New Rep.*, 104 (1941), 281, Malcolm Cowley suggests this reading.

9. "The Rhetoricians," *New Rep.*, 104 (1941), 221-22.

10. Ezra Pound, *Literary Essays* (London, 1954), p. 6.

11. "Conrad Aiken: The Poet," *Atlantic* (1953), p. 82.

12. "What is Poetry?" *N.Y. Times*, 1915, p. 45.

13. "Idiosyncrasy and Tradition," *Dial*, 68 (1920), 377.

14. "Small Excellencies: A Dissertation on Puns," *Any Number Can Play* (Cleveland, 1957), p. 248.

15. R. P. Blackmur, "The Composition in Nine Poets: 1937," *The Expense of Greatness*, p. 222.

16. William Van O'Connor's characterization of Aiken as "the greatest of the modern cosmic ironists" is, as is clear, only half accurate; for Aiken perceives the irony of existence, but, except in poems like "Poverty Grass," is not in the tradition of "post-Renaissance ironists who saw in a seemingly infinite universe no possible sanction for man's 'sentiments, faith, and morality.' " *Sense and Sensibility in Modern Poetry* (Chicago 1948), p. 132.

FIVE: —AND CULTURE: THE POET AS SAGE

1. "Why Poets Leave Home," *Scribner's Magazine*, 89 (1931), 84.

2. See C. P., 860-61 for the final version of this section. In the handwritten version of this poem, the spaces in lines 8 and 9 were left so that Aiken could later insert words to fill out the metre.

3. Stanley Vestal, *Kit Carson* (Boston and New York, 1928), p. viii.

4. *Under the Volcano* (New York, 1947), pp. 51, 135.

5. Cf. Marcello Pagnini, "The Myth of William Blackstone in a Poem by Conrad Aiken," *Wake* 11, pp. 70-71.

6. "Rolling Blackstone," N.Y. *Times Bk. Rev.*, Dec. 7, 1947, p. 6.

7. "The Poetry of a Supreme Technician," *New Rep.*, 133 (Dec. 26, 1955), 19.

8. "Wisdom of the Blood?" *New Rep.*, 54 (1928), 252.

9. Quoted from Robert N. Wilson, *Man Made Plain: The Poet in Contemporary Society* (Cleveland, 1958), p. iv. This poem appears in a slightly different and incorrect form in *Ushant*, p. 247.

10. "The Poets Are Awaiting," *Publisher's Weekly* (1954), p. 777.

11. *The American Imago*, 5 (1948), 173-81.

12. "Goethe; Or, the Writer," *Representative Men; Works* (New York, 1903), IV, pp. 285-86

13. "The Uses of Great Men," *Representative Men*, p. 19.

14. *The Victorian Sage: Studies in Argument* (London, 1953), pp. 9, 296, 16-17.

15. For instance Frederick J. Hoffman, *The Twenties* (New York, 1955), p. 213; Edwin Muir, "Fiction," *Nation and Athenaeum*, 41 (1927), 373; F. C. Flint, "Recollections of Two Artists," *Yale Rev.*, 42 (1953), 301.

16. "Recent Verse," *Hound and Horn* (1930), p. 454.

17. For instance, Dean B. Lyman, Jr., "Aiken and Eliot," *MLN*, 71 (1956), 342-43; Joseph Warren Beach "Conrad Aiken and T. S. Eliot: Echoes and Overtones," *PMLA*, 69 (1954), 753-62; Babette Deutsch, "Orchestral Poetry," *Dial*, 70 (1921), 343-46; Louis Untermeyer, "Conrad Aiken," *Modern American Poetry* (New York, 1950), p. 438.

18. " 'What Shall We Do, What Shall We Think, What Shall We Say,' " *Poetry* 99 (1962), 312.

19. "Shakespeare; Or, the Poet," *Representative Men*, pp. 189, 191; "The Uses of Great Men," *ibid.*, p. 35.

20. "The New Elizabethans," *Yale Rev.* (1922), p. 635.

21. "Fertilizing Poetry," *Poetry Journal*, 4 (1915), 33, 34.

22. "The Impersonal Poet," *Poetry Journal*, 6 (1916), 64-66.

23. "Goethe; Or, the Writer," *Representative Men*, pp. 281, 269.

24. "A Plea for Anonymity," *New Rep.*, 84 (1935), 155.

25. *The Victorian Sage*, p. 4.

26. "Wisdom of the Blood?" *New Rep.* (1928), p. 252.

27. "Idiosyncrasy and Tradition," *Dial* (1920), p. 376.

28. Irving Howe, "A Craft and a Calling," *New Rep.*, 141 (July 27, 1959), 27.

29. *The Victorian Sage*, p. 7.

30. "The Poets are Awaiting," *Publisher's Weekly* (1954), p. 776.

31. "Magnifying the Moment," *Dial*, 84 (1928), 329.

32. Lewis Nichols, "Talk With Conrad Aiken," N.Y. *Times Bk. Rev.*, Oct. 26, 1952, p. 26.

33. "Goethe; Or, the Writer," *Representative Men*, p. 286.

34. N.Y. *Evening Post*, Apr. 20, 1929, p. M11.

35. Malcolm Cowley, "Conrad Aiken's Autobiography," *New Rep.*, 127 (Oct. 6, 1952), 21. I am indebted to Cowley throughout this discussion.

36. "On Hallowe'en," *American Imago*, 5 (1948), 217.

37. *Poems* (New York, 1915), p. 29.

38. E. A. Wallis Budge, *Amulets and Superstitions* (London, 1930), p. 46.

39. Harriet Monroe, "A Potential Artist," *Poetry*, 13 (1918), 102.

40. "Industrial Poison Seen in Lyric Spring," N.Y. *Evening Post*, p. M11.

41. *The Education of Henry Adams* (New York, 1931), p. 420.

A

doxes in, 168; freedom from myth, 170; "tough-mindedness" of, 172; *caritas* in, 183; use of *Mourt's Relation* in, 197; self-extension in, 199; called *The Quarrel* in *Ushant*, 232

correspondence theory, 130-131; in *Time in the Rock*, 139; in "Li Po," 247. *See also* language

Costumes by Eros, 67, 94

"Counterpoint and Implication," quoted, 16, 52

Cowley, Malcolm, Aiken's letters to, 5, 100, 253; on *And in the Human Heart*, 170, 256n; on *Ushant*, 233

Crane, Hart, *The Bridge*, 102; and *The Kid*, 196

Crist, Lucien, "Disenchantment" dedicated to, 21

"Crystal, The," 241-244; quoted, 241, 243, 244, 245; commences in a visual experience, 17; success of, 207; method of, 240; Note to, 240; present and past in, 248

crystal, theory of, 197; in *The Kid*, 200, 240-241

Cummings, E. E., idiosyncratic language of, 175; quoted, 211

D

Dante, cited as an objective poet, 217

"Dark City, The," and Aiken's early poetry, 69; quoted, 70; portraits true in, 82

Darwin, Charles, 160; William James Potter on Darwinism, 210

"Dead Leaf in May," quoted, 108

"Dear Uncle Stranger," quoted, 87, 187; mirror image in, 46; *caritas* in, 184

determinism, in *Punch*, 59, 62; rejected in *Landscape West of Eden*, 145

De Quincey, Thomas, influence on Aiken, 219

Deutsch, Babette, letter of Aiken to, 40-41; 257n

Dickinson, Emily, *Selected Poems* edited by Aiken in 1924, 92; "Laurel" quoted, 203

"Dilemma," quoted, 15

"Disciple, The," and *Punch*, 67-68; story of religious aberration, 81

"Discordants," Aiken identified with style of, 5; Aiken's first series poem, 102; Poems I, II, III, IV quoted, 103

"Disenchantment," 21-23; quoted, 22; early experiment in symphony form, 18

"Disintegration in Modern Poetry," quoted, 205, 206

Divine Pilgrim series, Aiken's general description of, 16; and the "symphony," 18-19, 188; increasingly analytic, 19; pattern of, 22; *The Divine Pilgrim*, 39; conclusion of, 55; and Aiken's college fiction, 70-71; and "Changing Mind," 88, 89; as a psychological novel, 94; as a series poem, 102; summarized in "A Basis for

House of Dust, The, 38-45; quoted, 41, 42, 43, 44, 45, 53, 57, 58; 1917-1918 Preface quoted, 39-40, 89, 247; 1948 Preface quoted, 39, 45; dramatic and lyric themes in, 15, 20; and "Disenchantment," 22; contrasted to *The Charnel Rose,* 23; theme of, and *Senlin,* 47; limitations of, 49; and *Festus,* 49, 53; self-revelation in, 51, 56, 204, 235; fortune-telling in, 55; and later work, 57; vicarious experience in, 65; autobiography in, 81, 88; letter form in, 92; monologue in, 109; psychology in, 178; and *Brownstone Eclogues,* 184

Howe, Irving, on Aiken's criticism, 224

Hoyt, Helen, on *Forslin,* 38

Hugo, Victor, cited as an objective poet, 217; Kostyleff's study of, 220

Hulme, T. E., "Romanticism and Classicism," 60-61; quoted, 60

Humboldt, Alexander von, visited by William James Potter, 210

Huxley, Aldous, 77, 214

I

identity, variability of, 31; in *Forslin,* 35-36; in "The Old Man and the Shadow," 46; in *Senlin,* 47, 48; in *Blue Voyage,* 97; loss of, in *King Coffin,* 154; Aiken on, 221-222

"I Love You Very Dearly," fac-

tual basis of, 83; quoted on self-revelation, 93

Imagism, Aiken's criticism of, 7, 17, 18; Amy Lowell's defense of, 14; influence on the long poem, 102; and "Improvisations," 103; view of language, 132

"Impersonal Poet, The," quoted, 217-219

"Improvisation, The," quoted, 177, 231

"Improvisations: Lights and Snow," and visual images, 17; series poem, 102; xiv quoted, 104

"Impulse," quoted, 81

"In Memoriam," quoted, 238

"Innocence," fortune-telling in, 55

Institute of Arts and Letters, 11

interior explication, in *The House of Dust,* 41-42; in *John Deth,* 64-65; summarized, 109-110; in the Preludes, 124-125; in *Preludes for Memnon,* 137-139; in *Time in the Rock,* 139-140; and duty of the sage, 228-229; in Aiken's criticism, 229; in "Changing Mind," 229; in "Cliff Meeting," 229-230; in *Blue Voyage,* 230

J

James family (William, Henry, and Alice), referred to in "Round by Round," 83, 86, 93

James, Henry, 214, 226; theory of consciousness, 44; in tradi-

K

Aiken's work, 4; on Aiken's criticism, 12; on *Osiris Jones*, 110

Morse, Samuel French, on Aiken's reputation, 4-5

Mourt's Relation, called *Journal of the Pilgrims* in *Conversation*, 86; used in "Mayflower," 197

"Mr. Arcularis," quoted, 61

Mr. Arcularis. A Play, acceptance of history in, 70; Preface quoted, 83, 117; 1952-1953 MS quoted, 118; quoted, 79; factual basis of, 83; and *Great Circle*, 118; circular pattern in, 160; Aiken on collaboration in, 216

Muir, Edwin, 257n

Murray, Henry A., psychoanalyst-friend of Aiken's, 26; Aiken's letter on *Ushant* to, 236

music, and the lyric theme, 16; as expression of emotions, 16; characteristic use of, 18; in *The Charnel Rose*, 23-24; in Aiken's early poetry, 51; variations in, 55; rhythm in poetry, 132; in *The Kid*, 201-203; in *Ushant*, 231; and language, in "Li Po" and "The Crystal," 245; and number, 247

myth, in *Punch*, 58; in *John Deth*, 58-59, 63-64; Freud's definition of, 64; and dreams, 64-66; and the self, 81; in Jean de Bosschère, 108; in *Osiris Jones*, 111; of consciousness, in *Landscape West of Eden*, 141; freedom from, 170

N

"Necktie, The," autobiography in, 31

Neo-Humanist criticism, Aiken's opposition to, 7

New Criticism, Aiken's opposition to, 8

Newman, John Henry, *Grammar of Assent*, quoted, 225

Nietzsche, Friedrich, influence on *Earth Triumphant*, 31; quoted, 66; concept of "Exceptional Man" in *King Coffin*, 149

"Night Before Prohibition, The," autobiography in, 83, 86; quoted, 86; and *Conversation*, 166

"1915: The Trenches," contrasted to *The Soldier*, 188

"No, No, Go Not to Lethe," 81; megalomania in, 92; fear of self-revelation in, 116; and *King Coffin*, 147, 148, 152

"Nocturne in a Minor Key," and "musical analogy," 16

Nocturne of Remembered Spring and Other Poems, Aiken's anonymous review of, 12, 13, 128; emotional symbolism in, 16-17, 40, 103, 176, 206; and *Forslin*, 23; and *Blue Voyage*, 97

"Nocturne of Remembered Spring," and "musical analogy," 16

Nonsense verse, and *John Deth*, 65; and *Osiris Jones*, 113; place of in poetry, 132

O

O'Connor, William Van, *Sense and Sensibility in Modern Poetry*, quoted, 256n
"O How She Laughed," autobiography in, 83; objectivity in Aiken's early poetry, 56; in *The House of Dust*, 58; in "Changing Mind," 89; in later poetry, 175, 204; exceptions to, 206-207; Aiken on, 205-206, 217, 221; and anonymity in "Changing Mind," *Blue Voyage*, and *Ushant*, 254n
"Old Man and the Shadow, The," quoted, 46
"Old Man Weeping, An," fragmentation of stanza in, 107
Oppenheim, James, as realist, 14
"Orange Moth, The," quoted, 84; parody of Holmes in, 86
originality in poetry, of Aiken's language and ideas, 176; Aiken on, 179, 211, 213-214, 217-219, 220; and idiosyncrasy, 211; for the sage, 211; Emerson on, 215, 216, 220; and tradition, 248
"Overture to Today," quoted, 234, 245

P

Pagnini, Marcello, 257n
"Pair of Vikings, A," autobiography in, 83
paradox, in *And in the Human Heart*, 172-173; in "Blues for Ruby Matrix," 181-183
"Parasites: To certain Poets," quoted, 221

Péguy, Charles, 6
Perse, St. John, Aiken on *Pluies*, 188
"Personal Anthology," quoted, 219
Peterson, Houston, *Melody of Chaos* written to defend Aiken's reputation, 3; range of, 9; biography in, 74; quoted on "Cliff Meeting," 87; quoted on "parable" poems, 108
Pfister, Oskar Robert, psychoanalyst, 26
Pilgrimage of Festus, The, 49-54; quoted, 50, 51, 53, 54, 69; Preface to quoted, 51; dissection scene in, 38; imaginative experience in, 55; chronology, 56, 57; form in, 58, 88; solipsism, 97-98; identity in, 105, 126; influence of Jean de Bosschère, 108; and *Landscape West of Eden*, 143; dilemma of, 164-165
Plato, the "Cave," 123; conception of language, 129-130; *Cratylus* quoted, 129, 139; *Phaedrus* quoted, 130; Aiken's use of, 131-132
"Plea for Anonymity, A," quoted, 221-222
Poe, Edgar Allan, cited as a subjective poet, 217
poetry and the poet, and politics, 7; and culture, 25; Aiken's definition of, 27, 136, 205, 206, 223-224; poetry and prose, 131-133; inferior poetry, 133; sentimentality in, 167; and traveller, 189; and evolution of consciousness,

nineteenth-century poets, 71, 219-220; John Holloway on, 208, 212; and problem of originality, 211, Emerson on, 216, Aiken on, 221; and renewal of awareness, 212; and culture, 223; in "Li Po," 247-248

"St. Ambrose: Early Morning," quoted, 184, 184-185

Sainte-Beuve, Charles, quoted by Aiken, 210-211

"Samadhi," in Aiken's development, 128

Sandburg, Carl, as realist, 14; Aiken's criticism of, 196

Santayana, George, "A Long Way Round to Nirvana" and *John Deth*, 65

Savoy, Bert, Aiken's knowledge of, 29

Scepticisms, 216; and Aiken's poetry, 12; use of psychoanalysis in, 134-135; spiral structure of, 229

Schwartz, Delmore, on Aiken's reputation, 4

"Scientific Approach to Criticism, A," quoted, 156

"Sea Holly," experiment in repetition, 107

Seldes, Gilbert, *The Seven Lively Arts*, reviewed by Aiken, 29

Selected Poems (1961), Preface quoted, 110

self-knowledge, in *Forslin*, 37; influence of Coleridge's "Self-Knowledge," 43; in *Festus*, 50, 51; in *The House of Dust*, 57, 58; in *Blue Voyage*, 97; and *caritas*, in *King Coffin*,

155; in "The Census-Takers," 185-186; in *Brownstone Eclogues*, 187; in *The Soldier*, 190; and the past, 240

self-revelation, in *The House of Dust*, 42, 45; in early poetry, 56; use of letter form for, 92-93; in *Blue Voyage*, 95; and myth, in *Osiris Jones*, 111; self-definition, 204; in modern poetry, 219

Senlin: A Biography, 45-49; 1949 Preface quoted, 34; quoted, 42, 45, 47, 48, 53, 54, 61, 249, 10; and "Laughter," 15; and the lyric theme, 20; and vagueness, 24; and *Festus*, 49, 53-54; identity in, 51; Aiken on "economy" in, 52; written in three weeks, 55; and predicament of Everyman, 56; ego in, 58, 105, 146, 198; vicarious experience in, 65; begins with tactile, 79; generic I in, 88, 91; communication in, 93; 106; compared to Preludes, 138; inconclusive, 140; and *Landscape West of Eden*, 142; and "Li Po," 249; Burton Rascoe on, 251n

series poems, Aiken on, 102-103, 120; 124; in *And in the Human Heart*, 167-169, 179

"Shaemus," quoted, 186-187

Shakespeare, William, 218; in "Mayflower," 198; Emerson on, 208, 215; cited by Aiken as an objective poet, 217; Aiken on the modernity of, 219; the "use" of, 248

Sheepfold Hill, 3

U

V